Growing Together

Preserving Marriage and Family
in the Face of Personal Change

Staying Together

JÜRG WILLI, M.D.

TRANSLATED BY
Vivien Blandford & Tony Häfliger

JEREMY P. TARCHER, INC.
Los Angeles

Library of Congress Cataloging-in-Publication Data

Willi, Jürg.
    [Koevolution. English]
    Growing together staying together : preserving marriage and family
    in the face of personal change / Jürg Willi ; translated
    by Vivien Blandford and Tony Häfliger.
        p.   cm.
    Translation of: Koevolution.
    Includes bibliographical references and index.
    ISBN 087477-589-2
    1. Marital psychotherapy. 2. Family psychotherapy.
    3. Interpersonal relations. 4. Change (Psychology) 5. Family—
    Psychological aspects. 6. Self-actualization (Psychology)—Social
    aspects. I. Title.
    RC488.5.W55413 1992
    616.89′156—dc20   9137303
                                                                  CIP

Copyright © 1992 by Jürg Willi

Jeremy P. Tarcher, Inc.
5858 Wilshire Blvd., Suite 200
Los Angeles, CA 90036

Distributed by St. Martin's Press, New York

Manufactured in the United States of America
10 9 8 7 6 5 4 3 2 1
First Edition

Contents

Preface: About My Personal Experience as a Basis for This Book

This book deals with an ecological view of self-realization. In it we human beings are depicted as relational beings who are interlinked with our environment. This environment, however, is not only nature but also and in particular our fellow human beings. Consequently the book focuses not on the development of the individual, but on the development of suprapersonal processes, of which the individual is a part, and on the coevolution of our relational networks.

Psychological-psychotherapeutic books can exert a great influence on people's codes of values and on their attitudes. The works of Freud, Jung, Carl Rogers, and many others have had a lasting impact on our culture, far beyond the realm of psychotherapy. Although many of these authors claim that their assertions are based on objective and controlled experience, I proceed a priori from the assumption that my professional experiences are to a large extent identical with my personal experiences. Therefore I consider it appropriate to inform the reader briefly about the personal-professional experiences on which my assertions are based.

For the purposes of this book I regard three spheres as important: the religious, the marital, and the professional. I was brought up a Roman Catholic, and, despite my outward detachment from that denomination, I still feel bound in many respects to the Catholic way of experiencing the world. From childhood on I was fascinated by what a Gothic cathedral represents visually: the world, the cosmos, as an all-encompassing edifice. The portal, the entrance to the nave, goes through a representation of world history, arranged in the shape of a shell: from the creation of the world via a depiction of the Old Testament, and the events in the life of Jesus, to the history of the church with its apostles, its fathers, and its saints. The portal is bordered on both left and right by Old Testament prophets who carry New Testament saints on their shoulders. In these churches everyone has his or her appointed place. Their relational spaces depict how the one emerges from the other, how one step supports the next, how one thing symbolizes another, and how, as a historical process, the church aligns itself toward God, toward the superordinate Whole. These churches filled me with a feeling of my relatedness to processes reaching beyond me; they gave me security and strength; and they inspired me to devote my energies to this historical, suprapersonal process.

That which is my concern is also contained in the Catholic Mass in the form of ritual. The Mass is a process in which those present align themselves as a community toward the divine Whole, and in so doing include all absent relatives, the sick, the deceased, the saints, and the entire church. The believers offer to the superordinate Whole the products of their labor—bread and wine—in order to receive it back as a gift, changed into the real presence of Christ, and in order to incorporate him into themselves. Through Communion, the taking of the consecrated bread and wine, those present become one organism united in God.

A further important and extremely happy experience is my marriage to Margaretha Dubach, which has lasted for over twenty years. Margaretha has always been a very independent person, who was never in danger of giving herself up for me or of merging with me. We are very different in many respects, and at the beginning of our acquaintance we had great difficulty in adapting ourselves to each other. Even now, short-term separations are apt to make it difficult for us to find our way back to each other again afterward. This is no doubt connected with the fact that our relationship has always retained enough tension that we have always provided each other with a challenge, and offered each other resistance.

Margaretha is a sculptress, who is increasingly gaining international recognition. We have given each other as much support as possible, both personally and professionally. Despite many deep points of contact, there still remain enough barriers and separate spheres where neither of us can feel totally understood by the other. This is also a constant challenge to us to seek each other in deeper areas. Although Margaretha is an emancipated woman, we live in relatively traditional sexual roles. Margaretha takes great pleasure in decorating a home, in cooking creatively; she knows how to make a bouquet of flowers like no one else, and how to astonish people with all kinds of little things and amusing surprises. She is a person who loves to give frequent presents to other people.

All these are qualities that are underdeveloped in me. I am good and reliable at organizing, and at mastering difficult situations in life. I also believe I have the ability to create basic conditions for furthering other people's growth, such as that of Margaretha and of our two sons. What I write in this book about coevolution within a partnership derives directly from the experience of our relationship. In all fairness Margaretha should be mentioned here as coauthor.

Yet another happy experience is my professional activity as a psychotherapist. As far back as 1965, I turned my attention to couples and family therapy; I was beginning to be interested in suprapersonal processes even then. In couples and family therapy I gained both practical and theoretical experiences that were fundamental for me and that, in this book, I would now like to enlarge beyond the therapeutic framework. Many of the examples given here are based on my experiences as head of the Psychotherapy Unit of the Psychiatric Hospital of the University of Zurich. The Psychotherapy Unit is a small one, with twelve to twenty-two beds, in which we primarily treat young patients with severe neurotic personality disorders. Most of our patients suffer from a lifelong flawed development, are despondent and depressive, and shun contact; they have given up on life and have withdrawn from working life as well. The patients enter voluntarily for intensive treatment lasting about three months.

As head of this unit, I myself have experienced a valuable learning process. The closer psychotherapeutic tasks are to personal experience, the more difficult it is to work in a team. Some members of the team believe we should be strict and consistent with the patients; others, however, would like to act in a kind and encouraging way. Some favor individual therapy; others favor group activities. Some would like a clearly structured daily timetable; others would like as much freedom as possible in the way life is organized in the unit. Some think that the nursing staff should not interfere in the doctors' individual therapies; others believe the nursing staff to be equally capable of practicing psychotherapy. All these differences in a psychotherapy team are further fueled by the patients.

I had to learn how to be head of this unit by learning from my colleagues, and I was increasingly able to accept criticism as a "favor," in the conviction that I could always learn something from it. Instead of constantly justifying and defending myself, I learned how to listen. We experimented with various "antiauthoritarian" leadership models in this unit. After many years we realized from experience that the patients, having been accustomed throughout their lives to passive subordination and dependency, are overtaxed by a unit that wants to assign them too much individual responsibility and activity. As head of the unit, I learned to define clearly my own functions and those of my colleagues, to keep myself out of areas of responsibility that I had delegated to others, and to check only the results there. The most difficult thing for me was to keep my distance from my colleagues, most of whom were among my closest friends, in order to avoid the unproductive rivalries that can so easily occur in personal involvements. I learned that keeping my distance at the same time enabled us to be more frank with one another, and more critical toward one another in the sphere of teamwork.

In the last few years, one of my most important tasks has been to develop the new specialty of psychosocial medicine. I have advocated more consideration of the psychological dimension in medical studies, on both national and local levels. Medical faculties have the reputation of being particularly authoritarian and inflexible; but they are also run by people, and people can change. I repeatedly found that stubborn opponents of any psychologizing of medical teaching would suddenly and unexpectedly support our concerns in a well-meaning manner, and that people who appeared particularly narrow-minded would suddenly become more open-minded, more yielding, and more humane. Psychotherapists generally tend to distance themselves from institutions, and to resist them from the outside. My own experiences, however, have induced me to fight and wrestle with institutions. The prerequisite for a successful struggle, though, is patience, tolerance in the face of frustration, and respect for one's opponents and their arguments. In this building-up process, which has been going on for years, I have been vigorously supported, above all, by my three senior consultants, Claus Buddeberg, Jakob Bösch, and Hanspeter Wengle, to whom I owe a great deal, as I do to Professor Hans Kind, director of the Psychiatric Hospital of the University of Zurich.

The writing of this book took six years. In the course of those years I altered many of my original views. I have frequently felt very much alone in my choice of this subject, and have repeatedly doubted my ability to master it. It often seemed to me like a disease I could no longer rid myself of. I found the reactions of the public particularly perplexing. When, on the occasion of the Lindau Psychotherapy Weeks in 1980, I expressed my thoughts for the first time in the form of a lecture course, the audience of about four hundred was enthusiastic. After three years of intensive work, I held a second seminar in Lindau on this subject, which this time earned me rather malicious criticism. In the summer term of 1983, I gave a course at the University of Zurich on this subject. About thirty people attended the first lecture; by the end of the term, only six were left. During this frustrating period the appearance of Fritjof Capra's book *The Turning Point* proved a great help to me. I sensed the possibility of relating my thoughts to those of other questing spirits, and thus of finding access to the listening and reading public. The great success of my lecture at the Lindau Psychotherapy Weeks in 1984 finally gave me back the self-confidence I needed to write this book.

In the writing of this book I am greatly indebted to various friends. In the first place I would like to mention Ruth Rabian, my secretary, who in all those confused years typed and retyped texts with great forbearance and patience. At the outset she had to write many things with which she personally did not agree. I am pleased to hear from her that I have developed myself and my ideas in a positive sense. Elisabeth Constam helped me greatly with the compilation of the bibliography and the notes. I would further like to thank my German-language editor, Hermann Gieselbusch, for his careful and critical reading of the manuscript, as well as (in alphabetical order) Annie Berner, Claus and Barbara Buddeberg, Elsie Freutel, Alice and Hellmuth Holzhey, and Hans Kind. Each of them, and in particular Annie Berner, grappled with the subject in a very personal way and gave me a great deal of important and critical advice.

PART I

The Age
of Narcissism

CHAPTER 1

How Narcissism Affects Our Relationships

In the last few years ecological awareness has rapidly spread to ever-greater circles of the population. If, in the postwar years and the early sixties, unlimited economic growth was everybody's dream, the realization that there are limits to growth set in with the oil crisis in 1973. People are no longer happy with aggressive expansion; it affords them less and less prestige. Indeed, they are beginning to impose voluntary restrictions upon themselves in order not to destroy the world of which they are a part. This kind of ecological thinking, however, has not yet had much influence on theories about human relationships. This is in itself astonishing, since today the ecological balances of human coexistence are as disturbed as those of nature. They are also being destroyed by the same basic attitude—the belief that each person has a right to unlimited personal growth, as long as there is no risk to other people's life and limb. Many people regard the resources of human adaptability as inexhaustible, and dismiss the already visible symptoms of social disintegration as side effects of our growth toward a society of absolute freedom. They do not believe that our capacities for social regulation might be overwhelmed.

Striving toward self-realization has been at the center of the spiritual evolution of our Western culture for some decades. Some people perceive in this the foundation of a transition into a new age; others regard it as no more than a pseudoscientific disguise for egoism. I believe that, all too often, efforts toward self-realization are viewed in isolation, as the concern of only that individual; their ecological effects on the person's family and friends are not sufficiently taken into account. If self-realization occurs only at the expense of our fellow human beings, then little that is positive can be gained from it. The value of self-realization must be measured not only by its effects on the individual but also by its effects on the network of relationships that constitute the person's social reality.

Another ecological consideration that is often given too little weight in evaluating endeavors toward self-realization is the question of extent. All too often interest focuses on whether this or that is right or wrong; but from an ecological point of view, the decisive question is, *To what extent and in which connections* is this or that right or wrong? Many medicines that are beneficial in small doses are toxic in large ones. During a revolutionary uprising, questions of extent cannot be discussed, because the mere asking of such questions is considered reactionary. I believe, however, that the time has come to reflect with more objectivity on the meaning and aim of self-realization in a society as seen from an ecological perspective.

HOW NARCISSISM AFFECTS HUMAN ECOSYSTEMS

Nowadays there is a great deal of talk about self-realization; people also talk a great deal about the increasing narcissism of our time (Lasch 1979; Wangh 1983). Questions about the connection between narcissism and the self-realization movement are rarely asked, however. This is actually astonishing, for we can define *narcissism* as "a concentration of psychological interest upon the *self*" (Moore and Fine 1968). The intense striving for realization of the self is therefore very similar to narcissism.

It is now established that narcissistic disorders spread with great rapidity in our Western societies—for example, as borderline cases of schizophrenic psychoses, as anorexia, as depressions, as drug addiction, as criminality. At the same time, theoretical interest in narcissism is greatly increasing, above all in psychoanalysis, with the work of H. Kohut and O. F. Kernberg. Both phenomena—the increase in narcissistic disorders and the increase of interest in them—are an expression of the psychological tendencies of our times.

Where, then, can the causes of narcissism and of the excessive interest in the self be sought? Kohut (1977) sees the cause of narcissistic developments in faulty behavior on the part of the mother. Mahler (1968) proposes that some mothers cannot bear the normal separation–individuation process; that is, they cannot empathize with the early endeavors of the infant to be independent. Kernberg (1975) and many other prominent psychoanalytical authors surmise that the roots of narcissism are to be found in early, developmentally conditioned defects.

And yet I would like to ask if there is not a tendency in all this to overestimate the influence of the mother. Why should so many mothers' empathy have changed so fundamentally in the past few decades that it has caused such decisive social changes? The narcissism of our time cannot be ascribed to a single, isolated cause. Rather, our culture as a whole has been moving in the direction of narcissism. The way was paved for this well in advance; it happened initially in imperceptible steps, but now the speed is increasing. We can make no clear distinction between narcissism as disorder and narcissism as paradigm. Pathological phenomena are merely the side effects of a total process.

The development of the narcissistic retreat into ourselves appears in all spheres of our culture. I would like to elucidate five such spheres: work, leisure, relationship toward the state, psychological self-experience, and partnership and family.

Work

Alienation from work was described 150 years ago by Karl Marx, and need not be dealt with here in any more detail. Unfortunately, the attempt to humanize work has not been able to check the process of alienation. It is the machine that determines the rhythm and organization of human labor, and not human beings, whom the machine should serve. Charlie Chaplin gave an unforgettable portrayal of this in his film *Modern Times*.

The increasing division of labor has increased our alienation from the products of our work. Practically all workers are nowadays involved in the manufacture of component parts, often without knowing anything about the finished product, let alone being able to have it at their disposal or even being able to buy it. They never get any feedback from the purchaser of the product, and thus never receive any affirmation of their work, which could best strengthen and structure their self-awareness. They have no way to influence the manufacturing process in a creative way, or to be stimulated or challenged by their work.

Today's changeover to the information age requires us to adjust our mental and linguistic structures to the laws of information processing, and enforces further alienation from work. Robots and computers do so many jobs so much faster, more precisely, and more cheaply that the areas of human employment that provide self-confirmation are steadily dwindling. Many professions offer people no way to identify with their work whatsoever, and challenge only a pitiful fraction of their personal potential. This leads to an inner detachment from work, despite the fact that work occupies the greatest part of a person's active life.

Leisure

If workers can no longer identify themselves with their jobs, they can (they think) compensate for this in leisure, which they can organize independently. Yet even leisure has long been monopolized by rational and economic thinking. The demand to satisfy as many needs as possible in as little time as possible, to enjoy experiences missed before, has alienated most people from being able to use their leisure time creatively. It has indeed become a question of utilizing time as efficiently as possible at as little cost as possible. Whether the time is spent on skiing, safaris, visits to cities, or travels to distant continents and peoples, the "great adventure" is so completely programmed and rationalized that encounters with nature or with foreign peoples feel no different from having it all served up as a TV feature in the comfort of our own homes.

The State

Life in the modern state also leads to increasing alienation. In the Orwell year, 1984, we were particularly aware of the extent to which information about us is being stored and will be retrievable at all times, while we ourselves, as individual citizens, have neither an overview of, nor even a right to avail ourselves of, our personal data. We felt helpless and at the mercy of political and economic decisions such as comprehensive economic restructuring, of unemployment, of misplanning in educational policy, not to mention the catastrophic impact that the Western economy has on the ecology of the Third World. We felt powerless in the face of the superpowers' maniacal arms race, not knowing if and when we should all be exterminated. For a long time ordinary citizens retained the belief that experts and politicians were invested with powers that ordinary citizens lacked. The experts, however, are in obvious disagreement among themselves. The politicians, too, are overtaxed by the complexity of the problems; they tend to make their decisions primarily with a view to the next elections.

All this alienation, all this powerlessness, all this lack of constructive perspectives on the future encourage us to withdraw into ourselves and away from identification with the state. There is an increasing feeling that I myself am the only thing I can be sure of, the only thing over which I exercise control, which I do not experience as a mere consumer article or some administrative action, and which is at my disposal alone. With the increasing alienation of the environment, I myself become my only source of authentic, vital experience.

Self-Experience

But even the journey into one's interior, the adventure of the discovery of the self, has long become a profitable branch of psychotourism. Journeys into your own interior are recommended as a way to have many profound experiences in a short time and at an acceptable price. Self-experience threatens to become a consumer good. Offers beckon from all sides and entice you with the prospect of being able to experience yourself with their help in a real, intensely creative, and holistic manner. There is an increasingly widespread feeling that the individual man cannot find himself through his own efforts and in his daily experiences. It is the same with the photo safari to Kenya: why trouble yourself with all the work, false starts, and detours of organizing a journey into the unknown wilderness when you can be supplied with what is supposedly the same thing without having to invest any time in preparations, and at an acceptable price? Thus self-experience will soon no longer succeed without guidance. Few people ask whether the "uniqueness" thus discovered does not alarmingly resemble that of all the others who subject themselves to the same arranged experiences. Rollo May, a prominent cofounder of American humanistic psychology, writes about this in *The Meaning of Anxiety* (1977). The psychologists, he maintains, have exploited the uneasiness and the spiritual confusion of our times, and have capitalized on people's immense need to understand both spiritual health and their own selves. May thinks that the enormous boost psychology has received in this century results not from the psychologists' brilliant achievements, but from the intense emotional problems that beset people nowadays.

Partnership and Family

One area remains in which we hope for authentic experiences free of anonymity and manipulation: partnership and family. Despite all the alienation in other areas of life, a return to actual and vital aspects of life should remain possible in this sphere. Yet family and marriage cannot simply be idealized. With extensive alienation in all other areas of life, the family is overtaxed by the demands made on it. The family is supposed to compensate us for all our frustrations in other areas of life. This leads to emotional overloading. The narcissistic rage at the fact that even the family cannot compensate for the frustrations experienced elsewhere, and that it also does not satisfy our needs for devotion and tenderness, understanding and self-confirmation, causes people to destroy the family, so that they can retreat into themselves even more. Nowadays the family is no longer necessary for physical protection, but continues to provide personal closeness, often so much that it is stifling.

The extended family of earlier times was not as romantic as people now like to think, but it was certainly different from the small family unit. It offered a wide range of relationships and hence extensive ways to regulate and compensate for proximity and distance. The desire for the small family unit was inherent in the development of occidental individualism. With it we had to accept the fact that this small family unit is less flexible in overcoming conflicts, and that it promotes overintensive interdependence of the partners.

Most parents these days, in deciding to have a child, also decide to devote themselves to developing the child's potential optimally, both in and out of school, and to creating the best possible conditions for the child's self-development. This is why middle-class and upper-class mothers take their children to piano, ballet, judo, or painting lessons on their afternoons off. This encouragement is not authoritarian; the children are not *forced* to attend ballet classes, nor are they beaten into practicing the piano. No, the parents develop such arts of seduction and manipulation that the children themselves *want* to take ballet lessons; the children do not simply do this, but *like* doing it or, rather, have to like doing it. The careful supervision of games is also part of this care. On free afternoons children's parties are organized, with competitions and prizes. But even on weekends the children are not left to themselves; indeed, they often could not find any playmates if they tried, because parents go away with their children to engage in sports, or visit their holiday homes. The better residential areas are often deserted.

Today's parents center their lives around their children. During the day children often do not spend one single hour without their parents. At night, too, their bedroom doors are left open, so that a child can be comforted at once when he or she has a bad dream. In the wake of antieducational theory, parents reject any kind of role behavior, and try to be the child's friend and companion.

Yet what children would often like today is parents who keep themselves at more of a distance, who more clearly define themselves as parents, who clearly say what their responsibility as parents is and what it is not, and who have clear expectations of their children. This would provide the child with structures within which he or she could feel secure and find his or her bearings. These would afford the child a clearly defined freedom within which he or she could develop independently of the parents. The child could have his or her own experiences with peers in play groups that are neither arranged nor supervised by parents.

As things stand, the child frequently cannot argue with the parents at all, because the parents anxiously avoid confrontation, do not dare voice their own expectations, and want only "the best for the child." Where there is so much "love" and "empathy," every quarrel with the parents is bound to create feelings of guilt in the child. Where there is so much proximity and involvement and so little room for confrontation, the child's only way toward self-apprehension is a narcissistic retreat into the self.

This uneasy proximity/distance problem is further aggravated by the ever-increasing divorce rate, which has doubled in the last decade, with the result that there are more and more people who, as children, experienced their parents' divorce. What, from the parents' point of view, may be a logical solution to their conflicts in the direction of liberation, independence, and self-determination is from the child's point of view an insoluble conflict. There are increasing numbers of children coming for therapy who are emotionally completely overtaxed by the divorce situation. They love both their mother *and* their father, and want to be with both of them not separately—once with mother, once with father—but together as a family. Suddenly they must divide their love into two loves that are mutually exclusive, because their love for one parent is always at the same time a betrayal of their love for the other parent. In addition, they sense that their parents are no longer able to exert their parental authority, but can be manipulated at will whenever the child threatens to withdraw his or her love from either father or mother. Parents are effusive in their search for the child's intimate proximity. They tell the child about their past and present intimacies, and seek consolation and advice from the child in their new love affairs. The children are forced to act as parents to their own parents.

In this impossible situation there is only one sensible last resort left to the child: retreat into the self. The child has experienced that love is dangerous. To all outward appearances the child has been abandoned by one of the parents to whom he or she naturally feels attached. At the same time both parents swamp the child with attestations of, and enticements to, love, though often only during those periods of parental access laid down by the court. The child is caught up in triangles full of ambiguities. Because of this, the child's ability to enter into relationships is so damaged that for his or her future life there can be only one consequence: rejection of any kind of tie, and preservation of absolute autonomy. These injuries are often so deep and overwhelming that they cannot be healed at all. The craving for love, security, and unconditional acceptance has to be disowned by many "difficult" youngsters. They then struggle for even more self-determination and independence. The feeling of total isolation and senselessness is covered up. What should find expression as trauma and despair is turned into and presented as something promising and worth striving for.

At this stage, the causes and effects of the retreat into the self have become a self-perpetuating process. The attempt to achieve greater independence and self-determination within the family, and in the spheres of work and leisure, often leads to frustrations, which in turn increase the tendency toward retreat into the self—now, however, no longer in the sense of a constructive step in personal development, but as a defense mechanism. The border between self-realization as a paradigm and narcissism as a disorder can be fluid, and there can be reciprocal influence between the two. I perceive obvious and intrinsic causes of today's trend toward narcissism in the narcissistic paradigm of our time.

For decades, committed exponents of endeavors toward self-realization have propagated the individual's claim to autonomy and liberation from the expectations and obligations imposed by family and community. Lasch (1979) argues that they have postulated a person who lives entirely in the here and now, free from historical continuity, who lives neither for ancestors nor for posterity, who does not want to exist as a link in a succession of generations stretching from the past into the future, who is primarily concerned with his or her own mental condition, who strives toward the fulfillment of his or her own emotional needs as the ultimate meaning of life, and who refuses to subjugate personal needs and interests to a community, a cause, or a tradition.

This strong concentration on the development of the self has already produced statistically measurable effects on human ecosystems. Our Western society is developing into a society of singles, of lone wolves. The paradigms have drastic consequences for people's relationships with one another and with their environment. Today we are in danger of bringing about our own downfall, not only by the destruction of our own natural environment but also by the destruction of our most elementary community structures.

There is something wrong with a society that cannot maintain appropriate familial structures, and that cannot see a purpose for human life in the succession of generations and in reproduction. The protection of human ecosystems, particularly that of the family, seems to be as urgent today as the protection of our natural environment.

Just as the environmental-protection movement no longer merely raises a warning finger, but aims at a learning process that will help us to perceive, respect, and admire the complex regulating systems of nature, so I hope this book will promote in you, the reader, an awareness of being involved in space and time, so that you will strive for coevolution with your fellow human beings, not merely out of a sense of duty, but out of affection and joy.

REJECTING RELATIONSHIPS

Whereas emotional disorders in Western civilization once reinforced relationships, the disorders now common instead reject them. "Narcissus: a new socialization type?" educational theorists ask (Häsing, Stubenrauch, and Ziehe 1981). They have discovered that young people turn away from social reality and refuse to wear themselves out for it or even to adapt themselves to it; instead, they turn toward their own egos. Young people behave as if they were disconnected from the external world and no longer let themselves be seduced into interaction, be it satisfying or full of conflict. With an ideology of spontaneity, they demonstrate an abandonment of sociopolitical commitment and lay claim to an immediate and unrestricted satisfaction of their needs in the here and now. This satisfaction sets their productive energies in motion for a short time, but as soon as it encounters a reality that obstructs this motion, it turns first into blind rage and then into paralyzing apathy. "We want everything, and now!" was sprayed on many walls during the Zurich youth movement of 1980. According to Döpp (1981) this new narcissistic socialization type is characterized by a symbiotic relationship with the mother, which retains archaic traits of fusion and of immediate satisfaction of needs, of a striving for satisfaction not by means of actual relationships but through the primal experience of an "intrauterine" narcissistic feeling of well-being, a self-image diffusely extended into the cosmic and aimed at omnipotence, bound up with feelings of guilt in the face of which the ego feels helpless and powerless, so that these feelings can only be repressed. Another aspect of this turning away from external reality is the avoidance of all situations that could result in narcissistic insults— in particular, avoidance of competition with peers. This attitude of refusal serves to protect an extremely vulnerable self-esteem. The result is a melting, diffuse, unbounded self, which can concentrate only on its own interests and tends toward escapism.

The educational theorist H. von Hentig (1976, p. 52) has discovered that nowadays children go to school with an alarmingly undeveloped capacity for solidarity, inversely proportional to their need for security, belonging, and reliability. In Hentig's opinion, children should be able to experience what strong, lasting relationships and self-established orders in groups can achieve. It is not so much education and educational opportunities, not "activities" and motivation, not emancipation and academic thinking, but reliance and friendliness that, today, are children's fundamental requirements, to which we ought to devote ourselves first and foremost.

For decades now a shift in the relative frequencies of syndromes has been detected in psychotherapeutic practice, a shift that corresponds to the increase in this narcissistic socialization type. The syndromes that have increased, such as addiction, anorexia, and borderline disorders, reflect the social situation.

Addiction

An increasingly distressing problem consists of all possible forms of addiction, whether they be traditional ones such as alcoholism, nicotine abuse, and drug abuse (analgesics, sleeping pills) or the more recent drug problems (cannabis, heroin, cocaine, and so on). In the addict, a socially widespread attitude is expressed: that in this society (denounced as *Scheissgesellschaft*, "shitty society") a person has an absolute right to immediate well-being and to compensation for all frustrations, all this independent of concrete social relationships and without frustrating confrontations with other persons. The drugs used are supposed to induce a feeling of expansiveness and release. Therapists lament the addict's lack of readiness to form a therapeutic working alliance, lack of perseverance, and inability to tolerate frustration.

And yet, what must up to now be counted among the most effective "therapies" for addiction problems? *Not* professional aid, but intensive, supportive communities: from Alcoholics Anonymous, which brought about a revolution in the treatment of alcohol problems, to the current religiously oriented communities for drug addicts, as well as addictive (often symbiotic) love relationships. According to an investigation by D. Zimmer and A. Uchtenhagen (1982), thirty-three out of one hundred drug addicts in therapeutic communities referred to their partners as the most important persons for them, but only four mentioned the therapist in that role. Almost three-quarters of the men and over half of the women considered their partners as the most important motivating support in their treatment. Don't these addicts demonstrate the necessary corrective to our present narcissistic culture? What makes us ill is the lack of a binding affiliation to a community with distinct structures; what cures us is the acquisition of just this affiliation.

Anorexia

Things seem quite different for today's greatly increasing number of anorexics (Willi and Grossmann 1983). This disorder primarily affects women, and consists of a refusal to eat, which can lead to death from starvation. Here, too, there is a basic attitude that rejects relationships and help. Anorexics refuse all forms of dependence. This defense mechanism causes them to reject even their dependence on physical needs, such as hunger and sexuality. They reject any type of binding relationship, and refuse to accept the role of an adult woman and mother. This aid-rejecting syndrome can drive therapists to despair. Many therapists, particularly female ones, try with infinite patience, empathy, and maternal commitment to establish contact with anorexics, but all too often without success. In their angellike way, anorexics are superficially friendly and apparently accessible. In reality, however, they remain withdrawn into themselves, and in therapy their conversation with the therapist is purely formal. They demonstrate to the therapist the inefficiency of his or her efforts, often by losing more weight just as the therapist believes that he or she has gotten closer to the patient. No wonder, then, that anorexia was often diagnosed as a psychosis; this seemed to justify the ineffectiveness of psychotherapy.

In the past few years, however, new approaches have arisen, especially from family therapy (Minuchin, Rosman, and Baker 1978; Selvini-Palazzoli et al. 1975). One aspect that is important here, as I myself have found in the treatment of anorexics, is that they cannot be won over to a therapy by means of empathy, kindliness, or tolerance; on the contrary, anorexics must be fought with. This fight provides anorexics with a way to maintain their autonomy in a relationship. It leads to clear boundaries. Of course, this fight must be waged in a fair way. According to my experience it proves to be successful if, in the process, the therapist clearly defines his or her understanding of the roles, and proves to be absolutely reliable, transparent, and calculable. The therapist must prove to the anorexic that he or she does not primarily want to be loved, but demands what is necessary for therapy, independent of the anorexic's sympathy, without expecting more than this in the way of a personal relationship.

Many anorexics admitted to me only years after they had recovered that they had originally hated me because of my authoritarian attitude, but had nevertheless always known that the path I was taking was the only one that promised success. Thus anorexics, too, demonstrate by their behavior during illness what the defect is that compounds their illness, and what they need in order to recover. They miss and need relationships that involve neither manipulation nor stifling intimacy. They provoke in the therapist the form of relationship beneficial to them: a relationship of benevolent respect for the distance that is necessary for them to develop freely, a relationship that is at the same time unconditional, can endure stress, and is reliable, a relationship with distinct rules and structures.

Borderline Disorders

Another syndrome whose incidence has probably increased in the past few decades is that of the so-called *borderline disorders*. Since these disorders do not present a clearly definable syndrome, their increase is difficult to prove statistically. Frequently these patients show no clearly outlined symptoms, but only diffuse feelings of dissatisfaction and discontentment with themselves and the world; they experience their existence as having neither meaning nor aim; they suffer from an inner emptiness, lack of energy (adynamia), depressions, and violent fluctuations of self-esteem. Their self-concept is frequently flawed, which proves problematic, particularly in relationships. Owing to a lack of boundaries between themselves and those they relate to, they merge with the other person and are afraid of being manipulated at will by him or her. They are often not properly aware of whether what they feel, think, and speak is felt, thought, and spoken by themselves or by the other. In relationships they particularly protect themselves against ties. They frequently destroy a relationship as soon as it gets "too close for comfort." Thus they are inclined to keep out of any binding (and hence also therapeutic) relationship, and to retreat into themselves time and again.

The borderline-disorders syndrome is extremely complex. I do not intend to present a comprehensive view of it here. However, since not all readers will be familiar with this syndrome, I would like to present my thoughts on the issue by offering one patient as a concrete example.

A patient comes to our Psychotherapy Unit because of inexplicable states of panic, which occur primarily in crowds, particularly in restaurants and supermarkets. She experiences similar panic when she is alone in her apartment. In these situations she feels as if she were disintegrating. She can no longer feel parts of her body; it is as if her arms, hands, temples, and legs were numb; she often has the impression that she consists only of her torso, that her limbs have dropped off. She also has the feeling that her apartment is beginning to change, that the frames of her pictures are assuming different shapes, that objects seem to be swinging to and fro, and that she can no longer judge the distance between herself and her surroundings. She experiences all this without ever having taken drugs. She is seized with panic during these states, and suddenly no longer knows who and where she is.

These so-called depersonalization symptoms appeared in connection with the breakup of an eight-year-old love relationship. She had never experienced such symptoms before. She had, however, a tendency to cling too closely to her partner. After the relationship had broken up, she lost all support and direction. The psychiatrist she consulted advised her that in future she should look for support not in relationships, but only within herself. During therapy the psychiatrist behaved in a very reserved and inaccessible way, and in a professional manner refused to give her any directives, since he was of the opinion that she ought to find these herself. The patient tried hard to find support within herself by increasingly withdrawing into herself and by rejecting all relationships. She felt quite good in this isolation as such, because she experienced it as increasingly strenuous to pay attention to other people and to bear the frustration of not being fully understood by them. Nonetheless, these increasingly distressing depersonalization symptoms had not occurred before therapy was started.

In our Psychotherapy Unit we treat many such borderline patients. In the course of many years of work, we have worked out a concept that accords with the experiences of other university hospitals, and that has proved a success with these patients. The unit is run according to a clear daily schedule, which is binding. Morning is the time not only for individual therapy but also for group activities, in which all unit members participate. In the afternoon the patients leave the unit in order to work in their jobs. The distinct structure of life in the unit favors the patients' discovery of their own structures. Many patients with disorders similar to those just mentioned rediscover themselves in the conflict with these fixed structures of life in the unit. It is not our concern whether the patients like to observe the structures; our concern is simply that they *do* observe them. Whenever they defend themselves against the structures, we analyze this problem with them; and while we do not threaten them with dismissal if they do not obey the rules, we ensure they know that as soon as they transgress again, there will be another conflict and more friction.

This therapeutic attitude has also been developed in practice. Originally we attempted to follow the general trend and to treat patients in as antiauthoritarian a manner as possible; we appealed to them to organize, and be responsible for, their own daily schedules; we tried to further their "autonomy" by giving them freedom. This procedure proved unsuitable, however. Here, too, it was the patients who provoked in us the therapeutic attitude that proved beneficial, although patients frequently fight it at the beginning, and although it does not earn us any sympathy at first.

Relationship-Rejecting and Relationship-Creating Neuroses

It would appear, however, that not *all* psychological disorders are on the increase nowadays. Apparently some are at present decreasing, among them especially hysterical neuroses and compulsive neuroses, probably also phobic neuroses, and particularly cardiac neuroses. Previously these constituted a major proportion of the disorders we treated in patients. Nowadays they have become rather rare. If we now attempt to find a common denominator between addiction, anorexia, and borderline disorders on the one hand, and hysterical, phobic, and cardiac neuroses on the other, we can say that the former are *relationship-rejecting*, the latter *relationship-creating*, neuroses.

Hysterical symptoms such as paralysis and stupors, as well as hysterical demonstrative behavior, intensify the attention and care given by the social environment and therefore ensure that the patient is looked after more closely. Phobic neuroses, particularly agoraphobia, have a very similar effect: often the disorder becomes so acute that the patient can no longer be left alone for a single minute, and can leave his or her apartment only in the company of a person important to him or her. It is well known that the symptoms of cardiac neuroses occur in a situation of imminent separation (Richter and Beckmann 1969). The complaints, often occurring like fits, usually vanish as soon as a doctor or some other health professional appears. Hysterical and phobic patients often tend to cling to therapists and caretakers, and must often be admonished by these to be more independent and more autonomous.

Things are quite different with addicts, anorexics, and borderline patients. They reject relationships, especially with therapists. Although they, too, provoke the attention of the environment, they do it as if they had no greater desire than to condemn their environment to utter impotence. Psychotherapists, the professional helpers, in particular are often rejected. The question that arises for the therapist is how to reach these patients at all, and how to win them over into a working alliance.

Whereas in relationship-creating neuroses the fear of loneliness predominates, in relationship-rejecting neuroses it is the fear of a relationship that is of prime importance. These patients avoid or reject every kind of tie, since they sense in it a form of exploitation and surrender. They prefer to have no relationship at all, rather than run the risk of abandonment, frustration, and injury. And yet these patients are not fundamentally different from those with relationship-creating symptom formations. It is rather as if their defense had been doubled. Basically they, too, profoundly long for reliable relationships, security, and a sense of belonging; but because relationships seem to be too dangerous to risk, they retreat into themselves, even to the point of self-destruction. For example, one of our patients reported that she kept waking up from the same dream, bathed in perspiration: "I'm pursued by people and can save myself by suddenly flying through the air. I am flying high above everybody so that no one can do me any harm anymore. And then I'm horrified because I realize that I can't return to the ground. I try again and again but I can't do it, until fear makes me wake up."

The retreat into the self serves as self-protection in an increasingly alienated environment. I believe that experiences from therapeutic practice can result in insights that can be understood by everyone, and that stimulate us to correct our course. I am, of course, aware of the great complexity of alienation in all spheres of our culture, with its compulsions and interactions. I also see, however, a way to contribute to the necessary course correction by modifying certain paradigms. It is a pity that today many "cures" are offered that really only create the evil they are supposed to combat.

CHAPTER 2

Levels of Self-Realization

D espite their diversity, the self-realization endeavors of the postwar period reveal a meaningful, graded development. The economic boom of the 1960s resulted in an increased distance from a preoccupation that had once been of prime importance: the safeguarding of existence. The compulsion to buy began to be questioned; people began to turn to qualitative rather than quantitative aspects of life. The awareness of the individual's comprehensive dependence on institutional compulsions became more highly developed. Weary of material affluence, people increasingly began to rediscover their untapped personal potential: their suppressed receptivity to experiences, self-responsibility, and creativity. There was a rebellion against all institutions, against the state, the universities, schools, the health service, the law, the church, but also against the predominance of the economy. If institutions were supposed to exist for the benefit of citizens and individuals, then people demanded that they should show more respect for, and accept the participation of, the individual.

At first it was a question of liberating the individual from compulsion and repression, and of concentrating personal powers on inner life, on personal development, on the access to his or her own way of experiencing things, on personal emotions and experiences; it was also a question of becoming able to decide things oneself and to assume responsibility for oneself. This phase of intense concentration on oneself was followed, at the end of the 1970s, by an opening toward the self in its cosmic implications. The individual partially surrendered his or her boundaries so as to perceive the self as part of the universe. For the continuation of this development, a third stage is now due: the concentration of our powers on the creation of our common world, of which every one of us is part but which is also part of each of us. If for demarcating self-realization the perception of ourselves was the focal point, if for transcending self-realization it was the extension of cosmic consciousness, then for the stage of ecological self-realization that imposes itself now, it is making our own powers and our own consciousness available in a process that transcends us temporally and spatially.

Each cultural change has ecological effects that exceed what was originally intended. In addition, each cultural change has side effects that at first are not sufficiently taken into consideration, and that must be dealt with in a phase of consolidation. In this chapter I would like to discuss such side effects of achieving and transcending self-realization, without, however, questioning their positive possibilities. Many of these undesired side effects call for correction, which could be made by means of the paradigm of ecological self-realization.

THE CONCEPT OF THE INDIVIDUAL

The self-realization endeavors of Western culture are not a phenomenon of the last few decades, but can be traced back far into occidental history. In the history of Western consciousness, it was in approximately 2000 B.C. that an increasing process of separation and distance between self and nature was taking place. For reasons still largely unclear, the Hebrew and Greek cultures were chiefly responsible for the beginning of this development. Christianity represented a further stage in the appreciation of the individual. In Christian thought, the individual human being can and must make a free decision for or against God. From this time on, religious faith is no longer identical with affiliation to a nation. Every human being is given the responsibility to decide, in his or her unique life, for or against faith, and will be judged according to his or her own personal conduct in that unique life.

The appeal to the individual to decide freely gained little acceptance during the Middle Ages, however. The Catholic Church developed into a global organism whose structure finds expression in the architecture of Gothic cathedrals. It is a large community of saints, a great teleological process whose hierarchic structure assigns a place to each individual. The individual's responsibility is limited; his or her personal failure and sinfulness are offset by the deeds of the saints, who mediate between God and the faithful. The world was experienced organically; people lived in small communities; individual needs were subordinated to community needs. It was the aim of medieval science to comprehend the meaning and the role of things within a world order willed by God, not to dominate them and to forecast their development. Scholars asked about the *meaning* of the various natural phenomena, and strove for an understanding of the natural order and for a life in harmony with this order. Science was pursued to the glory of God.

In the Renaissance of the fifteenth and sixteenth centuries, antiquity was rediscovered, and likewise its image of the world and of man reborn. The Reformation stood for a revolt against the centralism of the church, and ascribed the highest authority in all questions of faith and life to the Gospel, the word of God. The individual believer should encounter God directly, and should be answerable to God in the freedom of his or her conscience. The community of the saints, the church as a large organism of which the individual is one part, was destroyed, and its right to exist questioned. In contrast to the Middle Ages, the Renaissance emphasized the importance of life on this earth, proclaimed the universal development of personality, and showed a keen interest in the individual and in individual character. The new way of seeing oneself, and the self-awareness reinforced by this (humanism), manifested themselves in new forms of art and literature. In painting it was the spatiophysical, individual representation of humanity in perspective that became prominent.

The worldview changed radically in the sixteenth and seventeenth centuries. The idea of an organic, living, and spiritual universe was replaced by the image of the world as a machine. Ever since Copernicus had disproved the geocentric worldview of Ptolemy and the Bible, the Earth was no longer the center of the universe. Human beings were deprived of their proud position as the central figures of the Divine Creation. The human as a microcosm and the world as a macrocosm were no longer meaningfully related to each other. Scientific language had become a mathematical description of nature. Galileo demanded the restriction of research to the material properties of bodies, to figures, measures, and quantities. Other properties of objects, such as color, sound, taste, and smell, were disqualified as being subjective projections of the mind, which had to be excluded from the domain of scientific research. Personal experience was banned from the sphere of scientific research. Descartes wrote that "all science is certain, evident knowledge. We reject all knowledge which is merely probable and judge that only those things should be believed which are perfectly known and about which there can be no doubts" (Capra 1982, p. 42). Among the natural sciences, analytical and reductionist thinking spread, according to which all complex phenomena can be understood by being dismantled into their component parts. Much was gained from enlightened thinking as a basis of natural science and technology, but equally much was lost as a result of it, in the understanding of the human situation and of human relations with society and with nature.

The Enlightenment, which as an intellectual movement derived from the Renaissance, had its greatest influence in the seventeenth and eighteenth centuries and reached its socio-political peak in the American Declaration of Independence (1776) and in the French Revolution (1789). Human reason was elevated to the level of a guiding principle. The general validity of natural things superseded religious obligations. The various philosophical trends shared the common aim of "maturity" or of the "autonomy" of thinking. Philosophers expressed human confidence in a fundamentally good nature (Rousseau, Pestalozzi). In legal and political philosophy, in-alienable human rights to freedom, property, and equality were derived from a rational law of nature. The absolute sovereignty of the church was increasingly criticized; the idea gained acceptance that the state was based on a free agreement of citizens, and that its function was the protection of the individual's right and of his claim to free development. In the sphere of religion there was a partial relinquishment of revelation in favor of a rational religion, with a tendency to equate religiosity with morality.

INDIVIDUALISM

Is individualism an adequate basis for psychotherapy? In the context of this book I am concerned with the effects of Cartesian thought on Western understanding of the nature of interhuman relationships, partnerships, and human systems. Here, as in the natural sciences, the reductionist way of thinking prevailed. Knowledge was sought in an atomistic manner, by dismantling psychological facts into their smallest constituent parts, on the assumption that knowledge of the sum of the parts would equal knowledge of the whole. According to Descartes's "*Cogito, ergo sum*" ("I think, therefore I am"), the only thing of which a human being could be certain was the certainty of himself as a thinking entity. Since, according to positivism, only that should be believed about which there can be no doubt, the individual is logically the unit about whose existence there is certainty and from whom all scientific psychology must be deduced. The Cartesian distinction between mind and matter encouraged the idea of an isolated ego existing inside a body, the body itself being nothing other than a machine. Descartes said that in his thoughts he compared a sick human being and a badly made clock with his idea of a healthy human being and a well-made clock (Capra 1982). But Descartes not only discovered an unbridgeable opposition between mind and matter; he also heightened—without directly intending to—the opposition, essential to psychology, between subject (*res cogitans*) and environment (*res extensa*). Through *cogito, ergo sum*, the I becomes the point of departure from which everything else must initially be doubted. Thereafter, humans could no longer experience themselves as embedded in nature and society, as inwardly connected with what they perceived, but had to devalue this experience as purely subjective. The experience of the person as *part* of the world became transformed into an experience of the person confronted by his or her surroundings.

For describing relationships between people, Cartesian thought led us into a dead end from which there is no known way out, even now. Using an argument by analogy, Descartes spared himself the difficulty of formulating how people relate to each other. According to this argument, understanding the experience of other people is possible in the following steps. Initially I am merely certain of my self-awareness, my thinking, my ego. I experience my own movements of expression as imbued with self-awareness. Now I apprehend the very same movements of expression in other people. I can deduce from this that the other person, too, possesses self-awareness. With this, Descartes justifies a standpoint of extreme subjectivism, by ascribing real existence only to one's own ego and one's own mental states, whereas everything else exists only in the imagination or can be inferred by means of analogy (Böckenhoff 1970, pp. 35–37). As a solipsism (Latin *solus* = alone, *ipse* = self; thus, I myself alone), an epistemology was developed in the nineteenth century according to which the I alone contains perceptive consciousness, and all other "I"s as well as the entire "external world" are merely imagined by it. This philosophical movement thus tried hard to base the whole world on the experience of the individual. A fellow human being is seen as the "alter ego," another I, an I that is locked in the other's body just as my own is in mine. The dualism of subject and object resulted not only in a diminished experience of environment and nature but also in excessive subjectivism and individualism. As a result of Descartes, only the experience of the individual can be described as humanly valid experience; it becomes the measure of all things, the only "actual." Thus the German philosopher Edmund Husserl perceived, around 1910, that "initially only the sphere of individuality is originally given, from which all other subjectivities are excluded as foreign. The cogitum as a monad at first constitutes the other as an 'alter ego.' There is no real connection between the monad which I am, and the other. The other is a reality for me. The interior of the other, however, will never be accessible to me. We live side by side, like monads."

This extreme subjectivism is also reflected in the psychoanalysis of Sigmund Freud. His interest was directed at the inner life. External behavior, conduct, and works as such received little attention, except as projections of interior processes. Intrapsychic reality, the functioning of the spiritual apparatus, is regarded as the essential mental-spiritual reality. The environment, external reality, is significant only insofar as it serves to embody interior processes, and to represent them symbolically. Originally, an essential therapeutic objective consisted of a process of becoming aware. Unconscious ideas, particularly repressed sexual experiences and fantasies, are to be consciously admitted. Freud believed that a person is healthy if his or her ego is sufficiently strong to mediate in the conflicts between the id (the representatives of the drives), the superego and the ego-ideal (conscience), and the environment. Early psychoanalysis assumed that relationships with external objects would be self-regulating if a subject could first clarify his or her internal relationships to objects. In order to do that, however, subjects must first succeed in becoming independent and autonomous in the face of their environment, and in regulating their internal conflicts and their current situation themselves.

But why is this independence so difficult to achieve? Why do other persons in their lives regularly try to fight back against being excluded from the therapeutic development process? Maintaining that the family and friends only impede the patient's cure, most individual-centered forms of therapy develop a defensive, if not openly hostile, attitude toward them, particularly toward the family. The members of the family are predominantly represented as having bad qualities. This defensive attitude toward the family had already been displayed by Freud: he tried to keep family members out of his patients' therapeutic processes. Apart from father and mother, to whom it quite strikingly ascribed the same qualities time and again, psychoanalysis showed little concern for developing better comprehension of the current human environment. In recent decades, however, psychoanalysis has paid more attention to the social environment, and has referred to its autonomy-impeding qualities, such as exploitation, repression, and abuse of power.

Psychoanalysis continued to concentrate on the treatment of pathologically impaired autonomy development, but the 1960s saw a real mass movement of self-realization; this was in the wake of humanistic psychology, originating in the

United States. Americans such as Maslow, Goldstein, and Buehler, along with many others, substituted simple, easily comprehensible hypotheses and appeals for self-realization for the European tendency to reflect and to propound complex theories (particularly in existential philosophy) that, because of their highbrow literary language, were accessible to only a small circle of elitist insiders. The novel and decisive elements that allowed propagation of these new hypotheses were techniques that supplied interested parties with opportunities to work on self-realization, not merely in terms of book learning and theory, but by means of exercises and self-experience. Sensitivity training must be mentioned in this context, as well as Rogers's encounter groups, Perls's gestalt groups, and Lowen's body-centered bioenergetic exercises.

The course that self-realization has taken can be represented in terms of three stages, which correspond not only to the historical development of the last few decades but often also to an individual's personal development. The course proceeds from achieving self-realization to transcending self-realization to ecological self-realization.

ACHIEVING SELF-REALIZATION

Starting from therapeutic observations of patients, intensified by public communication and literary representation of self-observations, the self-realization movement of the sixties and seventies concentrated on the concept that we had erected a façade of social conventions that had to be demolished so that real emotion and the true self could reappear.

Telling the True Self from the False Self

Thus Carl R. Rogers, in his fundamental work, *On Becoming a Person* (1961, pp. 166–75), lists the following goals that a person must strive for in order "to be that self which one truly is":

Away from Façades
Away from "Oughts"
Away from Meeting Expectations
Away from Pleasing Others
Toward Self-Direction
Toward Being in Process
Toward Acceptance of Others
Toward Trust of Self

The goal is the dissolution of the "false self" (Winnicott 1965).

People became aware of the fact that from childhood they had not been loved for their own sakes, but for their ability to fulfill their parents' expectations. According to Alice Miller (1981), analysands therefore arrive at the question as to whether their parents' admiration for them as gifted children was meant for their good looks or their capabilities, or for themselves. They ask themselves what it would have been like if they had been naughty, ugly, irascible, jealous, lazy, dirty, or smelly. They come to the conclusion that "it was not really I that was loved but what I pretended to be. Have I been deprived of my childhood? Were my abilities simply abused?" The child develops a false self because he wants to be loved; he erects a façade with which he can attain recognition. The environment may regard the false self as the true, whereas the true self is considered false. The mother professes to have known her son longer and therefore also better than he has known himself, and thus to know better than he what he can feel, think, and want. A human being thus acquires the feeling that the true, inner self cannot be made actual, and that the externally presented self is false (Laing 1960, 1961). The false self serves to protect and conceal the true self (Winnicott 1965). This self is false because it represents itself as particularly well adjusted, pleasant, kind, efficient, and altruistic. This altruism, however, has nothing to do with true love and care, but instead results from the fear of not being accepted, of making a bad impression, of being alone, or of assuming any responsibility.

In the course of the development of the true self, more individuality, genuineness, self-assurance, and self-determination is aimed for, more wholeness of personality. The self is apprehended as the essential core, as a person's original basis and source, as an autonomously controlled process inside the psyche. Nobody can say what his or her own self is. Everybody can only experience it. In order to encourage this experience, a suitable method is looked for outside the framework of therapy, in groups assembled ad hoc, whose members detach themselves from the reality of their own development and self-perception through an exchange of experiences. The feedback of the group members' emotions and impressions plays an important part. The ways toward one's self, toward the experience of one's own essential core, are also sought in creative work, in the observation of one's own dreams, in meditation, and in listening to the messages of the body. The body is often deemed to be a divine voice; it is assumed that the body cannot tell lies, that it will instruct us to live according to the nature of the self. In many circles, *self-realization became the actual goal and purpose of life.* The self is heard like an inner voice: it provides us with values and norms; it guides us internally and gives us support. The salvation and development of the self looked more and more like a religious path.

Whatever seemed to limit and threaten the self had to be destroyed. The true self cannot be developed as long as a person is controlled from outside (Maslow 1968)—that is, depends on others for his or her self-definition. Often the first step toward achieving self-realization consists in a defiant attitude of refusal. Thus Maslow (1968, p. 168) postulates that an authentic human is defined by his or her very own intrapsychic laws, which are independent of the environment: "The danger that I see is the resurgence . . . of the old identification of psychological health with adjustment, adjustment to reality, adjustment to society, adjustment to other people. That is, the authentic or healthy person may be defined not in his own right, not in his autonomy, not by his own intrapsychic and nonenvironmental laws, not as different from the environment, independent of it or opposed to it, but rather in environment-centered terms." It is necessary to get away from expectations, from the heteronomy of one's own self; it is necessary to refuse radically to fulfill role expectations or comply with institutional obligations.

What Total Independence May Mean

From a cultural point of view, the claim to authentic experience, access to one's own needs and emotions and their articulation, and the appeal for autonomy and independence were certainly an important step toward the differentiation of the individual. The women's movement in particular has strongly identified itself with the idea of self-realization. Many women readers may therefore take exception when, in the following, I subject certain side effects of these self-realization endeavors to scrutiny. I hope, however, that it will become clear that I do not advocate a return to the old social forms, in which women had to give themselves up and lower their expectations in men's favor; rather, it is precisely progress into the next phase of development that I postulate. I regard the phase of establishing personal boundaries and refusing unreasonable demands as a frequently necessary transition stage. Developments often pass through intermediate stages that are not themselves the goal of the process.

I support every woman's right to self-responsibility and independence, to be free to listen to herself, to apprehend herself, and to articulate her own concerns; and every man's as well. I merely have misgivings when radical self-assertion and defiant setting of boundaries are supposed to be the alternative to adaptation and self-denial. Self-assertion and refusal are psychologically equivalent to adaptation and self-denial, being merely their opposites. They have in common the theme of dependence, which for self-denial and adaptation is sustained by the fear of loneliness, whereas for self-assertion and refusal the same fear is covered up.

How does the idea of self-realization affect human communities? In the positive sense, it stimulates increased self-responsibility, more genuine participation, and a more perceptible personal commitment. The self-realization movement has always emphasized that its cause had nothing to do with egoism. A fully realized individual is also capable of love and relationships. At least for a while, however, strong self-centeredness and focusing on self-development can result in serious restrictions of social perception, which has a destructive effect on human communities. Frequently, too little attention is paid to what the consequences are if a man in a self-realization workshop, detached from the reality of his daily relational systems, feels encouraged to enforce his own claims, to separate himself from his environment, and to achieve independence. In a human system, as in every other ecological system, the modification of one element necessarily causes a modification of all other elements.

If a man's attitudes have been changed in a workshop, these changes are no longer his personal, private affair when he returns to family or partnership. Rather, these changes regularly trigger off feedback mechanisms in the partner, the purpose of which is to neutralize the disturbance in the homeostasis (equilibrium) of the system. The partner as a part of the relational system is usually not infected by the returnee's enthusiasm, but tries to eliminate, reduce, or absorb the disturbing stimulus. Not infrequently the returnee finds himself in the dumps, goes through an aggressive phase, or, for the sake of peace, accepts the same kind of life that he had before. Sometimes the returnees attempt to organize themselves as a group, and to continue to confirm each other in their efforts to hold their own and assert themselves at home.

Uncoached by a trainer, the person who remained at

home spontaneously tends to do the wrong thing. She tries to make fun of the changes in the returnee, or to insist on her customary rights, or to be defiant, to threaten, or even to become violent. Whatever she does to preserve the previous system is bound to be wrong. Sometimes it seems as if the returnee needs these destructive reactions by the partner in order to define and justify himself in his self-assertion. Not infrequently, the result is the dissolution of the relationship, after the person who remained at home has exhibited unreasonable reactions.

Even with only a little knowledge of ecological systems, we can see that within a relational system an abrupt, unilateral change favors destructiveness, particularly if the feedback mechanisms that regulate the relational system are prevented from working by negativity and detachment. The same goals could often be constructively achieved if, with more patience and consideration, the partner could be won over to co-evolution, so that both could change the relational system together. Since the returnee, though willing to change, is often struggling with his own fears and insecurities, he may be overtaxed when, in his new beginning, he is also supposed to consider the effects on his partner. The problem could be overcome more easily, however, if the workshop leaders paid more attention to it.

Assuming We Are Good

What might happen if we assume we are naturally healthy and good? One of the most important concerns of humanistic psychology was to detach itself from the psychoanalytical tendency to pathologize humanity, and instead to regard humans as basically healthy and positive. Thus A. H. Maslow (1968, p. 46) reproaches the Freudians for "seeing everything through brown-colored glasses." Carl Rogers (1961) perceives the innermost core of human nature as positive, fundamentally social, forward-looking, and realistic. Christian tradition spread the basic view that man was essentially sinful.

Freud and his disciples had submitted arguments in the sphere of psychology that the id consisted primarily of instincts that, if they found expression, would result in incest, homicide, and other crimes. Rogers (1961) is profoundly convinced that hostility and other antisocial emotions are a consequence of a deeper urge toward love, security, and a sense of belonging. The optimistic and affirmative way in which Rogers encounters his clients and his readers has something liberating about it, particularly for us Europeans, who tend toward pessimism and brooding: we heave a sigh of relief and learn to derive pleasure from ourselves.

And yet: where has all the evil gone? Has it dissolved into nothing? No, it cannot do that. There has been criticism of Rogers's forced optimism from among his own ranks of humanistic psychologists. Rollo May (1982), in particular, reproaches Rogers in an open letter for repressing the demonic and evil. It was inevitable for humans to express their diabolical possibilities, their greed for power, revenge, anger, and rage. Rogers said that it was cultural influences that constituted the main factor in our diabolical behavior. Thus culture becomes a bearer of evil. But who makes up culture if not we ourselves? Culture produces our selves, and our selves produce culture. Rogers did not want to recognize the diabolical demon. If we merely project the diabolical onto culture, then it becomes the failure of culture, not our own failure. Therapy can easily fail if client-centered therapists cannot deal with their clients' negative and aggressive emotions, or cannot even create an atmosphere in which their clients can voice such emotions, since a confrontation between therapist and patient is thereby made impossible. Genuine maturation, however, presupposes an emancipation process in therapy that frequently runs parallel to an aggressive argument.

The assumption that their selves are good, peace loving, positive, and healthy, if only the environment does not frustrate them and thus render them egocentric, evil, aggressive, and destructive, can be particularly helpful for those who have a lasting tendency toward destructive self-accusations. The same assumption can also provide therapists confronted with aggressive, destructive, and reserved patients with the certainty that their patients' core is positive, and that their negative attitude is merely a protection against frustration and injury. The danger of this assumption, however, lies in the tendency to project evil exclusively onto the outside, onto the environment, onto others.

In contrast to this, the term *self* as used by Jung seems to me to be substantially more extensive, more complex, and closer to reality. According to Jung, the self consists not only of its conscious but also, and in particular, of its unconscious aspects, of the dark sides of human nature, of the Shadow. Darkness is as much a part of the self as light. As the dark becomes conscious, more of the self is actualized, and more of the Shadow integrated. Jungian psychology does not offer a general solution to the problem of evil. It considers possible neither an ultimate explanation of the origin of evil, nor its extermination. The power of evil is considered more comprehensive than can be imagined when the conscious alone is taken into account. Evil that remains unconscious is no less dangerous than evil carried out consciously. Therefore Jungian psychology is skeptical of the "Christian" idea that evil can simply be overcome by good. In addition, the distinction between good and evil is often extremely difficult, especially when the motives and effects of a behavior remain unconscious. Thus, according to H. Barz (1981, p. 73), good carried out consciously may cause evil in the unconscious (perhaps even in the unconscious of another person). If we intend to take seriously the bonds linking everyone through the collective unconscious, we will not blame only those who are unconsciously or powerlessly at the mercy of evil for the execution of evil. Rather, we will try to bear, consciously, our own share of evil through the integration of the Shadow. Jung (1960a, vol. 12, p. 46) is convinced that "we may miss not only happiness but also our decisive guilt, without which a person cannot attain wholeness." Thus Jung perceives the great danger that arises when a man projects evil onto persons to whom everything bad can be ascribed, so that he himself remains "clean." Jung particularly sees the danger of missing the opportunity for comprehensive self-realization owing to a lack of integration of the Shadow.

Effects on Our Families

Why is it so hard to see how self-realization endeavors affect our families? The problem of integrating self-realization into interhuman processes exists above all in marriage and family. Human relational systems are ecological systems that consist of self-regulatory circles. Systems can change their organizational forms. Their processing and transformation capacity, however, has limits. In ecological systems no part can change unless all other parts change in their relationships toward one another. If self-realization depends on unbounded growth by the individual, then the regulation and transformation capacities of human ecosystems will soon be overtaxed.

As Marilyn Ferguson says (1980, p. 391): "Whatever the cost in personal relationships, we discover that our highest responsibility, finally, unavoidably, is the stewardship of our potential—being all we can be." Such statements can easily be understood as invitations to inconsiderate striving for maximal personal development.

Today, great environmental consciousness has been developed in other arenas. Human beings can ruthlessly win through against nature, exploit it, and defeat it, but after a while it becomes evident that the victors are as vanquished as the defeated. We may destroy ecological systems, but in doing so we destroy ourselves. In our relationship with nature, we have become aware that we must treat its systemic self-regulation with the highest respect, an attitude the Native Americans used as a guiding principle for their way of life more thoroughly than any other culture has done. In complete contrast to this, we have remained totally unable to recognize similar ecological systems in human relationships, or to understand that we must exercise care, respect, and circumspection whenever we attempt to interfere with them.

The weak point of many a self-realization endeavor is in the creation of long-term relationships. In his plain and honest manner, Rogers (1980, pp. 85–86) himself wrote openly about such difficulties in his relationship with his wife. In his books he repeatedly remarks on his rebellion against any form of control and obligation, on his wife's jealousy, and on her being hurt. When he was about eighty years old he wrote about his wife, Helen, who had been suffering from cancer for five years.

> She is making remarkable progress in fighting her way back, often by sheer force of will, to a more normal life, built around her own purposes. But it has not been easy. She first had to choose whether she wanted to live, whether there was any purpose in living. Then I have baffled and hurt her by the fact of my own independent life. When she was so ill, I felt heavily burdened by our close togetherness, heightened by her need for care. So I determined, for my own survival, to live a life of my own. She is often deeply hurt by this, and by the changing of my values. On her side, she is giving up the old model of being the supportive wife. This change brings her in touch with her anger at me and at society for giving her that socially approved role. On my part, I am angered at any move that would put us back in the old complete togetherness; I stubbornly resist anything that seems like control.

In their relationship with nature, people are beginning to pay attention to the types of interference by which ecological systems are being destroyed. This happens when the natural self-regulatory circles are broken. Human ecosystems, however, are also destroyed when their natural regulatory circuits are broken. The recognition of self-regulatory circles is tantamount to the recognition of the partners' interdependence. My own behavior and that of my partner mutually condition each other. Within a partnership I cannot change my behavior independently of the partner. A unilateral refusal to cooperate, or the claim to be permitted to act independently of the partner, in a partnership destroys the natural self-regulatory circles, and encourages the destructive behavior in the partner by means of which he or she tries to reestablish some balance in the relationship. Such behavior is often characterized by claims of ownership and the effort to remain in control. In this manner he or she will undermine the partner's self-esteem and steer the common process in a negative direction.

Mutual Exploitation Is Not True Partnership

A partnership based on the satisfaction of needs ends in mutual exploitation. An aspiration often expressed in the context of achieving self-realization is the wish to renounce the expectations of the environment, and to apprehend and meet one's own needs. For many people this is an important step in their development. It may result in conflicts, however, which can turn into an insoluble dilemma in the relationship with a partner.

I may decide to concentrate exclusively on my own needs, but then realize that I cannot satisfy my needs without my fellow human beings. If I can satisfy my needs only with my fellow human beings, then I must by analogy assume that the same is true for them. How, though, can I avoid being turned into a mere object being used to satisfy others' needs? I see all relationships in terms of exploitation, and am thus caught in a dead end with no escape.

A patient, after many years of marriage during which she lived only for her husband and family, fell prey to a depressive crisis as her children left home. With her analyst's support, she now wanted to assert herself with regard to her husband, and live so as to meet her own needs. In their sexual relations, however, this maneuvered her into an insoluble dilemma. She desired attentive and tender foreplay, in which the husband was perfectly ready to participate. Her husband's visible sexual arousal gave her the feeling of being desirable. Per se, this was an important intensifier of her sexual stimulation. But suddenly it would strike her: "There, he only wants to use me to satisfy his sexual needs. I'm only his sexual object." She then rejected him, while feeling frustrated herself. She wanted her husband to desire her without desiring her. Eventually he reacted with partial impotence.

Particularly in eroticism, where intense needs are operative, self-centered perspectives on both sides may regrettably result in exploitation. But this is also true in other relationships: the helper exploits the helpless, the parents the child, the teacher his or her pupils, the lecturer his or her audience.

No long-term or love relationship can be based on the satisfaction of needs. The continual weighing-up of who satisfies whose needs more at what time, of who is more exploited and suppressed by whom, of who must give up more for whom, and of who must adapt more to whom becomes too troublesome in the end.

If in a relationship our only function is to satisfy the narcissistic needs of the other, we feel abused. As a being-in-need—according to Alice Holzhey's criticism (1983)—I am ultimately interested only in myself. I interpret the world as a totality of objects, and take interest in something only because it promises to satisfy one of my needs. Each behavior toward something thus basically becomes a relationship with myself. I depend on the world to satisfy my needs. Within the framework of the need principle, interest is interest in oneself; development of an interest in an object for its own sake is inconceivable.

In this sense, work, for instance, is not valuable as a task, as devotion to something that is valuable in itself, but only inasmuch as it satisfies my needs as a working person. The meaning of work is reduced to the satisfaction of the need for recognition and self-realization.

A nurse from the general ward applied for a job in our Psychotherapy Unit. In the course of the interview I asked her about her motivation. She replied: "I would like to experience myself dealing with emotionally suffering people." Working with us would primarily have furthered her self-development, by enabling her to experience herself in the company of patients, joining the therapeutic team and exchanging ideas with colleagues.

The same applies to interpersonal relationships if, in loving another person, my main concern is to satisfy my own need to be loved. I would be assuming that what the other person means to me depends only on me, not on the other person. The degree and duration of the commitment to a relationship are assumed to depend on how my needs are satisfied by it. A relationship that is no longer satisfactory would have to be dissolved: it would appear pointless to remain in a situation that no longer satisfies my needs.

The predominance of the need principle has caused the rapid destruction of nature. Nowadays many people are filled with fear, sorrow, and rage in the face of this destruction. But what is it they are sorrowful and enraged about? The fact that natural resources are running short? Or the fact that nature has been relegated to being a mere resource for the satisfaction of human needs? The fight for the preservation of unspoiled landscapes, for the rescue of endangered plants and animals, derives from the fear that we may lose a relationship with nature in which we experience nature as being intact, even virginal. A peculiar need seems to appear here, one that does not fit the usual pattern of the satisfaction of needs: the need for a nature that exists not "for us" but "for itself," not as a disposable object, but as something that is unavailable (Holzhey 1983).

If we transpose the growing environmental consciousness

onto the human environment and its systems, we can see
how destructive it is to regard a partner as merely a resource
to satisfy our own needs. The "love object" does not exist
"for itself," but offers itself to the subject for possible use.
On the other hand, according to Holzhey (1983), the subject
can counter the power of the objects and the danger of self-
dissolution only by actually possessing those objects. From
this perspective the (now generally deplored) inability to tolerate frustration in relationships can be understood. The subject will find it intolerable if the desired person is not freely
available. Whenever a desired object refuses to be available,
the subject feels threatened and experiences himself as powerless. In order to escape emotional fear and impotence, he
often responds with excessive rage. Whatever limits the possession of objects must be classified as "other," as "unavailable," and must be destroyed (Holzhey 1983).

Thinking in terms of needs turns people into consumer
goods; partners become interchangeable. The illusion is created that we have a right to the satisfaction of our needs, and
that we have a right to react lovingly if our needs are satisfied,
but furiously and aggressively if they are frustrated. In the
ecological sphere this illusion has already been proved utterly
inappropriate. Increasing opportunities to satisfy our needs
create even greater needs and even less willingness to mod-
erate our claims. Insofar as dyads are seen in terms of needs,
our behavior in them will not differ from our behavior in
the material sphere.

The radical claim to have our needs satisfied, and to be
liberated from all ties, dependence, human expectations, and
obligations, has maneuvered many people into, of all things,
an increased (because addictive) dependence on others who
satisfy their needs. But this kind of relationship is not a positive process. It is filled with mistrust and despair. Many feel
caught in an insoluble dilemma: how can I enter into a relationship without being obliged to meet my partner's expectations? Is there not a danger that my partner's needs will

be satisfied more than mine are, and that I am therefore exploited? If I need to satisfy others' needs, then how can I protect myself from exploitation? And if I need to communicate with my partner, then how should I handle the situation if my partner apprehends me only from his or her point of view, and tends to create a fixed image of me that fences me in or distorts me? (Max Frisch has dealt critically with this problem in all his books and plays.)

Being Satisfied or Exploited or Objective

According to Maslow (1968) every individual has basic needs that can be satisfied only by other individuals—needs such as security, a sense of belonging, love, esteem, recognition, admiration, and so on. But our need to have these needs satisfied makes us very dependent on the environment. A man in this position of dependence can certainly not be said to be the master of his fate and the captain of his soul. Rather, he would have to be described as *heteronomous* and dependent on the approval, affection, and goodwill of others. "In contrast," Maslow says (1968, p. 32), "the self-actualizing individual, by definition gratified in his basic needs, is far less dependent, far less beholden, far more autonomous." Growth-motivated people do not even remotely need other people; rather, they are obstructed by others.

As a solution to the dilemma between the claim to interpersonal satisfaction of needs and fear of dependence, Maslow recommends a completely "need-disinterested or desireless perception" of other human beings. The need for love Maslow (1968, p. 39) describes as a "deficit need. It is a hole which has to be filled, an emptiness into which love is poured." A healthy individual, however, does not suffer from such a need, and does not need love in this sense. He or she develops a need-free love.

Such statements must be considered in terms of how they affect the life of communities and interpersonal relationships. The only alternative posited is that between independence and self-determination on the one hand, and dependence and heteronomy on the other. In contrast to this, I ask: are we not existentially involved in interpersonal relationships and therefore in interdependence? Must interdependence be regarded as so negative? After all, we are not passively at the mercy of our environment but can influence it actively.

Who is not overtaxed by the demand to live independently of love, affection, and human recognition, and to satisfy basic needs without needing, or being needed by, anyone? There are differences, however, in the manner in which people obtain the love, recognition, and affection they need. Self-confident, vigorous, and healthy people can remain relatively independent in some relationships, or they can postpone the satisfaction of their affectional needs. They succeed in this not so much because of an inner ability to regulate themselves, but rather because of compensating support they have in other relationships. This secure backing enhances their self-confidence and their ability to withstand stress. Neurotic and immature persons, on the other hand, are continually afraid of being dropped, rejected, or hurt; this attitude tends to make them appear greedy and blackmailing, or else arrogant and reserved, in an unadapted manner. This façade in turn provokes those around them to hurt, reject, and frustrate them, which is what they were afraid of in the first place. In my opinion, however, we each depend on our fellow human beings' affection, because this is an existential dimension of human life.

TRANSCENDING SELF-REALIZATION

We cancel loneliness by transcending it. Detachment from inter-human relationships, obligations, and dependences brings not only freedom and autonomy but frequently also loneliness, even isolation. In Europe, the existential philosophers underlined the individual's extreme loneliness. Sartre, in *L'etre*

et le néant, said, "Man is condemned to himself"; he is condemned to freedom. This sense of loneliness and of the absurdity of life, which was borne with heroism and at times
also with self-pity, did not fit the American paradigm of
optimism, of the right to happiness, of the solvability of all
existential problems. Yet how can we retain our laboriously
conquered autonomy without simultaneously having to suffer from isolation and a sense of absurdity?

One solution can be found in the transcendence of the
self. Jung's idea of self-development (individuation), in particular, aroused considerable attention in the United States
of the 1970s. It was Jung who introduced the term *self* into
analytical psychology. For him, self differs from the ego;
indeed, they represent opposites. The ego is empirically discovered to be a "consciousness complex"; it comprises all
that I know about myself and regard as belonging to me, all
that I can discover about myself without any great difficulties.
The self, however, is much more comprehensive and holistic
than the conscious ego. It signifies the entire personality,
consisting of both conscious and unconscious contents, and
thus has its basis in transcendental being. Jung (1960a, vol.
6, p. 513) also speaks of a superordinate personality or a
superordinate whole, which is represented in symbols such
as the mandala, the circle, the square, the quartered circle,
and the cross. According to Jung, the person relating to the
transcendental center will experience a process of individuation and a development toward unity and wholeness, *no longer
being isolated, but becoming one*. Only subjective consciousness
is isolated; if this becomes related to its center, however, it
is integrated in the Whole. The center of the self is the center
of the universe. The self is a psychological construct that is
meant to express a being that we cannot recognize within us,
that we cannot comprehend as such because it is beyond
human understanding. According to Jung, it could equally
well be described as "the God in us." Thus God is not the

Intangible, the Completely Other; God, too, is experienced in the experience of the self. Jung emphasizes that if the process of individuation is confused with the ego's becoming aware of itself, or the ego equated with the self, then individuation is turned into mere egocentrism and autoeroticism. The self includes not just the ego but also our fellow human beings and the whole world.

A large part of the self is therefore unconscious, and ultimately based in the transcendental, the cosmic, and the religious. This view corresponds to experiences that people on a spiritual quest had in the United States and in Europe in the 1970s. Meditation, as well as drugs, provided experiences in consciousness expansion and in the transcendence of the self into the cosmos. If the humanistic psychology of the sixties and early seventies taught people to utter the two magic words *I* and *no*, two new terms were added in the late seventies: *whole* and *trans*. The previously one-sided concentration on the realization of one's own personality was now supplemented by holistic, cosmic, and universal perspectives, by transcendental meditation, by transpersonal psychology, by transcultural experiences, and so on. Experiments were conducted with various techniques, such as the isolation tank or hyperventilation, in order to expand human consciousness, to advance into so-far-unknown internal spaces of the psyche, and to have occult and mystical experiences.

John Lilly (1972, p. 23), for instance, writes about his LSD experiences:

> I am in a large empty place with nothing in any direction except light. There is a golden light permeating the whole space everywhere in all directions, out to infinity. I am a single point of consciousness, of feeling, of knowledge. I know that I am. That is all. It is a very peaceful, awesome, and reverential space that I am in. I have no body. I have no need for a body. There is no body. I am just I. Complete with love, warmth, and radiance.

The samadhi tank developed by Lilly is a graphic symbol of the new trends of the 1970s: completely shielded from the outside world, from aural stimuli, from visual stimuli, but also in a state of incorporeality produced by weightlessness in the salt water, a person can experience his own "central core."

Lilly writes (1972, p. 46),

In the first tank experiment with LSD, the first space I moved into was completely black, completely silent, empty space without a body. The blackness stretched out to infinity in all directions. The silence extended out to infinity in all directions, and _I remained centered at a single point of consciousness and of feeling_. There was literally nothing in the universe but my center, myself, and the blackness and the deep silence. In a shorthand way, I called this "the absolute zero point." This became a reference point to which I could return in case things got too chaotic or too stimulating in other spaces. This was _the central core of me_, my essence in a universe with no stars, no galaxies, no entities, no people, no other intelligences. [My italics.]

Lilly's concern, and that of others, too, is the liberation of ourselves from the prison we ourselves have erected, and the transcending of the restrictive limits of consciousness, for "there are no limits in the sphere of the spirit." There is mention of states of perfect consciousness, of highest stages of consciousness, of correspondence between consciousness and the universal spirit.

Transcending All Limitations

In passing from achieving to transcending self-realization, the following has changed: whereas the self-defining self wished to define its boundaries, the transcending self stands for the dissolution of all limitations; whereas the self-defining self wants to be regarded as unique, and different from its environment, the transcending self wants to be experienced as a part of universal consciousness.

Transcending self-realization would like to abolish all temporal, spatial, and physical limitations of self. This results in transcendental experiences in time: in prenatal experiences, but also in the abolition of limitation through death. Whereas the existentialists still spoke of "being until death," it is now assumed that physical death will not terminate consciousness. Thus a kind of religiosity is being revived, which, however, is closer to Buddhism than to Christianity, since it pursues the idea of the inner God, of the God in oneself, and does not want to regard God as a personal opposite. There is renewed interest in extrasensory perception, parapsychology, telepathy, precognition, telekinetics, spiritual experiences, and so on. There is also a renaissance of astrology as an expression of the correspondences between self and the stars. In the Enlightenment, particularly owing to Copernicus's correction of the geocentric concept, astrology had lost its significance.

The new movement expresses an aspiration toward re-unification with all life, with the cosmos as a whole, with mankind as a planetary family. There is a new interest in ethnology, in so-called primitive cultures, in old wisdom, in ritual, and particularly in mystic traditions. In this view, the self is not limitable but infinite. It can be narrower or wider only in its consciousness. It is a stream of infinite consciousness, which formulates itself variously in each self. The teachings of Buddhism, particularly of the Zen school, of Taoism, and of Sufism, have become highly influential in the West.

Transcending the Self in Buddhism

In my view it is Lama Govinda who most lucidly describes what can be gained from the perspective of the transcending self (Govinda 1976). Govinda is of German extraction. Before he wrote down his life's work in 1977, Govinda devoted himself to more than sixty years of meditation, largely in Sri

Lanka and Tibet. He communicates the Buddhist path in a manner that we Westerners can comprehend. The Tantric Buddhist does not believe that the world exists independently of himself, that a subject is divided from the object, or that the self is set against a nonself. The internal and external worlds are warp and weft of the same fabric, in which the threads of all forces and of all events are interwoven in an inseparable network, a network of infinite mutual relationships.

Every form of life and every form of consciousness is contingent, and depends on the totality of everything that has ever existed. The more we are aware of this infinite interdependence, the freer we become, for we liberate ourselves from the most fatal of all illusions, the illusion of a permanent, separate self. As long as we persist in the illusion of a divided and separated self, we oppose ourselves to the nature of life. If we see the world from the perspective of our limited and small self, of our wishes, desires, and needs, then we make it into a prison that separates us from our fellow men and from the sources of true life.

Whatever is set against the continual transformation of all forms and of all consciousness condemns itself to death. Self and death share the characteristic of being delimited. However, if we accept the fact that life is something contingent, there will be no limitations, provided that we acknowledge the all-embracing totality of such a contingency through reciprocal relationships. This teaches us modesty as a result of our mutual dependence, but it also opens our eyes to the universality of our true nature. By overcoming our egos, we do not lose our selves, but we enrich and extend our personalities, which in this way become the expressions of a greater and more universal life. We then learn to apprehend ourselves as the conscious focus of an infinite universe. We are like the lens that focuses the universal forces, making the sun appear in an image the size of a dot.

The universal needs the individual in order to realize itself.

As we become conscious of our universality, the universe is made conscious in us.

That is a summary of some of Govinda's essential ideas. Meditation on these thoughts leads to a more profound connection with all living and animated beings, and relativizes the importance of our own separate existence and of our being as a self. We feel related to our environment and to our contemporaries as the vehicle of a universal consciousness that is crystallized and articulated in us. This does not reduce the claim to self-responsibility and self-recognition, but augments it; yet it frees us from the separating and mortal aspects of a dividing self-comprehension. It relates us to a superordinate Whole, a universal spirit that connects us all and works in all of us.

Govinda, on the other hand, sharply criticizes those in the West who—now succumbing to the other extreme—effusively and irrationally seek universal relatedness by removing everything individual. Thus he criticizes those for whom the removal of individual boundaries is an escape from individuation, or who think that drugs and other forms of intoxication could effect an extension of consciousness while bypassing conscious cognition. Attaining at-one-ness does not mean losing our individuality. It does not abolish the individual's identity, but robs it of its absoluteness, and modifies it into a higher relativity. The recognition of universal relatedness conveys to the individual the meaning of his or her existence. In Buddhism individuality and universality are not mutually exclusive qualities, but two complementary sides of reality that become one in the experience of enlightenment.

True Self-Realization Is Universal Realization

According to Capra (1982, pp. 285, 291), "the new vision of reality . . . is based on awareness of the essential interrelatedness and interdependence of all phenomena—physical, biological, psychological, social, and cultural. . . . we are in-

separable parts of the cosmos in which we are embedded."
If I am part of the universe, then there cannot be any external
influences. It is the cosmos as a whole that is evolving. The
same spirit works in matter, in plants, in animals, and in
myself. The cosmos is a gigantic organism in which everything is reigned over by the same spirit. There are no unbridgeable differences between matter and energy, and
between energy and spirit. They are only different manifestations of the whole (Capra 1982). Now, if we presume that
we alone have spirit and think of only our own survival, then
we will inevitably destroy our environment and thus also
ourselves, as we must now learn from bitter experience. From
the point of view of systems theory, there are no autonomous
entities, only organizational patterns that an organism has
assumed in interactions with its environment.

Our environment is neither static nor passive, but a system capable of life. The main interest is therefore shifted from
the evolution of an organism to the coevolution of organism
and environment (Capra 1982, chap. 10). If I accept that spirit
is immanent not only in man but equally in all other manifestations of the cosmos, if I even accept that there are higher
spiritual manifestations of which our spirit merely represents
a subsystem (Bateson 1972), then my attitude toward my
natural surroundings will be fundamentally changed. If, however, we ascribe spiritual phenomena to ourselves alone, then
the environment will appear to be without spirit, and we will
feel that we have the mission to exploit it.

Knowing that we are an inseparable part of the cosmos
will fundamentally change our relationship with the environment, and will reinforce the environmentalist movement.
The idea of protecting the environment, however, should no
longer be restricted to our relationship with natural ecological
systems, animals, plants, earth, water, and air, but should be
extended to human ecological systems, such as family, community, state, and society, which, after all, are basically much
closer to people. If we observe how our economy, our "Third

World aid," and our tourism destroy the human ecological systems in the Third World, then we recognize the same erroneous attitudes as in the exploitation of nature. The consequences for the cultural ecosystems of those peoples are hardly less cataclysmic; yet so far they have been taken less seriously. The self-destruction, too, of our own human ecological systems, particularly of marriages, by self-centered paradigms is registered only statistically, in terms of the divorce rate.

In recent decades people have had to relinquish the idea that there are independent constituent parts of matter, because of findings in subatomic physics. Equally, the idea of independent organisms has been jettisoned in biology. Why, then, should things be different for psychological processes in human beings? Living organisms as open systems keep themselves alive and functioning by interacting with their environment. The whole biosphere—our planetary ecosystem —is a dynamic and integrated texture of living and nonliving forms (Capra 1982, chap. 9). Should things be different for the human psyche? Is the consciousness of individuals not equally part of a dynamic and integrated network of the consciousness of others and of all people? Up to the present day, this texture has not been studied or described in any significant depth.

Knowledge of the network of human consciousness could cause us to reach the same conclusion that we have reached about people's relationship with nature: *if we strive for self-realization or evolution without allowing for the coevolution of our psychological-spiritual environment, we damage our surroundings.*

How Transcending Self-Realization May Affect Partnerships

Humanistic psychology has recently come to denounce the "ego trip." Efforts to establish one's own boundaries by means of self-realization are again being reevaluated. There is no mention yet, however, of the need for increased interhuman relatedness; so far, it has been more a matter of surmounting one's own ego. Thus Walsh and Vaughan (1980) describe a transpersonal personality model. They refer to Buddha, who said that attachment is the origin of all suffering and that release from suffering is a consequence of the dissolution of this attachment (nonattachment). The root of attachment, and thus the root of all unhappiness and pain, is desire. This kind of psychotherapy means to aim not at a modification of personality, but at a disidentification with one's own personality. Our personal dramas are—so it is said—a mere luxury, which impedes our full functioning capacity. If we no longer identify with our own drama, then we can detach ourselves from our emotional baggage and free ourselves from suffering and problems. The ego is basically an illusion. If no identification with anything can be maintained, then there is no more difference between I and not-I. We experience ourselves as nothing and everything. Through continual meditation, we reach an indeterminate state in which thoughts and emotions continue to pass through our brains; we, however, do not identify ourselves with them. The aim of this is the release from the tyranny of determination and limitation.

The transposition of such Buddhist ideas onto Western reality raises the question of the extent and contexts of their application. I can see a certain danger that they may be taken too literally. In some of my acquaintances, such efforts toward disidentification resulted in a serious reduction in their work and social capacities. They became adynamic, emptied, and in consequence appeared to face their environment in alienation and without perceptible commitment.

ECOLOGICAL SELF-REALIZATION

What I intend to present as ecological self-realization has been formulated by Govinda (1976, p. 243) with masterful conciseness:

- Underdeveloped man strives for the finite for the sake of its usefulness.
- Thinking man strives for the infinite for the sake of its freedom.
- Perceptive man returns to the finite for the sake of its infinite love.

Achieving self-realization prepared the individual to be guided not from the outside but from inner experiences. Transcending self-realization embeds the inner experiences in a suprapersonal, universal relation. Ecological self-realization is a matter of synthesis—of personal actualization in a universal relation to the real, historical environment. In this chapter, ecological self-realization will be described especially in terms of encounter philosophy.

Ecological self-realization denotes a type of self-realization that occurs along with and in human relational systems—that is, as a process of coevolution in a shared world and environment. I need to approach this concept gradually. First I must deal with the question of the extent to which self-realization is an interactional process in human relationships. The ecological perspective also finds its roots in occidental thought—in early Greece, for instance, or in the Christian relationship paradigm; it is further grounded in Buddhist thinking and in the philosophies of possibly all cultures and religions. The problem is to make old wisdom comprehensible to a different world with new points of reference. In contrast to the self-defining and transcending forms of self-realization, ecological self-realization can succeed only in relation to other people, by participation in suprapersonal human processes.

Form

The infinite needs a finite form in order to manifest itself. Lao-tzu describes the method of Tao as "finding the great in the small, and much in little." Every manifestation of life is ruled by a world order that can be experienced, not globally and in the abstract, but only in the concrete and individually. The universe never appears to us as a whole, but only in concrete aspects. The universe per se is neither this nor that manifestation, but the potentiality of all forms.

According to Govinda (1976, p. 125), existence means restriction. But restriction does not mean confinement. It is the finite that gives meaning to the infinite, for the infinite can be expressed only in terms of the finite. If an existence wants to assume a shape, then it cannot be *all* shapes. The preciousness of form resides in the restriction to uniqueness in time and expression. It is precious because it is transitory, like a flower, which blossoms and wilts but nonetheless expresses the eternal character of all flowers and of all life. It is the preciousness of the instant in which atemporal eternity is present. It is in the preciousness of individual shape that the infinite reveals itself. Universal relatedness is not the relationship with an abstract whole, but the organic connection of all that exists and lives, in whose every shape the whole is expressed.

Shape

The self must assume a limited shape in order to manifest itself. Just as the universe is neither this nor that manifestation, but is the potentiality of all forms, the self is not this or that form of expression, but is the potentiality of all forms of expression. The self cannot be apprehended as an abstract, but only in its concrete aspects, in its presence. My self is contained in each of my forms of expression, but is not conclusively defined and made recognizable as my own by any of these. Just as the self can be apprehended only in its concrete aspects, consciousness is comprehensible only in terms of the contents of consciousness, and not per se.

In order to actualize itself, the self must assume a shape. The infinite self can actualize itself only in the finiteness of its concrete expression. In order to apprehend itself, the self must join in the interplay of suprapersonal relational processes; it must assume a shape in the interplay of constantly changing shapes. The self can assume only that shape which it is offered and granted by superordinate interconnections. Each representation of the self results from relatedness, and is always also part of the greater system, part of the others.

According to Govinda, the mutual interpenetration of being results in a reorientation of our thinking. We must free ourselves from the rigidity of the idea of substance, from the idea of a division between identity and nonidentity. Where all is in flux, such terms cannot suffice. Shape and non-shape are not mutually exclusive, but are two aspects of one reality.

The discovery that I and all the people I have relationships with share the same nature will affect the way my relationships are created. The shape in which another person appears to me, and the shape in which I can present myself to him, is always a result of relatedness. No one exists independently of others. Everyone comes into existence only in relation to other people and other things. Thus all that appears in me or in a partner derives from a simultaneous act of the imagination. It derives from a common ground that connects us.

In a world viewed in this manner, self-development cannot take place independently of fellow human beings; rather, it results fundamentally from relatedness and therefore from mutual limitation.

Self-Realization as Seen by Religious Philosophy

According to the Greek philosopher Heraclitus (sixth century B.C.), the unity of opposites is the great law according to which multiplicity continuously develops from the one original energy (Störig 1969, vol. 2, p. 125). All development occurs in the interaction of opposing forces. In Heraclitus's opinion, the harmonic wholeness of the world is achieved in a struggle or, as we would call it today, in competition. With this theory of the combination of opposites, Heraclitus created the model for the dialectical theory of development that was further elaborated more than two thousand years later, particularly by Hegel (1770–1831). According to Fichte, one of Hegel's predecessors, the world as a whole, as well as the ego, can develop only in the face of resistance. The ego must oppose itself to a nonego. After the first thesis has been posited, a second follows: the antithesis, which contains a contradiction to the first. Ego and nonego do not, however, remain mutually exclusive opposites, but are in need of a third, of the synthesis.

In Hegel's view thesis and antithesis are not restricted in the synthesis, but *aufgehoben*, in all three denotations of this German participle: "canceled out"; "preserved"—that is, kept alive in a higher unity; and "lifted onto a higher level," on which they no longer appear as mutually exclusive opposites.

The perspective of thesis, antithesis, and synthesis was recognized as an active principle in the development of the history of peoples as well as of individuals. Hegel's active principle of thesis/antithesis/synthesis was further developed by Ludwig Feuerbach (1804–1872), one of Hegel's critical disciples, into the active principle of the I/You/We. Hegel dealt with dialectics, Feuerbach with dialogue. Feuerbach posited the You instead of the antithesis, and thus provided crucial stimuli for a later philosopher, Martin Buber (1878–1965).

Feuerbach said, "True dialectic is not a monologue of the solitary thinker with himself, but a dialogue between me and you." Ideas derive from human conversation. Just as two people are necessary for the physical begetting of a human being, so two people are necessary for spiritual begetting. The community is the first principle, and the criterion of truth and generality. "What I perceive alone, I doubt; what the other perceives as well, only that is certain." For what is shared by all is true. We can achieve objectivity in thinking only if our thoughts can be rethought or thought at the same time by others, or if "you become humble enough to be an object for others." I can be certain about something only if it is also accessible to others. Factual knowledge is always preceded by the knowledge of a You. Consciousness of the world is conveyed to me through consciousness of you. We are human only by being human for others. "Only in the face of others can we become clear about, and aware of, ourselves." In Feuerbach's view, a human being existing completely in isolation would be lost in the ocean of nature, unable to distinguish himself from anything else, and thus with no sense of self.

For Feuerbach, the real I is only that which faces a You and which in itself is a You for the other I. My own thinking presupposes an object, a You. I am and think and feel, as a subject, only in relation to an object. I exist in relation to another being and am nothing without this relation. We can experience an object only through the resistance it offers us. I can become aware of myself only through the resistance of the other. *Where there is no You, there is no I.*

Feuerbach perceives the unity formed by partners not in their fusion, but in the realization of their difference. The You needs a real otherness, for I cannot establish the difference by encountering something in myself, or something identical with me, but only by encountering someone *other*. A concrete You is therefore called for, who is different from me but willing to join me in a synthesis, in a We-ness. "Our human essence is contained only in the community, in our unity with one another—a unity, however, that is based only on the reality of the difference between me and you."

These thoughts were developed further by such German-speaking philosophers as Buber, Ferdinand Ebner, Max Scheeler, and Ludwig Binswanger. Instead of considering the I to be an unarguable fact and using it as a starting point in their search for the remaining reality and for what is common to humanity, these *encounter* philosophers start with *We* or

You.[†] In part, this philosophy of the You was a reaction to the isolation of the I brought about by the Industrial Revolution and by the catastrophe of the First World War, both of which occasioned a rethinking of the bases of human social life. The Industrial Revolution had modified not only people's relationship with themselves but also their interrelationships.

I and You

"The I shapes itself against the You," Buber said. The encounter philosophers of the twentieth century sharply opposed the solipsism that developed as a consequence of Cartesian dualism—the separation of subject and object. They queried *cogito, ergo sum* as an axiom of our own self-certainty. Without our fellow human beings, without communication, we are in no position whatever to think and thus to prove our existence. Buber in particular continued to ask how far the I comes into existence only in the encounter with a You, in the reciprocity of a concrete human relationship. "Relationship is reciprocity. My You works on me just as I work on my You. Our disciples educate us; our works develop us" (Buber 1973, p. 19). For Buber, not only is human contact a characteristic quality of human existence; he maintains that human beings come into existence only in a concrete human encounter.

In this context, *between* is a key term for Buber. Actual reality lies between You and me. It is the between, the spirit, the logos, or love. My origin and yours lies in this between. I and You result from the between of an encounter. Only

---

†Certainly the terminology of "I and Thou" has become standard in translating Buber, but it was a bad translation from the start and should be abandoned. Using *thou* to translate the German *du*—the *familiar* form used to address children, spouse, friends, and (Buber stresses) God—might have made sense four hundred years ago, but it does not work now. Americans hear *thou* only in readings from the King James Bible, suppose that it is a *polite* form (like the formal German *Sie*) appropriate for addressing God as King, and so miss Buber's point entirely.—Ed.

this between creates me and You. In this encounter there is no fusion. Rather, I and You confront each other. I and You are in action together. It is not that one is active in order to conquer and to dominate, and the other passive in order to obey and to adapt. The focus is not on I who only use You the better to perceive and realize myself. Nor is the focus on You who are compassionately helped by altruistic me. The focus is on the in between, on the sphere in which I and You can occur. "To be human means to be the being facing you. . . . Every individual is oriented toward, and depends upon, the other" (Buber 1973, p. 19).

In this context I am your You, and we exist in our common presence by withstanding and confirming each other. The other is an exacting claim for me, a challenge. "I come into existence as against You; becoming I, I say You. All real life is encounter" (Buber 1973, p. 15). The I develops by participating in interhuman processes. This does not diminish my responsibility for myself, although it relativizes it—puts it into proportion and restricts it in its particularization. What realizes itself as my I does not lie in my sphere of influence.

Buber says, "All reality is action in which I participate without being able to make it my own." Self-realization must also be understood as action in which I may participate, but which ultimately I cannot have all to myself. This action results from the in between, from the participation in interhuman processes. "Whoever is in a relationship participates in a reality—in an existence that is not internal and not merely external. All reality is action in which I participate without being able to make it my own. . . . The I becomes real by participating in reality. Where there is self-centeredness, there is no reality" (Buber 1973, p. 65).

If self-realization results from encounter and from establishing historical reality, then the paradox arises that the more I actualize myself, the less autonomous I can be.

Buber distinguishes between personhood and autonomy as two poles of human existence. Autonomy is approximately what is aimed at in an individualistic paradigm. The *person* is able to expose himself to life and to human relationships, and to enter into them. The *autonomous individual*, however, is at pains to set what is its own apart from others, and to keep it as something special.

> The autonomous individual appears by contrasting itself with other autonomous individuals. The person appears by relating to other persons. . . . The person becomes aware of himself as participating in existence, as co-being, and thus as being. The autonomous individual becomes aware of himself as being such-and-no-other. The person says, "I am"; the autonomous individual says, "I am like this." "Know yourself" means to the person, "Know yourself as being"; to the autonomous individual, it means "Know your essence." By contrasting himself with others, the autonomous individual distances himself from being. This does not mean to say that the person in any way surrenders his particular existence, his otherness; he just does not use it as his own focusing point. . . . The person perceives his self; the autonomous individual deals with that which he owns: his manner, his race, his works, his genius. The autonomous individual does not participate in any reality, and does not gain any. He contrasts himself with the other and seeks to possess as much of it as possible, through experience and use. . . . All his extensive and multilayered essence, all his studious "individuality," cannot furnish him with any substance. [Buber 1973, p. 65–67].

Buber's existential philosophy was further developed, by Ludwig Binswanger (1881–1966) in particular. He dealt with the relation of I and You within the spatial structure of loving togetherness, of the We. Within the We-space, I am I and You or, seen from your point of view, also I and You. At times I am I, at times I am You. Within the We, I exist only insofar as You exist, although I am not You. "As You are not, unless I am, the highest spatial principle is We. Only because I and You, as belonging to each other, are already contained in the We, do I belong where You are, can I be where You are, can a place for me emerge where You are, can the fact that You will be or are here be decisive for my Here" (Binswanger 1962, p. 29).

This gestalt of the We does not, however, result in a dissolution of I and You. In love, the I is limited by the You. This limitation refers me back to myself and provides me with an opportunity to grow with its help. Self-discovery results from the limits the other sets for me, but also from the limits I set for the other. By accepting and acknowledging the limitation of myself through your presence as a gift, I am referred back to myself. But also, the more I can limit your self, the more I myself in turn grow with your help, as you yourself grow with mine. That which I am, I am not by means of myself, nor simply by means of heteronomy through the partner, but only by means of the process of *We ourselves*. I cannot reach love by means of my own existence, nor can I become able to be whole through love, for love means precisely the renunciation of "one's self-perfection" (Binswanger 1962, pp. 137–38). Today's idea of holism and self-development with the paradigm of androgyny—the integral sexual development of the individual who does not need a male or female complement—provides no basis for a love relationship.

According to many of today's paradigms, a relationship is based on mutual acceptance and benevolent support in integral growth. In contrast to this, I agree with Binswanger, and understand the I as something that is in need of interaction with partners for its self-development. Thus the desire to be whole appears to be an obstacle to love and consequently an obstacle to self-perfection. The creation of a We gestalt presupposes a sense of *not* being self-sufficient.

Binswanger says (1962, p. 138), "Where no You expects . . . or demands anything from me any longer, I am . . . erotically dead." If partners in a love relationship expect things from each other, they do not fence each other in in the process, but reveal that they desire each other, that they mean much to each other, and that they want something from each other. Mere benevolent acceptance and mutual support makes love stale. Love is a game, struggle, and conflict, too. The partners do not need only each other as complement or completion; rather, it is the orientation of the conflict toward a third party that provokes the emergence of two persons.

In the sphere of psychotherapy and psychology that today may be described as applied philosophy, thinking in terms of I and You has not been widely disseminated, perhaps because the German-speaking philosophers tended to idealize relationships with words that sounded too beautiful. Down-to-earth proof in reality and practice was often lacking. However, one of the few points on which all the various schools of therapy agree is in regarding the therapeutic *relationship* as the healing agent. Carl Rogers in particular has described the therapist's compassion, genuineness, and appreciation as essential qualities in this respect. Nonetheless, the therapeutic relationship is shaped by the command to treat the patient, and therefore does not correspond to a free dialogue between I and You in the reciprocity of partners.

The dialogue principle was further developed, particularly in the sphere of Protestant and Catholic theology. I do not propose to deal with this in detail. A connection seems to exist, however, between transcending self-realization and a religiosity that predominantly derives from Buddhism, whereas the dialogue point of view is more developed in Christian thinking. Since our culture has developed from Christian roots, it is amazing how little Christian thinking has influenced the more recent, religious tendencies of self-realization.

Self-Realization and Christian Religiosity

It can be observed that in the Western Hemisphere interest in religion is rapidly growing, while at the same time interest in Christian denominations is rapidly diminishing. It is assumed that the rigidity of institutional structures is a major reason for the weakening of the churches.

I think that the problems are more fundamental. One aspect that goes against the grain of many religious seekers is the personification of the divine in the shape of God, the Lord and Father in Heaven. This enhances the popularity of those churches in which experience of self and experience of God are equated, in which self-development is tantamount to becoming God. Buddhism says, "Look into yourself, you are Buddha!"; Hinduism says, "Atman [individual consciousness] and Brahman [universal consciousness] are one"; Siddha-Yoga, "God dwells in you as you"; the Upanishads, "Whoever understands himself, understands the universe."

Christianity, however, approaches us with a Gospel, a message that does not result from and in us, but that is written down as a unique historical fact and as such may annoy, displease, attract, or repel us. Much is said in it about faith in the message, in the sole truth revealed in it, in the sole savior Jesus, and in the sole God the Father. *The idea of faith in a personal God contains the idea of a dialogue, of an interactional relationship between God and man.*

In both the Jewish and the Christian scriptures, God is not described only as a being that is above and beyond everything, or as centered in the human self; rather, God is described as a being directly affected by relationships with people. God grants people the freedom to love Him; at the same time, however, He gives them responsibility for their relationships, as well as the opportunity to become guilty of rebellion against Him. In Jesus, God is experienced in a particularly impressive manner and thus becomes one's brother, one's neighbor. Jesus is not described as an illustrious monarch, nor as one enlightened, but as somebody underprivileged, as an instigator who was executed. Jesus is in need, and seeks help; he is at the mercy of fear and pain. He is not at rest in himself, whole, or without needs, but rather is related to his Father, whose orders he must obey. He does not strive for wisdom and the development of his own consciousness, but puts himself entirely at his Father's service.

In Christian teaching, the relationship with one's neighbor occupies a central position. What was revolutionary about Jesus was that he used, as an example of brotherly love, one of the hated Samaritans, who were a remnant of Israel that had rejected the Judean reforms under Josiah, whose very existence challenged the legitimacy of Judaism. This *heretic*, in Jesus's parable, responded in an exemplary manner to someone in need, to a man left half dead by thieves, whereas the Jewish priest and the Levite (temple servant) did not respond at all (Luke 10: 30–37). In other parables there is a wealth of acts of love, not only *toward* despised people but also *by* despised people, whose acts of love are regarded as far more genuine than those of the righteous.

Jesus himself demonstrated who his neighbors were: the least of his brethren, outcasts, sinners, publicans, usurers, harlots, the sick, children, even his enemies. And why these instead of the religious establishment? Neither justice nor lawfulness is described as decisive: only the genuineness of a personal encounter is decisive. The humiliations that the despised had to bear made them particularly responsive to such personal encounters. These were the people who needed Jesus most. Interactionally speaking, it was they who made it possible for him to become Christ and to begin the process of salvation.

The life of Jesus in the Gospels consists of parables and of incidents resulting from daily encounters. The Gospel is not a philosophy of or instructions for the path toward enlightenment. What happened resulted from the combination of Jesus and the people in his life. It is in encounters with people that the "actual" takes place. Jesus applies the term *neighbor* precisely to those who were at a distance from his audience.

The encounter with God is an incident, an interaction, an action directed at a specific person. No instructions for meditation are provided here, and only a few for prayer; rather, it is pointed out that God also encounters us in our fellow human beings and in the human community. Jesus, speaking in God's voice, says, "For where two or three are gathered together in my name, there am I in the midst of them" (Matt. 18: 20). My neighbor is everyone to whom I can do good and respond. I love my neighbor because God loves him or her. I love God in my neighbor, whom I encounter in the least of my brethren. In the encounter with a fellow human being, with a You, something divine takes place. Neither cosmos nor universe is in the center, nor is the self; rather, the process of human relationship is now central.

Our Own Imperfection Helps Create Relationships

The New Testament shows us that we do not have to be perfect in order to create perfect works. It is often our own inadequacy that informs our actions with intensity and tension. Many artists and scientists who accomplished significant works were far from perfect and mature as persons. Yet it is precisely the suffering caused by our own imperfection that may motivate us to create works that embody what we desire but cannot personally achieve.

Fundamentally, life consists of instability, disequilibrium, and change. Surmounting this disequilibrium by being modest about our own needs is difficult for us average human beings, and perhaps not even really worth aspiring to. Many people are motivated by precisely this sense of their own imperfection to do something for their fellow human beings. Their work can be valuable even if in their activities they are not free of egoism and personal limitation. Frequently their fellow human beings shape and correct their actions by demanding that the acting person subordinate ambition, rivalry, and jealousy to the common goal. In this way it is the common process that redirects our personal acting and feeling, even if we could not do this by our own efforts. Aggression, envy, and jealousy show, as much as love, compassion, and human interest do, that we relate to other human beings. "You will know them by their fruits" (Matt. 7: 16). Imperfect, neurotic, "sinful" people can still do good.

In my view, self-realization should be judged by its effects, by its sense and use for the development of the whole. From the perspective of suprapersonal processes, an individual's immature and imperfect aspirations can contribute toward a useful and balanced whole through corrective interactions of the relational system. This helps the individual experience an ability to become productive together with others, despite his or her own disharmony. "And thus the desire for perfection may grow out of inadequacy, that desire which is creative power itself and which we mean when we speak of the divine in us" (Govinda 1984, p. 105).

Ground Rules for Ecological Self-Realization

In order to be able to view those elements that justify an ecologically understood self-realization, we must start with the following assumptions.

The self cannot be comprehensively defined. Some qualities of the self can be circumscribed, however. The self is not something that can be completely actualized or of which we could ever become completely conscious. You can never say, "I now know who I actually am" or "I have now become completely myself." The term *self* describes my essential core, which as such, however, defies comprehension. *Self* means potential—the possibility for development innate in a person. H. Schmid (1981, p. 143) speaks of an "entelechial self," which can be in conflict with the real, really lived, self. (*Entelechy* is that which contains its aim, *telos*. *Entelechy* thus denotes a force inherent in an organism that determines its direction of development. *Entelechy* or *entelechial* means the same thing as "actualizing the form.") Just as a chicken, another animal, or a human being may develop from an egg cell, depending on its internal plan, every person contains a development plan, as it were, which during development indicates a certain course like a compass.

Genetics offers an analogy to what may be meant by the term *self*. Genetics distinguishes between genotype and phenotype. The genotype is the totality of all information stored in the chromosomes of an organism. This genetic information as such is inaccessible to any conscious experience. What it consists of can be observed only in its effects, only in the way it is actualized. The genotype can develop itself only in interaction with the environment. Depending on the nature of the interaction with the environment, the same genotype can produce different phenotypes (the gestalt that appears). *The genotype comprises the entire spectrum of an individual's possibilities for development.* What is actually developed, however, cannot be decided by the individual alone; it results only from interaction with the environment.

The genetically limited behavior spectrum of a living thing is called its "reaction norm." The genetically caused behavior spectrum of people is much wider than that of animals. But people possess a kind of inner reaction norm; in the depth of their being they can sense a kind of direction or plan for their development. This internal compass indicates only generally what is suitable and what is not. Possibly it would be more accurate to say that it indicates what is *not* suitable. Whatever your own self is, it cannot be experienced in the abstract. You can experience your self only in concrete expression, and particularly in its borderlands. You can feel how your body resists you by means of exhaustion or illness, even if you are not willing to accept your limitations. You can also feel when something is not in agreement with what, deep inside, you sense as your way and your treasure of experience, when you choose a behavior that merely pleases others or avoids a conflict.

It is particularly through the nonself, through the suppression of self, and through transgressing the borders of your own development spectrum that your self becomes perceptible; it does not, however, become perceptible as such. "We can see here again how the usual advice, 'Be yourself,' is misleading, for the self can be felt only as a potentiality; anything more definite must emerge in actual behavior" (Perls, Hefferline, and Goodman 1973, p. 430).

Another important observation is that we cannot develop and differentiate the self by ourselves. The self is not something that dwells in us and can be discovered, as it were, but something potential that must be developed and differentiated. The self can appear only in concrete interactions with the environment. The self is developed through support but also through limitation and provocation by others. The self does not exist as such; rather, it can be perceived in an individual's behavior patterns and actions, and is also contained in these. The self appears in action and realization. The word for *realization* in the German language, *Verwirklichung*, etymologically derives from the Indo-Germanic root *uer-* (meaning "to turn, bend, wind"), which is related to the Greek *ergon*, and thus to the German *Werk, werken, wirken*, and to the English *work*. Because the self is realized only by being called upon through interaction with others, the shape in which it is realized will depend not only on the person but also on who those others are. It is the partners who provide the self with space in which it can be realized. It is the partners who make it possible for someone to develop some of his or her own potential.

This recognition need not make us feel defenseless and resigned about our partners, or think that we are hopelessly dependent on them for our own self-realization. Rather, this recognition can also stimulate us to persuade our partners to provide us with more room for development. This, however, presupposes that we are ready not to want to assert ourselves defiantly against others, but to aspire to coevolution, to a development of the self within the framework of a common and simultaneous development of other people and suprapersonal processes. The environment is more likely to permit our own development if it experiences this development as a contribution to a process in which it is included.

Viewed in this light, the self is not transcended in an unknowable and noncommittal cosmos; rather, the person transcends the realization of the self so as to participate in interhuman processes. This transcendence is not an expression of a noble, ascetic, or ethically superior attitude, but an expression of the rational observation that the more I become myself, the more I develop what is my own as part of what is different and transcends us.

Self-realization understood in this manner is not based on the development of individual personality as opposed to that of others in the person's network of relationships. Mere self-assertion against my partner can result only in short-term advantages; in the long term it will destroy the system that provides a framework in which I can develop myself. Self-realization understood in this manner does not depend on a retreat from society and on setting up firm boundaries between myself and others (although such retreats may be sensible at times, in that they allow me a chance to take stock and see which way my development is heading). Self-realization understood in this manner refers to people and incites a response, and is therefore experienced as significant. It relativizes the sense of uniqueness and individuality of my own self-realization. I cannot assume the sole responsibility for whatever parts of my self have taken shape, because they have done so only as part of processes in which other people have been involved. In striving for ecological self-realization, I can encourage suprapersonal processes by putting what is my own at their disposal. Self-realization understood in this manner is not its own measure, but is measured according to its effects.

CHAPTER 3

An Ecology of Personhood

In the preceding chapter I pointed out how the various paradigms of self-realization are based on philosophical-ideological and religious views of man. Ecological self-realization is philosophically rooted in dialectics and dialogics. In practical psychology and psychotherapy it has attracted little attention. The various forms of group therapy—encounter groups, sensitivity-training groups, and so on—remain strongly individual-centered in their approach. The groups are specially assembled for therapy. Outside the therapy sessions there are no binding relationships between the participants. Therapy or training aims at making the individual participants aware of their personal interaction patterns by means of the group situation; it aims at pointing out the defenses that arise from this situation, and at offering participants opportunities for corrective emotional experiences and for behavioral change. Encounter groups additionally aim at offering new forms of communication and of instinctive experience to people who suffer from the general malaise of the times or from a sense of isolation.

A suprapersonal psychotherapeutic perspective arose only after the application of systems theory and cybernetics, particularly in couples and family therapy. In this perspective the focus is no longer on the person, but instead on the relations within the human system of which the person is part. Questions about the structures, organization, and hierarchy within the family as a system are dealt with, as well as communication patterns and regulation processes. The linear-casual approach is replaced by the circular, by a way of observing reciprocity, mutual conditioning, and determination.

INDIVIDUAL OR PERSON

The terms *individual* and *person* assume two different definitions of human nature. What *human nature* is defies conclusive cognition and generally valid definition. Every definition that has been offered is an expression of a culturally restricted understanding of human beings. In this book, a human being is to be understood as a relational being, as part of suprapersonal ecological systems. What is meant here can be explained with the help of the terms *individual* and *person*, although the usage of these terms is not uniform and they are often used as synonyms. *Individual* derives from *indivisible*, which is a translation of the Greek *átomon*, which denotes that which cannot be divided further, and hence the monad, the single being. It manifests a tendency, appearing with the Greeks, toward analytical, categorizing, and thus also reductionist thinking. In scholastic philosophy, the meaning of the term *individual* changed from "indivisible" to "idiosyncratic." The individual was contrasted with genus, with general behavior, with the collective. In biology an individual describes a single member of a species. The term *individual* always denotes a single member of a class.

In Western civilization the term *individual* has developed

into a criterion of social distinction. Each human being has a unique, unmistakable individuality, which remains relatively constant in different situations and times, and in spite of different roles. Thomas Hobbes (1588–1679) regarded it as a function of the state to protect individuals concerned with their particular interests. The English philosopher John Locke (1632–1704) described individuals as the natural proprietors of their persons, who opposed society antithetically. Today, the term *individual* also denotes the single human being in contrast to society. Thus a sociological encyclopedia (Fuchs et al. 1973, p. 293) defines *individuation* as the "development of a particular individual personality structure that should enable the individual to hold his ground against society's adaptation pressure by means of autonomous, nonstandard behavior." The terms *society* and *collective* are used mostly without differentiation to mean "anonymous, unchangeable mass." Jung says that individual is whatever is not collective, whatever pertains to one person and not to a larger group of individuals. "The individual . . . exists only . . . insofar as an awareness of idiosyncrasy exists—that is, insofar as there is a conscious difference from other individuals. Along with the physical, the psychic individuality is given as a correlate" (Jung 1960a, vol. 6, p. 477).

Collective and *society* are barely distinguished from family systems or partners, as in Jung, for example: "Man cannot exist without oxygen, water, protein, fat, etc. Like all those, society is one of the most necessary conditions of existence. It would be ridiculous to claim that man lives in order to breathe air. It is equally ridiculous to say that the individual exists for society. *Society* is a mere expression for the symbiosis of a group of people. An expression as such is not imbued with life. The natural and only being imbued with life is the individual, and this is the case in the whole of nature." Or: "An assembly of one hundred highly intelligent heads is in its totality one great blockhead, since each gift,

whether intellectual or moral, is ultimately individual differentiation." Individualism is that philosophical view according
to which only the individual exists as an independent reality,
collectivism being the opposite view. The individual is therefore the indivisible, the inseparable, the self-contained, and
the unique.

From a Marxist angle, the overrating of individualism is
regarded as the basis of capitalist thinking. According to this
criticism, psychology as well as psychotherapy is guided by
the paradigm of the single, isolated, competitive, and consuming individual. Therapy is meant to enable an individual
to be more assertive, to compete more effectively, and to
hold on to gains more tenaciously. Willingly or unwillingly,
ideas of profit and exploitation are connected with this. Yet
this critique, too, remains caught in the polarization of individual and collective.

I would like to make a clear distinction between *individual*
and *person*. The etymological derivation of the term *person*
has not been settled, but according to Yannaras (1982, p. 16),
the word is the equivalent of Greek *pros-opon*, which means
"I turn my eyes, my gaze, or my face toward somebody, I
am opposite somebody." The word originally denoted a direct relationship. The word *person* is defined in terms of a
relationship and not as an individuality, not as something
bounded, standing outside a relationship. The person is a
being in the face of a concrete other. The Latin expression
persona denoted an actor's mask in the theater. After Cicero
the term assumed the connotation of "character mask" or a
part played by somebody in life, and of the (great or slight)
dignity to which those who play these parts are entitled. (The
derivation of the term from *per-sonare*, "to sound through,"
is uncertain; it may be a mere popular etymology based on
phonetic association. Nonetheless, this interpretation of the
term *persona* was assumed as early as the first century B.C.)

The following observations are relevant to my further
arguments.

- Fundamentally, the person is understood as being engaged in a relationship.
- One part of the person is his or her real appearance. The person is audible and visible, or rather, is heard and seen by fellow human beings. The person's essence sounds through his or her manifestation, but this essence as such cannot ever be apprehended. The person assumes concrete forms by interacting with the environment. Appearance and sound are what can be apprehended as person. Whatever can be perceived about the person as he or she has appeared always contains a statement about the human being who perceives it.

A SELF-ORGANIZING SYSTEM

For many of the aspects that I propose to describe in this book, the paradigm of systems theory is particularly apposite. Some aspects of systems theory that are relevant to the present personality paradigm will be summarized here, and treated in more detail later on.

A *system* is a whole, organized by the interaction of its parts and able to regulate itself. Within the system each part is influenced by all other parts, and itself influences these parts.

Living systems are largely open toward the outside: they continually exchange matter, energy, and information with their environs, and maintain a quasi-stationary state, a fluid equilibrium. According to James Grier Miller (1978), they contain nineteen qualities or subsystems, which are necessary for their survival. One is that, despite their openness, systems must demarcate themselves against the outside, and must have effective components that hold the system together and protect it against the outside. Incoming matter, energy, and information must be selected, distributed, and transformed; they are stored, processed, eliminated, or produced in a new form, and emitted. Additionally, a living system can not only repair itself but also reproduce itself—that is, produce similar

systems. Anabolic and catabolic processes are going on continuously and simultaneously. The structure of a system is
not rigid but must constantly be re-created. A cell, for instance, is continuously being renewed, and does not consist
of the same molecules for any length of time. Being an *autopoietic* system, it is capable of a certain autonomy despite
its interdependence with its environment. In 1973, the Chil-
ean biologists Humberto Maturana and Francisco Varela
coined the term *autopoiesis* (self-organization), by which they
mean the capacity of living systems to renew themselves
continuously and to regulate this process so that the integrity
of the organism is safeguarded.

The structure of the system is constituted by the spatiotemporal order of its processes. If these processes change, as
happens in evolutionary processes, for example, then the
structure of the system concerned will also continuously
change.

An important advantage of this perspective lies in the fact
that biological, psychological, and social processes can be seen
as operating according to the same organizational principles.
Naturally, they interact intensively with one another. For
psychosocial processes, the exchange of information or ideas
is of central interest. *The concept of the idea is of crucial significance for this book.*

Information is defined as everything that makes a difference
and can be communicated and perceived as a difference. This
is how the term is defined in computer language. An idea,
too, has an informative aspect, but its significance for us far
exceeds this. The Greek word *eidos* means "what has been
seen, the image." Greek *idein* denotes "see, look, recognize,
know." Sight and recognition presuppose a personal relation
to what has been seen and recognized. We have a relationship
with what we see. We individually attribute more or less
significance to it. We identify ourselves with the ideational,
and appropriate it. The ideational may become the most important purpose in life. The concept of the idea must therefore

not be restricted to a rational content. Rather, ideas are constructs that concern people holistically and emotionally.

In contrast to a theme (Greek *thesis* means "that which forms the basis"), ideas are usually purposive and tend to demand actualization. An idea is not (or at least does not remain) the property of one person, but has a relationship-creating and relationship-maintaining quality. Ideas keep families, groups, nations, religions, and communities united.

As a psychological person, I am an information-processing or, as I propose to call it here, an idea-processing system. I take up ideas selectively, transform them, associatively connect them with other ideas, process them, express them again, or produce new ideas. As an idea-processing system I coordinate the ideas into a whole. In such a person, continuous anabolic and catabolic ideational processes are going on. The psychological structures are not rigid but must be constantly re-created by ideational processes. My structure as such a person is the spatiotemporal order of my ideational processes. I must always regulate these processes so that my integrity and identity are safeguarded. Existing ideational structures must be renewed continuously.

As an idea-processing system, I am in a constant state of disequilibrium. Equilibrium amounts to spiritual standstill and to stagnation of mental evolution. Disequilibrium keeps the autopoietic ideational processes going and stimulates a continuous exchange of ideas with the environment.

Here is a summary of some qualities relevant to an ecological-systemic understanding of the person:

- As a living system I constantly exchange matter, energy, and ideas with my environment.
- As a person I can regulate the psychological expressions of energy and ideas in processes, can organize them into a whole, and can regenerate, repair, and reproduce them.
- Anabolic and catabolic ideational processes are going on constantly and simultaneously. Like a cell, as a person I keep on reproducing myself as an idea-processing system.

In doing so, I show the dynamic of a structure that as a whole is stable, but at the same time is never at rest. As a person I am a self-structuring ideational process.

- As a person I experience myself as a purposive process of growth and development. I evolve as a system and change my own structure. Structure results from the interaction and organization of ideational processes. Just as a cell does not consist of the same molecules for any great length of time, so I do not consist of the same ideas for any great length of time.

- As a person I am always in a state of ideational disequilibrium. By constant exchange of ideas with my environment, I can create a quasi-stable but never rigid structure for myself.

- As a person I experience myself as one and the same unity in different situations and at different times (identity in time and space). I have a relationship with myself and with the ideational processes whose vehicle I am. I identify with my ideas to varying degrees.

UNREALISTIC THERAPIES

Many psychoanalytic and individual-centered forms of therapy claim that fantasies and inner life have more significance for the general condition of a person than outward reality does. External reality has more of a trigger function, which stimulates and reactivates processes within the psyche. *The external world is, to a large extent, considered to be a projection of the internal world.* The subject perceives his surroundings and reacts to them according to his own interests, skills, habits, and affective states.

The way in which a human being perceives the environment may be regarded as a "projective test." As he behaves in a Rorschach test, so a man will respond to those environmental stimuli that are connected with his inner situation, his *fears, needs, and instincts.* This view is a logical consequence of Descartes's theory that I can be sure only of myself.

I must therefore assume that the external world is my projection.

Actually, the inverse perspective would also be possible. From a holistic view of the universe, the interior of a human being could be a projection of the whole; the individual man would thus be the receptacle or the vehicle of forces working on him but centered outside him. The individual is here apprehended as one charmed, as one possessed, as a vehicle of an evil spirit, as a magician, a sorcerer, a shaman. This view is widely held in many cultures. This becomes particularly clear in terms of how the nature of dreams is understood. In our own culture, dreams are perfect examples of intrapsychic productions. In antiquity, however, dreams were regarded as divine revelation (the Bible), as the messengers of the gods (Homer), or as divine admonition (Socrates).

For understanding the neurotic's mental functioning, Freud (1940b, vol. 11, p. 383) demanded that fantasy and reality be equated. "It remains a fact that the patient has created such fantasies for himself, and this fact is no less significant for his neurosis than if he had experienced these fantasies in reality. Such fantasies possess psychological as opposed to material reality, and gradually we begin to understand that in the world of neuroses, psychological reality is decisive."

Now, Freud had not assumed that fantasy and reality are equally able to cause neuroses right from the start. Until 1896 Freud had adhered to the so-called seduction theory about the genesis of neuroses. This theory attributed central significance to concrete family influences in the shape of sexual seduction and overstimulation of the child by the parents and their representatives. The rejection of the seduction theory occurred, according to Freud's own testimony, during the profoundest crisis of his scientific career. Not concrete, traumatizing seductions but purely intrapsychic fantasies or repressed and repelled desires were now supposed to be the cause of his patients' neurotic symptoms. This insight has subsequently determined the perspective of psychoanalysis as depth psychology—as the psychology of intrapsychic and largely unconscious depths (Stierlin 1978, p. 172). Marianne Krüll (1978) puts forward the thesis that Freud's rejection of the seduction theory could be related to his own concrete childhood experiences. The seduction theory could have forced Freud to trace his own neurosis back to events in his own childhood.

Freud's crisis (1896/97) followed the death of his father, Jakob. When, in the course of his self-analysis, he began to throw light on his prehistory, his piety after his father's death prevented his criticism of his own father from becoming conscious. Once Freud had rejected the seduction theory, he at first felt relieved. He could now release his own childhood experiences from repression. But he was dealing only with his cover memories. The fantasy theory of the universal Oedipus complex left their backgrounds unanalyzed. The search for the background and the geneses of the fantasies led Freud to increasingly more recondite mystification of the experience on which they were based (the idea, for instance, of a phylogenetic legacy of patricide in the original tribe). Thus it became possible for Freud to circumvent the taboo, established by his father, against researching the past, by replacing the seduction theory with the theory of the Oedipus complex. In this manner the real parents became mere figments of the child's imagination.

It is difficult to tell how the history of psychoanalysis and of psychology in general would have changed if Freud had not been restricted by such taboos. I suspect, however, that the tendency to withdraw into oneself and to deal with one's own fantasies was favored by the times, and was thus further developed in theoretical concepts that diverged from Freud, such as those of Jung. Generally, depth-psychological concepts tended (and partially do so now) to concentrate largely on the productions of the unconscious, on the person's dreams and fantasies, and to pay little heed to external realities. These were largely accepted as conditions that merely demanded adaptation. The dialogue served by psychoanalysis was above all the interior dialogue (Stierlin 1978). The main concern was an improved relationship of the analysand with himself, and with the repelled, repressed, and conflicting parts of himself.

How Dreams Differ from Reality

From a purely intraindividual angle, there is seemingly no essential difference between whether a seduction occurs only in fantasy or in reality. The difference becomes crucial, however, as soon as we regard the same phenomenon interactionally. If a child was indeed seduced by an actual person, then the perpetrator, too, will continue to occupy himself with the seduction situation in his own fantasy life. He may possibly feel guilty, fear discovery and accusation; he may avoid the child concerned, threaten the child, and so on. The incident of the seduction will have real consequences, even if it is not discovered as such, even if both partners never speak about it, and even if it is not talked about later. Such consequences will not be caused to the same extent, however, by a seduction experienced only in a fantasy.

This poses the epistemological question about how far subjective experience apprehends a difference between dream and reality. Repeated attempts have been made to prove phenomenologically that the dream was not realistic, that it was formally characterized by certain distortions of experience that branded it as a dream. Even Perls, Hefferline, and Goodman argue (1973, pp. 443–44),

> how, awake, do you know that you were dreaming and are not now dreaming? . . . it is not by special "connotation" of "reality," as if reality were a detachable quality, but by integrating more awareness into the actual situation, more consistency, more body-feeling, and especially in this case more deliberate muscularity. (You pinch yourself to

see if you are awake; not that you may not be dreaming also
of pinching yourself, but that this is more evidence, and if
all the available evidence of this kind coheres, it makes no
difference whether you are awake or dreaming anyway.)

I consider it a great merit of Medard Boss to have pointed
out (Boss 1953) that, phenomenologically, there is no perceptible difference between existence in a dream and existence
during wakefulness. As far as subjective, present experience
is concerned, there is no conclusive difference between dream
and external reality. There are differences, however, in terms
of the ecological effects. *Whatever has real consequences is real.*

If I dream that a certain person has died, then I am relieved upon waking to realize that it was only a dream. If this
person has really died, however, I will realize this not only
once but repeatedly and in the same manner for days, months,
and years. If this person is close to me, then his death has real
consequences in my life, which go far beyond the fact of his
absence. Thus people who have been bereaved frequently say
that in the first days after the death, they were still under the
impression that it had only been a dream and that the deceased
would suddenly reappear. Only in the course of time had
they learned to accept that the deceased was really dead. External realities create facts that decisively influence my further
personal development, but at the same time also my fantasies,
aspirations, and ideas. Yet what is real and therefore has real
consequences cannot be deduced from the temporal alone,
but must be deduced also from the spatial continuum. A real
incident will frequently not only concern myself but also be
perceived by others in a similar fashion. External realities mold
our history much more compellingly than fantasies and dreams.

The Appearance of Reality

An undifferentiated perception of external reality makes it
appear overpowering and immutable. According to Freud
(1940b, vol. 8, pp. 230ff.) each neurosis tends to force the

patient out of real life. The neurotic turns away from external reality because he or she finds it intolerable. The extreme form of this turning away from external reality manifests itself in a hallucinatory psychosis. These observations of Freud's are one-sided. It is certainly true that on the one hand neurotics tend to seek the fulfillment of their pipe dreams— which remain unfulfilled in real life—in hallucinations, dreams, or fantasies, and to withdraw from external realities in this process. But Freud still paid too little attention to the circularity of hallucinatory satisfaction and frustrating reality. A hallucinatory withdrawal will have consequences for external realities. The person's tendency to withdraw will make these realities even more frustrating and overpowering, so that it is easy for a vicious circle to come into play: the more frustrating and overpowering external realities are, the more a person will retreat into hallucinatory satisfaction; and the more he or she retreats into hallucinatory satisfaction, the more overpowering and frustrating external realities will become.

This one-sided focusing on internal as opposed to external realities also has therapeutic consequences. If in the treatment of claustrophobia, for instance, a therapist exclusively concentrates on the patient's fantasized fear, then he may perceive in the symptom the formation of a compromise between desire and defense. He may, say, bring out unconscious rape fantasies, believing that it would be curative for the patient to become conscious of these. According to ecological viewpoints, however, the therapist will work substantially more efficiently if he simultaneously includes the external realities in his concept—that is, the manner in which the patient organizes his environment. He will then exhort the patient to oppose his tendency to avoid all fear-inducing situations. After all, a protective attitude does not alleviate his fears but reinforces them, so that the patient increasingly retreats from all realities that might induce fear. It is a prerequisite for the alleviation of fear that the patient be determined to reconquer the lost external territory and to hold on to gains in spite of the fears connected with this. The urgent aim of the therapy is not the alleviation of fear but the ability to *endure* fear, the ability to cope with the tasks in external reality in spite of fear. Each concrete success in an active change of the environment boosts the ego and encourages personal development.

The neglect of external reality and action is also evident in the *Vocabulaire de la psychanalyse* (*Vocabulary of Psychoanalysis*), by Laplanche and Pontalis, which is today's authoritative psychoanalytical dictionary, where there are no entries for *action, behavior, external reality*, or *work*. The basic attitude of complete concentration on internal realities, while ignoring external realities, remained unchanged even when in recent decades a new tendency appeared: the tendency, based on the writings of Wilhelm Reich and Herbert Marcuse, to regard society with its conditions of dominance and exploitation as the cause of internal conflicts and of neuroses. The opinion arose that first society would have to be changed; intrapsychic conflicts and individuals' neuroses would then disappear, since needs could now develop, and regulate themselves, freely. The instinct renunciation (described by Freud) that culture demands from us was replaced by Reich's and Marcuse's formula of unnecessary instinct renunciation; adaptation to society and culture was replaced by liberation from society and culture (Stierlin 1978, pp. 176ff.).

But who is this society? In most of its outward aspects, society is not an anonymous mass. Society appears to us as people with whom we interact; we, too, are society. Society was turned into an undifferentiated hodgepodge of power and repression, and in this abstract form became a suitable scapegoat for the concealment of one's failure in social interaction. Doubtless the social criticism of recent decades was useful for raising our consciousness, but we need to discover not only what society—the others—are like, but also what I, as part of this society, am like. A person not only is passively at the mercy of a society but also shapes the human environment continually.

Those who assume an inherent opposition between individual and collective also assume that the products of the unconscious emerge from a part of the individual that cannot be influenced from the outside. Jung defines individuation as an intrapsychic process in the course of which contents that had been unconscious are processed, and in this way assimilated, by the psyche. If the individuation process penetrates further into the unconscious, it first reaches animus and anima, representing a man's female and a woman's male tendencies, and then arrives in the collective unconscious, which contains innumerable archetypes. The last stage of the individuation process is the *self*, which, infinitely remote from consciousness and *immediately linked with the all-encompassing cosmos*, directs as the center of the entire system the conscious and unconscious layers, including archetypal matters.

Now, if the self is immediately linked with the cosmos, why should it be something so individualistic, demarcated, unique, and unmistakable? Are not two tendencies inadmissibly mixed here: on the one hand the effort to listen to myself and to let an inner voice speak; on the other hand the listening-to-myself as a pretext for erecting boundaries between myself and the claims of the environment, and for rejecting them? Why should this voice articulate itself so defensively against the voices of other selves? Why should not a partner or partners be included in this "self"? Why should this voice not also *mean* the processes that are about to occur with me and my partners? Is it not rather the purpose of this listening-to-myself to sense what is harmonious, not only for individual and personal processes but also for collective and interactional ones? Won't this internal voice contradict the partner's claims only if those claims are foreign to the process and demand something that is not harmonious? Is it not much more likely that the cosmic and the collective express themselves in the individual's voice, and that the so-called individuation process extends my consciousness so that I am more open to, and can hear better, what the cosmic and the collective want to pronounce?

If our culture were not so individual-centered, what is meant by the individuation process would long have been in harmony with what in other cultures is experienced by people who retire into solitude in order to become utterly responsive to this inner voice. Many founders of religions did this (Jesus, Mohammed, Buddha), and so did many shamans. It was not their aim to find their own personal and unmistakable paths, but to become sensitive to what they wanted to absorb and then reveal as part of the society to which they belonged.

In both Freudian and Jungian psychoanalysis, the dream is the classic manifestation of the unconscious. While the dreamer is asleep, keeps his eyes shut, and is therefore shielded against external stimuli, his interior produces images and modes of experience that we might expect to be free of interactional influences and to be pure products of the unconscious. According to Jung, dreams are the expression of a process withdrawn from consciousness, which provides the patient with clues about where his real path is leading.

Now, Freud had already pointed out that there were so-called day residues in dreams—to which he attributed little significance, however. More recent research into dreams has shown how much even dreams are influenced by the dreamer's interactional, relational situation.

Christoph Fischer (1978) examined the manifest contents of the dream series of eight analysands, four being of Freudian and four of Jungian orientation; there were 240 dreams in all. All eight patients suffered from phobic neuroses. They were selected so that both groups were parallel in age and social data. The series of dreams were recorded, partially by the analyst, partially on tape. The contents of these dreams were then categorized according to certain criteria by independent colleagues, who had not been informed of the objective of the investigation. The dreams in the *Freudian series* are markedly more dynamic, more strongly charged with aggression and sexuality; their affective color is more pronounced; they express the desire for a partnership more often, and more often take place in active interaction with the environment; they are more frequently structured in a manner that makes one suspect that repressed instinctual desires had been the motor of the dream. In the Freudian dream series there are almost three times as many sexual acts and fantasies as in the Jungian ones, and far more experiences of failure. The dreams in the *Jungian series*, however, more frequently show abstract, mythological-irrational contents; they tend to take place more frequently in nature; they contain far more experiences of success.

According to their contents, 62 percent of all the dreams could be ascribed either to the Freud syndrome or to the Jung syndrome. From among those syndrome dreams, 72 percent were congruent with the relevant psychoanalytic orientation, either Freud or Jung. Incidentally, these dream syndromes correspond to the dream contents known to be typical of Freud and Jung themselves. It would appear, then, that the dreams of psychoanalytical patients reflect the dreams of Freud and Jung. These results contradict Freud's assumption that so-called day residues, such as the current relationship with the analyst, could not affect the organization of dreams. How otherwise would a distinction between these dream series in both form and content be conceivable? If dreams are predominantly produced by the so-called unconscious, then the products of the unconscious are obviously not independent of concrete relationships.

Our innermost self-perception, our most private feelings and fantasies, are therefore largely caused by interactions with persons close to us, and by *their* feelings and fantasies. From all this *it appears unlikely that we have any psychological spheres at all whose contents are not also of an interactional nature.*

Amazingly, the two pioneers, Freud and Jung, both communicated such observations themselves without, however, paying them any more attention. Thus Jung (1972) writes to the analyst James Kirsch: "As far as the patient is concerned, it is quite correct that her dreams are caused by you. The female spirit is earth awaiting seed. This is the meaning of transference. The less conscious always receives spiritual fertilization from the more conscious. . . . As soon as certain patients start treatment with me, the type of their dreams begins to change. In the deepest sense *we do not dream only from within ourselves, but instead from what lies between us and the other.*" It is a pity that as far as I know Jung never developed these thoughts any further.

Freud (1940a, pp. 307–8) speaks about how dreams can be influenced by the doctor's suggestion: "No proof is needed for the fact that the manifest contents of dreams is influenced by the analytical cure. After all, this follows from the insight that a dream continues from waking life and processes its stimuli. What happens in the analytical cure is, of course, also part of the impressions of waking life, and is very soon among the strongest, too. It is therefore no wonder that the patient dreams of things that the doctor has discussed with him, and whose expectation he has awakened in him." Thus many patients have dreams that "may have been fantasized at the doctor's suggestion instead of having been brought to light from the dreamer's unconscious." How can distinctions be made? When and how are such influences at work? Freud suspects that positive transference could be the motor of such dreams, which support the intentions of the analysis in this manner. Thus a dreamer in analysis could succeed better in bringing to light what is repressed than could a dreamer outside the analytical situation. The interactional situation is therefore suited to help the dreamer bring the repressed to light.

Freud (1940a, p. 309) thinks, however, that this influence does not affect the actual dream work, and he attempts to substantiate this by means of a (faulty) argument. He reports on a discussion with a patient who asked whether his dreams, which confirmed analytical interpretations, could not be an expression of his submissiveness to Freud. Freud replied by saying that the analysand remembered dreams that he had had before entering analysis. "The analysis of these dreams, which were free of the suspicion of having been suggested, resulted in the same interpretations as the later ones." The analysand did raise the objection that the earlier dreams had been less clear than the ones occurring during analysis, but for Freud the correspondence of the dreams before and during analysis was sufficient evidence of the slight dream-forming influence of the analyst. In my opinion, Freud overlooks the fact that remembering, formulating, and uttering memories can be influenced a great deal by the analytical situation and by positive transference (interaction). We never learn what the patient really dreamed in previous times; we learn only about those dream reminiscences that can now be formulated in the analytical situation and in the relationship with the therapist.

We have come across a seeming paradox, then: what I perceive of my "unconscious" is not free but influenced by the current, real relational situation. I can perceive more of the unconscious if I am in an interactional relational situation, and can penetrate more deeply into the unconscious than I could if I were all by myself. The discovery that the I shapes itself with the help of the You or, rather, results from what is in between is unexpectedly confirmed where it has been least suspected: in the products of the unconscious in the dream.

This provides a further indication that I as a person am not centered in myself only, and that a so-called self does not manifest itself independently of the environment, but rather, that I as a person am fundamentally part of processes that organize themselves in a systemic-interactional manner.

LANGUAGE AND UNDERSTANDING

We understand ourselves only by means of language that is also understood by others. Our feelings, fantasies, ideas, and needs cannot be perceived in the abstract. We become conscious of them only to the extent to which we can formulate our perceptions. Our self-perceptions must assume shape in order to become conscious and comprehensible. As long as something is not expressed in language, it remains shapeless and unstructured. A thought cannot be thought without language. Wilhelm von Humboldt (1968, p. 374) held that "language is not only the relation of an independently shaped thought, but in itself the organ that shapes the thought." It is not as if a thought first comes to my mind "as such," and only afterward is expressed in language; rather, every thought becomes comprehensible to me only in its linguistic formulation.

According to Maurice Merleau-Ponty (1966, p. 211) there is no extralinguistic thinking. "Only by being named can something come into existence or be changed. God creates things by naming them." It is peculiar, and not at all self-evident from the start, that the form into which I must shape my self-perceptions in order to become conscious of them and to tackle them is the same form in which I can communicate these perceptions to other people. The language I speak with myself is the language I use with my partners. I cannot make myself comprehensible to myself in a way that differs from how I make myself comprehensible to others; indeed, I often become comprehensible to myself only after talking with others. In itself it may seem possible that every person carries on an internal monologue in his or her private language, but this is simply not true. Every man is clear to himself only insofar as he can explain himself to others, too; it may even be argued that his efforts to explain himself to others are an aspiration toward clarity about himself. Humboldt (1968, p. 377) remarks about this: "Man understands himself only by experimentally testing the comprehensibility of his words on others." The searching movements of self-perception avail themselves of language and interaction, for to find myself means to be able to make myself understandable to others. "I comprehend myself only to the degree to which I succeed in making myself comprehensible to others. My own clear thought is the result of communicative efforts. Thus no man has immediate, privileged access to himself."

Every human process of becoming aware takes place in the creation of language and images, including myths, rituals, fairy tales, symbols, music, rhythm, miming, poetry, gestures, dance, "body language," and artistic creations in color and shapes. Consciousness may assume the shape of an image, and it may have the effect of an image. One particular kind of language is physical language, the language of the body.

BODIES AND PERCEPTION

We perceive ourselves as the bodies that can also be perceived by other people. K. Dürkheim (1983) speaks of a physique that I have and of a body that I am. I have a physique that helps me to be energetic and efficient, and to function in the real day-to-day world. The body that I am shows my integral being. It can allow my innermost essence to manifest itself in the world. *The body is the organ that can enable us to experience our actual essence. The body, not consciousness, is the organ that enables us to sense our innermost core. If we try to listen to ourselves, then we hear the actual much more clearly as body than as consciousness. The wholeness of the person sounds through the body.*

The body plays a central role in present-day psychotherapy and humanistic psychology. Bioenergetics (founded by Alexander Lowen, a disciple of Wilhelm Reich) starts from the assumption that neurotic energy blockages may express themselves both in emotions and in muscular tenseness, and therapy may thus tackle them equally from both sides. Bioenergetics concentrates on the study of human personality from the perspective of physical energy processes. The production of energy through respiration and metabolism, and the discharge of energy through motion, are the basic functions of life. The amount of energy a person has, and the way in which he or she expends it, determine how that person copes with life situations. In a way, biography may be gleaned from the body. Words can tell lies; bodies cannot. Disowned emotions and defense mechanisms result in unnatural posture and in muscular tenseness. Neurotic character structures and suppressed emotions have their counterpart in chronic muscular tension. These muscular tensions are frozen impulses to act, particularly those of an aggressive or sexual nature. The forgotten impulses remain intact but are not used. The totality of such muscular tensions constitutes a system of muscular armor that screens us from both external stimuli and internal impulses.

A holistic development also includes the perception of body language. Many people use their bodies like engines, which they expect to be in good working order without having any personal relationship with them. The body, however, is the place where we can most sensitively perceive what in our being presses toward manifestation, if we open ourselves to the messages of the body. Thus Dürkheim does not invite us to drop our shoulders in meditation, but to allow our shoulders to drop. The fact that the language of the body is often more direct and clearer than consciously spoken language is an important experience, particularly in psychotherapy. Much of the rage, anger, fear, shame, and desire that we experience but disown speaks to us in the language of the body.

The body is not only the place where our being manifests itself but also the place where we become visible to our fellow human beings. We may disown our anger, our rage, our fear, our shame, and our desire in front of other people, and keep it secret from them, but the body does not tell lies, and usually communicates our feelings to others in an unmistakable way.

Quite frequently situations arise in which we let the body speak for us because a conversation is too difficult or hopeless. We feel less responsible for the language of the body, and we are also made less responsible for it. If a man's body expresses reserve, rejection, or rage while he is declaring verbally how much he enjoys being with his partner, the verbal efforts toward an encounter may be perceived, but the body's message of rejection is also taken into account. Rejection expressed bodily is often more easily excused than rejection expressed verbally.

It is in the sphere of sexuality that the body most often utters what the partners do not dare express. A man's impaired potency is not merely an expression of his own insecurity, but is perhaps meant to communicate to his partner that he is neither willing nor able to join in like this; the contact may be too frustrating, or he may feel sexually misused, or it comes out of defiance or rage because he does not feel accepted in other ways. Quite often I have treated patients who reacted with impotence because, unlike themselves, their wives urgently wanted a child. The men did not dare oppose this desire for a child openly. The penis as the man's representative spoke to his wife. Many married women, on the other hand, react with so-called sexual aversion. Whereas previously they were sexually highly responsive, they now suddenly tolerate no physical contact whatever, and have a deep aversion to every kind of sexual act. Here, too, the body expresses a relational disturbance that is often verbally disowned. The relationship is no longer harmonious in a holistic and thus also in a physical sense. Insofar as the disharmony may not be expressed in words, it is expressed bodily.

Furthermore, it is also not rare at all for the body to speak as the *partner's* representative. Impaired potency protects and conceals the woman's sexual insecurity. Seemingly, the disturbance is exclusively the man's; in truth it may perhaps predominantly be the woman's. Or a man provokes a woman's sexual attitude of defense by proceeding too brashly. He then complains that she is sexually inhibited, but his impetuosity only serves to conceal his own sexual inhibitions. Just as happens with claustrophobia, agoraphobia, and cardiac neuroses, the person who shows the symptoms may be the one who suffers, but he or she is by no means always the one who is actually ill. Rather, the symptom results from the phobic atmosphere of the partnership, from constriction, clinging to each other, and fear of separation. Fairly frequently, the symptom occurs in the partner first, and is then seemingly taken over by the other. A wife whose husband had shown the symptom before and who was now herself being treated by us for this symptom said, "I am glad that it is I who am ill now, and not he, because I feel that I can cope better with it than he could."

It is therefore the connecting atmosphere, the "in between" (Buber) or, rather, the relational field that lets the body speak, and the body in its reaction not only speaks for its "owner," but also can be where a suprapersonal process manifests itself. It is as if a suprapersonal relational body were actualizing itself in the bodily instrument of one or other of the partners.

This idea is considered natural by many primitive peoples. According to Capra (1982, chap. 9) the prominent characteristic of the shamanic concept of illness is the belief that human beings are integral parts of an organized system, and that every illness is the consequence of some disharmony within the cosmic order. Correspondingly, shamanic therapy attaches great importance to the restoration of harmony and of the equilibrium of nature with nature, and in human relationships. According to shamanic traditions, humans are part of a living social group and a cultural religious system. The patient's individual psychological and spiritual state is less important. Men and women are not predominantly appreciated as individuals. Rather, their biographies and their personal experiences, including their illness, are regarded as a result of their membership in a social community. In some traditions, the social connection is so emphasized that an individual's organs, physical functions, and symptoms are inseparably linked with social relations and other environmental phenomena.

For us modern Westerners, such ideas sound unpleasant. We would like to regard our body as our most private space, as the most intimate place in which I can appear, as the place of my personalization and my self-development. Correspondingly we would like to protect our body from the influence of other human beings, and establish boundaries against them. In order to achieve this, I can withdraw so far from human relationships that the influences of other people and of entire relational systems cannot be "embodied" in my body. Or I can decide to commit myself actively to inter-human processes, and be glad to make my body available as a place where disharmonies in my commitment or in the common process can be manifested and then healed.

Merleau-Ponty argues (Böckenhoff, p. 251) that a child's original relational form is the perception of the mother's intentions in his or her own body, but also the perception of "my body with hers and thus my intentions in her body." In a strict sense, the body is not private. The consciousness of my body is the perception of my situation within the coordinate system of my environment. "As the parts of my body together form a system, thus from now on the other's body and my own are one single whole, the two aspects of one single phenomenon." The newborn boy is in a state in which he cannot distinguish himself from others. It is therefore impossible to say that a newborn child communicates with another, for communication presupposes a separation between communicants. Initially, therefore, there is a state of precommunication, in which the mother's intentions somehow work through my body, and my intentions through the mother's body. This original state remains at work in adult life, even in cases of high individual differentiation.

RESISTANCE AND DEVELOPMENT

We need challenge and resistance from outside in order to develop and grow.

> *What, wind, would you be*
> *Without the trees you thunder through?*
> *What, spirit, would you be*
> *Without the trees which are homes to you?*
> *All life needs something to withstand,*
> *All light needs dimness, flows*
> *Of air need trees or dunes of sand:*
> *An exercise, through which it grows.*
>
> CHRISTIAN MORGENSTERN

Just as light can manifest itself only through objects that resist it, so we experience our potential by means of the external resistance that lends it shape and permits it to crystallize. Govinda says, "Force as such is not creative. It becomes creative only when it finds resistance." The person can appear only because of the resistance of the environment. A sculptor becomes a sculptor by overcoming the resistance of the stone; a farmer becomes a farmer by toiling against the resistance of the soil and the weather; a doctor becomes a doctor only by fighting the resistance of illness and patient; a psychotherapist becomes a psychotherapist only by outwitting the resistance of psychological suffering.

The person develops skills only by mastering resistance. This can be observed in the development of the baby boy who gradually conquers his environment, tackling new and more difficult problems again and again. He learns to grasp things, to tear them apart, to bite them to bits; he learns to conquer space, to climb over obstacles; he learns to use objects. A child develops by dealing with objects. If a child receives little stimulation, as in an institution, for example, then developmental delays may occur. According to Piaget and Inhelder (1966), the developmental delay that René Spitz observed in institutionalized children is caused not merely by the lack of a mother-child relationship, but much more generally by the lack of stimulating interactions. Nowadays it is generally accepted that a child needs external stimulation in order to develop skills. What is criminally neglected, however, is the challenge of intellectual and mental skills in old age. We still act as if the more looked-after old people are, and the more they are relieved of all their difficulties and are turned into mere recipients of charity, into passive consumers, the happier they are.

In this context I would like to mention the tragicomic results of an investigation by Blenkner, Bloom, and Nielsen (1971). These three authors drew up a pilot program to improve the care of old people. The random sample consisted of 164 people over the age of sixty who did not live in their own homes and who, it was assumed, were no longer in a position to look after themselves, for which reason they figured on the lists of the welfare offices. The cases were randomly separated into a test group and a control group. Four highly qualified social workers were employed to go through a special care program with the test group, while the control group received merely the standard care of the local welfare offices. Unexpectedly, the mortality rate of the better-cared-for test group was higher than that of the control group after only a year (25 percent as opposed to 18 percent). At the end of the fourth year, this difference was even more pronounced, amounting to 63 percent as opposed to 52 percent. It also seemed a paradox that a much higher proportion of the test group (who received particularly intensive outpatient care) had to be housed in old people's homes: 61 percent in the fifth year, as opposed to the control group's 47 percent. Intensive care by social workers apparently accelerated the deterioration of competence and increased the mortality rate. Similar observations reveal that once people have been admitted into a home for the chronically ill, they soon begin to lose their mental abilities, and often die relatively quickly.

Analogous observations are known in the sphere of industrial psychology. The declared aim of a company is to manufacture products as efficiently as possible. Management, which is responsible for production, is largely guided by a view of people that was described as Theory X by D. McGregor (1960). According to this theory, the average man has an innate aversion to work and tries to avoid it whenever he can. For this reason he must usually be forced, guided, led, and threatened with punishment so that he meets the company's requirements. Moreover, he prefers to be led by the hand, would like to dodge responsibility, has relatively little ambition, and is concerned above all with safety.

On the basis of comprehensive experience as a company consultant, McGregor became convinced that the average man is not naturally like that, but that such behavior is a consequence of management behavior in the company. People whose work does not allow them to satisfy their own needs behave precisely as Theory X predicts: they become lazy and passive, shirk responsibility, resist change, are susceptible to demagogues, and make absolutely absurd claims about economic advantages. As Ulich demonstrates, a company produces not only goods and services but also human qualities and behavior. "The product of work is people" (Herbst 1975). If companies are to stand accused of damaging the environment by polluting air and water, should they not also be made responsible, Ulich asks, for the damage to personality development and mental health caused by working conditions? In factories that do not sufficiently challenge the work force, and in which work is routine, repetitive, and supervised by others, absenteeism because of illness is particularly high. Demanding activities keep intellectual abilities alive; undemanding ones let them go to waste.

A person needs resistance in order to be able to develop his or her potential. A person becomes a person only by overcoming the environment. On the other hand, a person creates his or her own environment. The result is a circular process: a man selects, and is involved in the creation of, that environment which enables him to bring himself and his ideas into existence. To a certain extent, he selects the material that puts up enough resistance to enable him to develop the skills he considers to be his most important. Thus it is the difficult stone for the sculptor, the difficult soil for the farmer, the difficult patient for the doctor that provides each the chance to prove his or her worth.

Nowadays there is a widespread tendency to deprecate the resistances and limitations of external reality, particularly for interhuman relationships. We speak of compulsion, suppression, and constriction. We develop not only because of the support of our aspirations, however, but at least equally because of the resistance that we are offered and that stimulates us to act creatively. A man *does not have* a personality, nor does he have such characteristics as intelligence, reliability, and diligence. He *is not* a personality, either, but he becomes a personality time and again; that is, he appears to be a personality only because of the challenges of his environment.

If the challenges diminish, then the person can no longer appear in the same way. If a personality keeps appearing in a similar way, which is then described as character or personality structure, this may mean only that he keeps being challenged by his environment in a similar way. If the familiar environment changed, then the familiar behavior would change, too.

Creativity

Creative work allows a person to develop fully. I as a person not only develop and regulate myself in an environment that I continuously create for myself from birth; I also perceive myself in my effects on this environment. Self-perception—listening to myself, sensing my inner being, perceiving my own feelings, fantasies, and needs—should, in my development as a human being, find an important complement in the creation of realities, of creative works in which I become visible to myself. Max Frisch says: "To write is to read oneself." By shaping what moves in me, I can encounter this shape and deal with it. The poet and painter Henri Michaux said something similar: "Just as I write in order to find something, I also draw in order to find something, to rediscover something, to be given back, as a gift, what I own without knowing it." Thus the painter often experiences the created work, the painting, as a responding reflection of his or her experiences, which manifest themselves visibly only through daily work with colors and shapes. The painting is extracted from dreams or from the unconscious and receives its full, visible presence only in the act of being painted.

We do not first have a picture in us, which we then paint; but the act of creation is itself the creative process in which we assume shape. It is as if we can encounter ourselves in the objectivization of the work, as if we become tangible and visible to ourselves in our work. In creative work we can capture forever certain otherwise volatile feelings and emotions, so that we can deal with them retroactively.

In this context it is a frequent experience that the work precedes the creator. A painter will create something intuitively and must then appropriate what he or she has created, must reflectively and consciously catch up with what has been created intuitively. Inner experiences are not simply reproduced in a painting. Paintings evoke by creating new significances and new contents of experiences. Creative work distinguishes itself crucially from fantasies and dreams in that it renders possible a certain continuity in the historical development of a person by consolidating that development creatively. Thus the creation is both an expression of the inner world and a stimulus for the inner world. Work and inner experiences stimulate each other circularly into a process. We can take our bearings from, and find support in, what we have created. Creative work is of central value for the discovery of identity, because in creative work I become visible to myself. This, too, represents a crucial distinction from fantasies and dreams.

Creative work and a critical examination of it can have a salutary effect on and reinforce a person's self-regulation. Frisch says: "I write out . . . of my personal needs. Possibly out of fear, which had already made cave dwellers into creative people: you paint the demons on the walls of your cave so that you can live with them." The creative work of art, too, can be an artist's attempt at reparation. An artist's inner danger is expressed in his or her work, and is simultaneously overcome by means of artistic creation. The work of art may become the supporting symbol between destructive and structuring forces. The work of art may help me to gain distance from my own fear, and to encounter myself.

Even if a human being has no special creative and artistic talents, the shaping of something by means of language is an act that allows inner feelings and fantasies to be apprehended and encountered. Language, as mentioned above in Humboldt's terms, is not the designation of independently shaped thoughts, but is in itself the organ that shapes the thoughts. Only by coming out of himself by means of articulated language, only by "uttering," can a man succeed in perceiving himself. In Humboldt's words (1968, pp. 374–77): "As spiritual aspiration forces its way out between a person's lips, its result returns to that person's own ears; the subjective, inner act is again perceived as external object." But like all creative work, the uttered word becomes a reality in the external world, a reality that becomes visible and available to other people in the same manner as it did to the utterer.

Words can move mountains, work wonders, start wars, result in murder and manslaughter, seal marriages, effect witchcraft and curses; words can trigger all kinds of intense emotions, and can critically affect the development of human beings. Freud, above all, discovered the powerful effect of language in psychotherapy. As long as I only think something, it is largely my private affair. What I pronounce, how-

ever, creates realities with real consequences. There is a
decisive difference between thinking that Joe Smith is an idiot
and calling him one. I may indicate that I consider him an
idiot by means of my stance, my facial expression, my gaze;
as long as I do not pronounce it, I can always deny and correct
it. As soon as I pronounce it, I place a reality in the world
that I can no longer undo. Joe Smith may be provoked into
wanting to insult me in turn; he may even decide to sue me
for slander. The word I have pronounced provides him with
the opportunity to get the upper hand. With creative work,
too, I create something external, objectify my essence. This
exterior may become independent and confront me, control
me, and deprive me of my freedom.

Realities created by people—works, paintings, words—
often gather their own momentum and, once detached from
their creators, become processes of their own, in which the
creators may participate but which they may no longer be
able to control, and which are no longer their own, either.
Images and ideas as works are no longer simply objects, but
may themselves become creative forces. Many revolutions
slipped from their instigators' influence and then developed
in a direction that had not been intended. Ideas require the
shape of the word in order to become comprehensible. Words
may be pregnant with significance and may trigger ideational
processes that spread epidemically and like an explosion, and
will survive as long as there are people who lend these ideas
strength, feed them, and develop them further.

Creative work, the created painting or the word, may
become part of my environment. It may give me an identity.
It may also tie me to a false identity. Through creative work
I become visible to others. Others may identify me with my
work, and see in it the image of my person. With our works
we lay down traces and signs through which we will remain
identifiable. A work of art can become a reality of its own,
which, detached from me, gathers its own momentum.

If we start from the assumption that a man can develop

his potential, his powers, and his skills only by means of the resistance that he is offered, and that his creative work has an essentially stabilizing effect on him and fosters his identity, we are bound to recognize the great significance of labor for human existence. Human alienation from ourselves and from our fellow human beings is the subject of one of Karl Marx's fundamental theories. The working man creates something, a product, which is no longer his own. In this manner he alienates himself from his work and ultimately from himself. "The worker's alienation from his product not only means that his labor becomes an object, an external existence; but it also means that his labor exists outside him, independently, alien from him, and confronts him as an independent power; and that the life that he has given to the object confronts him as hostile and alien." The division of labor also alienates us from our fellow human beings. "An immediate consequence of it . . . is the alienation of man from man. . . . What obtains with regard to man's relationship with his labor, with the product of his labor, and with himself is also valid for man's relationship with other men, and with another's labor and its product. . . . If the product of labor is not owned by the worker, if it confronts him as an alien force, then this is only possible because it is owned by someone other than the worker." Of course, it is the capitalists who are meant.

At present we are in a difficult phase of restructuring: the increasing rearrangement of labor by microelectronics. Technology has long ceased to serve us; we have, on the contrary, become the servants of technology and of the economy, both of which have become independent processes. We must adapt our working methods to the niches that microelectronics leaves for us to organize freely. For some people, microelectronics means a colossal challenge to organize this technological, information-theoretical, and social process of restructuring in a creative manner. For many others, however, work threatens to become mere supervisory activity, which may well be even more monotonous than assembly-line work.

This could result in a substantial reduction of working hours, or in massive, permanent unemployment; so there would have to be enough challenges outside gainful employment to safeguard human spiritual and personal development.

PERSONS EVOLVE IN RELATIONSHIP

Persons evolve as their relational systems evolve. The person and his or her environment are linked in a circularly developing process. A man creates an environment for himself and is active in it, examines it, familiarizes himself with its peculiarities, its rules, and its nature, settles down in it, works in it, changes it, adapts it to himself and also adapts himself to it, recognizes the limits set on the possibilities of its expansion, and perceives the room for development put at his disposal.

But the relational systems of which a person is part are also continually being transformed and developed. Just as the person's life is structured into different stages, so the "life of the family" also develops through various stages, from the family with small children to the family with schoolchildren to the family in the phase of detachment, and so on. School is a relational system structured in classes, which are usually renewed in a three-year rhythm. Youth clubs, such as the Boy Scouts and sports clubs, are relational systems preserved by generations that succeed one another every three to four years. The same is true of working teams, which are not developed continuously but in generationlike phases of organization, stabilization, dissolution, and reorganization. Leading staff are promoted or go into retirement; younger staff move up; new staff must get used to the work and partially adapt themselves, but on the other hand they change the company, bring along new ideas, and find their places in the systemic self-organizing work process.

Just as I create my environment for myself, so do relational systems create their members for themselves. The relational system actively interacts with the man who is part of it, examines him in his singularity, in his limitations and possibilities, tries to change him, to develop him, to limit and to use him, demands adaptation from him but also adapts itself to him. The development of the person and the development of the relational system are in a complementary relation of tension. They continually negotiate how much mutual influence they allow each other, where one sets firm limits for the other, where compromises can be made, where developments are of common interest.

Piaget and Inhelder (1966) have made a comprehensive study of the child's mental faculties in the child's interaction with his environment. They view the tendency to adapt to the environment in two forms: in assimilation and in accommodation. In assimilation, the environment is adapted to one's own organism. In accommodation, the organism adapts to the environment and its requirements. We must eat in order to survive. We must therefore accommodate ourselves in the environment in a way that lets us succeed in procuring foodstuffs. We must examine the environment, actively deal with it, observe its rules and regulations, and adapt ourselves to it. In a second phase, however, we must assimilate the foodstuffs. We must cut them up and prepare them chemically in such a way that they can be absorbed through the intestinal mucosa and be utilized by the body. Here environmental conditions, in the shape of foodstuffs, have to adapt themselves to the organism.

These adaptation processes can easily be generalized to the life of the adult. When a man first enters a relational system—say, a working team—this causes a disturbance. From his point of view, he must ask how far he can join the team without losing his own singularity—i.e., how far the team will adapt itself to him, and how far he must adapt himself to the team in order to become effective in it. In the course of a subtle process, both parties gain clarity about the limits of the readiness for mutual adaptation.

Whereas the infant usually relates only to the nuclear family, it is a characteristic of his further development that the relational systems of which he becomes part become increasingly varied, pervade and influence one another, and are interwoven like a network. Urie Bronfenbrenner (1979) has described this systemic network as follows. *Microsystems* are relational systems in which the person has direct relationships, plays parts, and carries out activities. These various microsystems are in turn interrelated into *mesosystems*. Examples of mesosystems are the relationships between family and school, family and neighborhood, or working team and in-house sports club. *Exosystems* are systems of which other members of microsystems are part, and which therefore have an indirect influence on the person. For a child, for instance, his father's working team is an exosystem. If the father has been humiliated or oppressed by his employer, this can affect the child's educational behavior. Events in the exosystem may influence the child's immediate surroundings, although the child is not part of this system. The *macrosystem* is the suprapersonal system as a complex of variously connected systems of a certain culture or subculture. Examples of macrosystems are the community, the country, the language area, and so on. The children of legal aliens, for example, may experience the conflict that their family's microsystem is not part of the macrosystem in which they live. This may result in identity conflicts, because they feel that they belong to two different macrosystems that are very difficult to integrate.

The person develops a history, which is represented by his or her effects on the environment. The person leaves behind traces and signs by which to recognize himself or herself and also be recognized by the environment. In his or her development there are phases of the stabilization and integration of the environment created, as well as phases of the dissolution and destruction of what was created, and of the re-creation of the environment. Changes in environmental conditions may stimulate as well as obstruct the person's development processes. Changes in the person and changes in the relational systems are interrelated.

Birth entails a comprehensive change in the child's relation to the environment. Previously the child lived in an environment with constant temperature, constant quality of skin contact, and relatively restricted changes in light and in intensity of sound; then suddenly he or she enters a world with various stimuli, with a much broader spectrum of quantitative and qualitative environmental influences. For the marriage partnership, however, birth also entails a profound change in the relational system. Previously, husband and wife were lovers and lived together in companionship; now they are parents. This makes the partnership substantially more binding and more responsible. Questions arise about division of labor in the family and at work. The births of children often result in a stronger role polarization between husband and wife. Often, too, their personal relationship with each other is changed. The partners can no longer just be a twosome and live for each other, but must essentially orient their relationship toward the child. Each partner must share the other with the child. The birth of the child changes not only the partnership but also relationships with all other systems. Frequently, the relationship with the parents' own parents is intensified, because they assume a new function as grandparents. The circle of acquaintances and friends is often changed, too, and is now more strongly oriented toward those who are also concerned with bringing up children. The birth of a child thus stimulates the development of young adults in an intense and comprehensive manner, and creates new and novel relational systems and networks.

The development of the person and the development of relational systems are interdependent. When the young woman breast-feeds her baby, she has her first experiences as a mother, just as the baby has its own first relational experiences. Breast-feeding maintains a special mother-child dyad for a certain time. After weaning, this symbiotic relationship is deprived of its special nature; the child's relationship with its mother need no longer differ in nature from that with its father or with other people. This alters the baby's reference system, but also its "relational capacity": it has the first presentiments of the subject-object division, a diffuse consciousness of I and You.

At the age of two to three years, the development of both the child and its family is again fundamentally changed. The infant begins to play with peers. Its behavior in these interactions is at first very clumsy; it may have difficulties in sharing with other children, in distinguishing between mine and yours; it is full of a conquering urge on the one hand, but on the other hand full of fear that everything will be taken from it; the child still finds it difficult to cooperate. On going to kindergarten the child must for the first time fit in with an organized group. She must learn that she is no longer the center of attention, that there are others besides her who also want to come into their own; she must learn to wait her turn. At the same time, however, more intense relationships with her peers are developed; the first peer groups are formed and meet without supervision of parents or school. The child is now in the relational systems of home, school, and peer group, which in turn are related to each other.

On entering school the child climbs on to a further fundamentally changed level of development and relationships. The time of play is over; she is required to fulfill concrete tasks and functions, which are compared with those of other pupils, and judged. Already the child must be able to fulfill certain social expectations; she plays a role that entails certain duties. Whenever she later completes another phase of her education or vocational training, her relational systems change with the increasing maturation of the person. If initially a teacher and a self-contained class formed a stable and familiar environment, the structure now becomes relaxed. Teachers concentrate more on the communication of knowledge. The acquisition of knowledge lies increasingly within the student's sphere of responsibility. Her performance is examined at less frequent intervals. Also, the parents' abilities to help the adolescent at school are more and more restricted. The peer group becomes more and more important to the adolescent. In puberty her body changes, and thus her relationship with her own and the other sex changes, too. She must be able to cope with her own sexual role.

This interaction between personal development and the development of the relational systems continues throughout life. In working life, changing positions in the course of our career also changes our professional relational system. If a man is promoted within a company, his relationship with the colleagues he has been familiar with changes more or less perceptibly.

Further fundamental changes in the relational systems and in personal development occur in old age. Although it is always pointed out that old people find it difficult to readjust themselves, they are nevertheless expected to readjust themselves more than they ever have before in life. The move to an old people's home means the loss of their own apartment and of the independent management of the household with all the duties, tasks, and responsibilities involved. It means the loss of relationships with neighbors, house owners, tradesmen, and so on, often also the loss of control in their own kitchen, along with the loss of the relational systems connected with shopping. The move to an old people's home is often linked with the loss of essential pieces of property that constitute a firm component of a person's identity: familiar pieces of furniture, paintings, a garden, flowers on a balcony. In an old people's home, the person lives exclusively among other old people; he or she must establish new relationships with them, which is often difficult, since many people do not want to identify themselves with the existence in an old people's home, and make this known by not getting involved in relationships with others.

Every change in the relational system represents a chance but also a danger for the person's further development. When a person's position in the environment is altered by a change in the area of life and in his or her role, this is called an *ecological transition* (Bronfenbrenner 1979). Ecological transitions may result not only from biological and psychic changes but also from changes in the environment. Such ecological transitions may induce fear. Many people try to avoid such transitions, sometimes by developing a critical illness, such as anorexia nervosa. Nonetheless, the person's further development necessitates change in the relational system. Thus ecological transitions are both cause and result of development processes, and indicate how person and environmental systems are in continuous mutual dependence and in a common evolutionary process.

In this chapter I have outlined an ecological paradigm of the person. This paradigm regards the person as a relational being, as part of relational systems with which he or she is in a continuous exchange and whose development processes are mutually dependent. There are no "intrapsychic areas" that function autonomously and independently of the environment. A person's "unconscious," his or her dreams, fantasies, and physical experience, too, are influenced and caused by interactions with partners and with relational systems. The person needs the resistance and the challenge of his or her environment in order to develop. We perceive ourselves in our creations, and form our identity from the traces that we leave behind. We are part of our relational systems, which in turn are part of us.

The person is an idea-producing and idea-processing being, connected with the environment by means of an exchange of ideas, and at the same time part of suprapersonal ideational processes. In subsequent chapters, the coevolution of person and relational systems will first be presented for the dyad, the person's relationship with a partner to whom he or she is committed in a long-term relationship. It will

then be presented in the larger perspective of familial evolution throughout the generations, and finally in the evolution
of suprapersonal ideational processes, of which the person is
an element, and which articulate themselves in the person.

PART II

Growing
Together

CHAPTER 4

Coevolution in
Our Relationships

I have so far spoken of environment, external realities, and relational systems in a rather general way. How does the matter stand, however, if we do not speak generally of environment, but start from the assumption that this environment is a You, a partner, who does not face me passively, who does not simply offer me resistance or passively permit me to impose a shape, but is as active as I am, both in encounter and in relationship? To what extent is this You an environment created by me? To what extent am I an environment created by this You? What happens if the creation of me and you is fused into *one single* process, if I influence this You both as myself and as this You's creation, and if this You responds to me both as a self and as my creation?

Since the thoughts presented in this book stem from practical psychotherapy, and in particular from couples and family therapy, concrete psychotherapeutical experiences will be examined more closely in this and the next two chapters, so that the foundations of these experiences become more comprehensible to the reader.

RECENT ATTITUDES TOWARD COMMITMENT AND DIVORCE

We live in a time in which both separation from a partner and dissolution of human systems are regarded by more and more people as an opportunity for individual growth. It is correct that transitions in personal development are at the same time always transitions to new or transformed relational systems, and vice versa. The dissolution of a relational system clears the way for creation of a new person within new relational systems. The positive appreciation of separation as a chance for personal growth has meanwhile been carried so far, however, that many people have come to consider divorce a sort of "achievement test" for emancipation. Many people can no longer discern the specific growth-stimulating opportunities of lasting long-term relationships. Dealing with the subjects of separation and individual growth seems to me to be less important today than considering how a person can grow within ecological human systems and within long-term relationships. Many people can no longer even imagine this; instead they are apt to ask how personal growth is conceivable *despite* a long-term relationship.

SHORT-TERM AND LONG-TERM RELATIONSHIPS

Short-term and long-term relationships have radically different properties. All psychological concepts, even individual-centered ones, emphasize the high value of human relationships for personal growth. The individual—it is said —needs interhuman exchange, interhuman encounter; every woman has sexual, erotic, and physical needs; every man needs an authentic relationship in which the feedback he receives from his partner enhances his self-perception and stimulates his personal growth. The capacity for intense interpersonal exchange, for the greatest possible closeness, openness, and acceptance, is nowadays being explored in many psycho-workshops. These relational aspects reveal the decisive qualities of any valuable relationship, whether it is a one-night stand, a fleeting love relationship, or a long-term relationship planned to last. A long-term relationship arising out of love, such as marriage, has above and beyond this completely different qualities, which, however, are largely dismissed as negative these days. Marriage—it is said—is a prison, linked with stagnation in growth, with claims to ownership, customary rights, dependence, and repression. Marriage as an institution is rejected because it means fixed role expectations, rules, limitations and compulsions, and because it is said to restrict personal growth. A long-term relationship, however, is not only the encounter of two individuals who consider themselves independent but also a system, which, by definition, possesses all the qualities of a system, including structure (see Lemaire, p. 122). With the long-term relationship, a shared, purposive process is initiated, which organizes itself systemically. I can choose freely whether I want to make myself part of a long-term relationship, whether I want to stay out of it, or whether I want to leave it. Within the relational system I will, in any case, not be free and independent, but will have to subordinate my personal growth to the laws inherent in the system. But how can a man subordinate himself to the laws of a system if his external circumstances in no way encourage him to take any interest in this system? In order to understand this, we must examine what people have to say whose long-term relationships were suddenly and unexpectedly broken up.

PERSONAL REORGANIZATION AS A SHARED PROCESS

It often happens that the structures and rules of a system can be comprehended only after they have been disturbed and destroyed. Basic medical research—for example, the investigation of the function of cells and organs—often made its discoveries when something healthy was destroyed. What can we learn from the observation of long-term relationships that have been destroyed through a partner's death? There is statistical evidence that the surviving partner often also meets a sudden death after a short interval. Direct statements by the people concerned strike me as more important than figures, though. In this context I would like to refer in particular to statements in Verena Kast's book *Trauern (Mourning)*. She quotes Augustine in his despair after the death of his friend: "For I felt mine and his soul as one soul in two bodies, and therefore life made me shudder, for I did not want to live as one halved" (Kast 1982, p. 14). She quotes statements made by bereaved people, such as: "It is as if he [the deceased] had been torn from me, without any prior warning—and I feel seriously injured, I'm an open wound, I'm bleeding, I'm scared of bleeding to death" (p. 19).

As Kast rightly emphasized, these were not immature persons who had given up and lost themselves in symbiotic relationships with their partners. Rather, these persons' self-experience was embodied in a shared relational space, in a system formed together. Kast (p. 16) says: "It is part of human life that self-experience substantially results from relationships with other people, that *we often experience as our selves what other people have evoked in us* and continue to evoke in us, and that our relationship with our depth, with our innermost selves, is molded by the relationships we have with people, particularly by love relationships." [My italics.]

Our partners not only provide us with feedback that improves our self-perception, and with support and acceptance in our self-development; the relational process as such actualizes us more intensively than we could actualize ourselves in isolation. We experience our selves through being evoked by other people. Our personal characteristics, emotions, and acts appear only, or at least most intensely, when they are made use of by other human beings.

If it is claimed, however, that those people who, after the loss of their partners, feel as if halved, as if cut in two, are *not* immature beings who had immature, symbiotic relationships, how are we to understand this? Does not the present-day view of human nature promote the idea of a person who is self-centered, integral, autonomous, and independent? Let us try to describe in phenomenological terms what happens when two partners form a long-term relationship.

It is significant that I will display only the behavior within a relational space that is seen by the other, and I will say only what the other is likely to respond to, precisely because it is only such behavior that the partner will react to. Thus I am more likely to display what the other can see, and more likely to say what the other is responsive to. Therefore the other can influence me in what I make visible and audible (*personare*) through his or her readiness to see and hear me. In my relatedness to the other person, I will thus change within the relationship. Am I still myself, then? Or must I give myself up for the other?

The other's seeing and hearing, however, does not take place only one way; rather, I can influence how he or she sees and hears me, so that in turn I can reveal and express myself to the extent to which I have made the partner perceptive and responsive. Thus I need not simply adapt myself to the partner; I can change the partner. Yet I do not draw my intention of making my partner perceptive and responsive solely out of myself; rather, this intention is again determined by my partner and by the process we share.

If a love relationship is often a question of experiencing each other both physically and emotionally, then the long-term relationship has the added characteristic of a purposive process, the making of shared history, which creates signs and leaves traces. A couple wants to work on, and create, something together. The relationship is not an end in itself; the partners do not suffice each other in their togetherness, but direct their relationship toward a third, toward a shared objective. Their relationship is not merely a mutual satisfaction of needs, with the added dimension of mutual exploitation, which would be hopeless in a shared process. It is no longer a question of knowing or of being known by another person. Rather, both partners create their common goal and their unique historical process out of the experience of I and You. The partner is a precondition for the perception of this common goal, and for the foundation of a common history in which both of us are recorded as I and You.

Within the relational system, the person is no longer independent, integral, and self-centered, in terms of either behavior or the way he or she feels and experiences things.

The partners' manifest personalities are a function of the common purposive process in which the behavior of the one results from the behavior of the other and from the suprapersonal whole. Not only behavior and the way each feels and experiences things personally, but even dream life is codetermined by the relationship. Equally, each codetermines the partner's feeling, thinking, fantasizing, and experiencing. Each will remain a center of his or her own energy, consciousness, processing, and responsibility, but the way in which each feels, experiences, and fantasizes is no longer mutually independent. Whatever one feels and experiences, he or she also feels and experiences as a part of both of them.

Those parts of the self that are involved in the relational system are reorganized by the suprapersonal whole of the dyad process. In a long-term relationship of husband and wife, these may be large parts of the self of each partner, but never the self as a whole. We are never part of only a single relational system, after all. Rather, we are involved in a multitude of fleeting or lasting, superficial or profound processes that we share with other persons. We must each be able to integrate our various personal involvements, to appraise them, and to relate them to one another. For the formation and maintenance of identity, we must attribute to all these involvements a significance that refers to the personal whole; we must put our self into a relation with them. Since, according to the concept of the interaction personality, constantly changing personal possibilities can be stimulated in every relational system, relational behavior often seems to be contradictory. Husband and wife often do not want to restrict their relationship to certain areas, but want to have the whole person involved in their love for each other. This results in a tension within the persons and within the partnership between those parts of the self that are reorganized into a dyadic whole and those that are not.

Systems theory has the term *supersummation*: the whole is more than, and different from, the sum total of its parts. This is also true of the dyad. The partners organize themselves, as parts of a dyadic whole, differently from the way in which they would organize themselves on their own. Both persons orient their organization at least partially toward the shared, suprapersonal process.

This whole formed by the partners could be called the *dyadic self* (the couple self), by which I mean approximately what Theodor Bovet means by the term *marriage person* or Ludwig Binswanger by *both of us* or Martin Buber by, simply, *We*. I mean *those parts of the partners' personal selves that are bound into the dyadic process and there unite themselves into a suprapersonal self*, which is different from both partners' personal selves. The use of the term *self* for a suprapersonal whole may be somewhat daring. I consider it justified, however, in that *the partners no longer perceive and experience large parts of their selves, of their actual essential cores, independently of each other*. Something like a shared development principle is formed, which is inherent in the couple. Only in this way is it comprehensible that the violent separation of two lovers can be experienced as a being-cut-in-two, as a destruction not only of the relationship but of somebody's own self, which loses its lifeblood, its energies, and its organization. What we observed in a relationship broken up by death is also true for divorces, often in a similar way. Here, too, we recognize what great efforts the partners have to make to reorganize themselves into persons on their own, detached from each other.

The holistic character of the shared process encompasses, in a love relationship, the two persons with their essential cores. As a rule, the formation of the common self entails a decision that in its absoluteness and seriousness is equivalent to a marriage contract. The dyadic reorganization of both partners makes them vulnerable to being damaged by separation to such an extent that a decision not to separate is perfectly appropriate. Nowadays, however, many people no longer want to be tied down by the binding nature of such a relationship, but claim that love is something spontaneous and would be destroyed by any definitions, rules, and structures, and could happen only here and now and in complete freedom.

There is a call for the freedom, in love, to decide for oneself at any time if and when one wants to have other, parallel relationships without having to establish if and when and how strongly these parallel relationships disturb the wholeness of the dyadic self. Many therapists tend to dismiss one partner's claim to absoluteness as a claim to possession, as inappropriate jealousy, as a fear of loss, or as an inability to let go. With increasing experience I have observed that this claim to absoluteness need not be a sign of immaturity, just as the above-mentioned feeling of self-loss in the breakup of a relationship need not be immature. Every human being has the choice nowadays whether to let a love relationship evolve into a long-term relationship or not. In any case, a long-term relationship has rules and structures peculiar to itself as a system. This fact is frequently denied today, and such denial of the system-inherent laws of the long-term relationship is a frequent cause of destructive partnership developments.

In order to protect oneself against being hurt by the partner (and hurt is inevitable where binding rules are not obeyed), each partner turns the long-term relationship into an endless border war, trying to hurt the other as much as one is hurt. By generating jealousy each wants to prove the other to be as dependent, weak, and powerless as oneself. Many painful and destructive developments are based on the partners' frantic compulsion to defend themselves against the formation of a common process, for fear of not being able to tolerate the dissolution of the relationship, a dissolution that is generally to be expected these days. Instead of being a reason for joy, the state of being in love becomes a specter that must be fended off (or at least controlled) enough to let each person leave the relationship undamaged at any time. I think the narcissistic partnerships that are so frequent today are based not so much on the narcissistic relational experiences of early childhood as on the narcissistic paradigms of our time.

COMMUNICATION

Communication in the partnership is never perfect. From what has been said so far, we could assume that the two persons' restructuring toward a common development process would ideally result in a complete adaptation or supplementation of the two personalities. This, however, is far from being the case. Even if a shared process includes both persons, *each of the partners still feels alone in his or her innermost being. Each senses that the partner's capacity for understanding is limited. The desire to be fully and completely understood by at least one human being cannot be wholly fulfilled.* Now that a long-term relationship is no longer an economic necessity but is primarily meant to serve the satisfaction of emotional needs, this limited ability of a partner to accept and understand the other is tolerated less and less. The standard reaction to it is *rage and resignation*; there is a belief that love gives us each a *claim to happiness.* But can happiness be planned? A long-term relationship is a historical process that is unique, in-eradicable, and unrepeatable. Whether or not the *development of this process is happy* can be determined by the partners only *within limits.* On entering into a long-term relationship, they decide *to want to create their world together and to realize themselves in this world.*

If a naive claim to happiness is inappropriate, then so is the demand that the long-term relationship serve the mutual satisfaction of needs. The claim to satisfaction of needs results in a continual *weighing up of who satisfies whose needs better* or, rather, of who *exploits* whom. An ideal equally difficult to realize is the demand that the partner be able to accept and support all of the other's feelings, needs, and actions without reservation, to understand and encourage the other *without making any restrictive demands or having any restrictive expectations.* If the partnership becomes an end in itself, for instance, by serving the ideal mutual satisfaction of needs or by serving comprehensive mutual understanding and acceptance, then this ultimate sense of not being understood in a partnership will result in *insurmountable frustrations.*

If, however, the aim of a long-term relationship is seen to be a common purposive process, whose creation *necessitates common growth in mutual challenge and stimulation,* then a complete correspondence of both persons would actually constitute a *danger. Evolution* does not result from complete correspondence but *from the tension of neither understanding, nor corresponding to, each other completely.* Complete adaptation, like complete nonadaptation, is fatal. *In ecology the natural habitat suits the species adequately* but does not completely define it. *The species adequately fits its natural habitat* but is not completely defined by it. This also applies to a partnership. Complete adaptation and complete nonadaptation are not tolerable in a partnership. *The partners must be adequately suited to each other,* without corresponding to each other completely. A certain amount of strangeness and incompatibility stimulates development and provokes a continuous search for each other.

That the desire (which frequently exists) for symbiosis cannot be fulfilled may demand that the partners do the work of mourning for the loss of this goal. That some desires are unattainable can also be interpreted positively, however: a continuous situation of not being understood by the partner contains a positive chance for improved self-comprehension. The partner's incapacity enhances my own capacity for apprehending and understanding myself. I learn to experience myself through my partner's resistance and limitation.

A woman recently wrote to me: "I do not think that personal development in a partnership must necessarily be restricted or become pointless because one of the two no longer cooperates or can no longer cooperate. . . . I believe and have experienced myself that it is precisely through the severe constriction and the seemingly intolerable pressure that enormous powers can be mobilized and greater maturity can be attained. I owe my own development in recent years, and many essential insights, purely to my endless difficulties, which have not managed to crush me, for the sole reason that I have tried to understand and to survive again and again." Each couple has areas in which the partners cannot find each other. Even in an intense love relationship each partner remains lonely in certain spheres. We might see a certain tragedy in this, but might equally well acknowledge it as a wise protection, which prevents the complete and exclusive fusion of two persons in their relationship. Being able to tolerate the frustration of remaining partially lonely even in love can, within certain limits, stimulate personal maturation and also make a person open to other relationships. As always in a systemic approach, the question is how to optimize the interaction of different factors. Many people feel lonelier and less related in marriage than single people do.

MUTUAL SHAPING

In a long-term relationship the partners shape each other. Within their relational space, the partners no longer think, feel, and act independently of each other, but are directly affected by each other. In the limited relational space of the system, the action of the one is the action of the other: life in a shared home, the furnishing of this home, the decision whether or not to have children, and how to bring them up—all these are realities in the common relational space. Within this space it is not possible for me simply to accept the other just as he or she is, or to support the other's behavior and activities unconditionally, because my own behavior and actions are directly affected by all this. How, then, are reasonable people at all prepared to take upon themselves such a restriction of their own development?

The Chinese symbol of yin and yang is often used for the representation of a love relationship. The space, the field in which yin and yang meet, is limited. It may be larger or smaller, but it is always limited. This restricted space is shared by the two polar centers. Where one expands, the other gives way and withdraws. The two poles do not face each other statically but are in a dynamic relationship. They complement each other. The shape of the one creates the shape of the other; the limits of the one are at the same time the other's limits. A love relationship is characterized by a tense, dialectical relation, in which the gestalt of the common self is subject to continuous confrontation. The partners shape each other by resisting and holding their own, but also by evoking and challenging. If a long-term relationship is understood in this way, then violent conflicts are part of it. Yet this continuous friction and sharpening can also lend each partner a profile, a shape that is being responded to.

According to Rogers's person-centered approach, the most important function of my relationship as well as my partner's is to stimulate my personal growth by means of acceptance and support. However, support is only *one* form of stimulating behavior. Often, resisting and holding my own ground have a more stimulating effect; provocation may cause furious and defiant reactions, but may also trigger crucial developments. This frequently makes it difficult for outsiders to evaluate marital arguments. Outsiders often consider a quarrel worse than the quarreling couple themselves do, since, despite all their rage and bitterness, they experience in the argument a stimulation to tense interaction. Siblings often reveal how stimulating an argument can be: when they are together, life is intolerable owing to their continual quarrels; if one of them is away on holiday, life is so boring that it is even less tolerable. How vital continual arguments can be for many partners in marriage is quite frequently revealed by one partner's intellectual deterioration after the other partner's death.

Frequently, differences of opinion between partners are not based on a genuine incapacity for mutual understanding; rather, one partner more or less consciously provokes the other into assuming an attitude that enables the first partner to assume a contrary attitude. The polarization of the partners' opinions and attitudes may stimulate the dialectical development of certain themes with which the two partners wrestle in their common process.

No matter how much each partner seems to want to reduce tension in a difference of opinion, often each prevents the other from making a concession, because this would break up the stimulating effect of the struggle. In the course of doing therapy with quarreling couples, I have often noticed that they do not respond to attempts to clear up their differences at all. I finally realized that if two people have arguments of such intensity, they must surely attach a great deal of importance to their relationship. I made the mistake of wanting to make them quarrel less. Only now do I realize that this would be dangerous, for less quarreling could be interpreted as a sign of decreasing interest or waning love. Quite often my verbalizing this insight causes both partners to smile, just as if I had caught them in a secret ritual.

According to Erik Erikson (1956/57), being responded to is an important prerequisite for identity formation. One partner will always be able to respond to the other only in a restricted manner, and so will always be shaped in only a restricted manner, in a long-term relationship. Many of a person's possibilities remain undeveloped because they are neither challenged nor given any opportunity to develop. Is it worth renouncing so many opportunities for further development and for the realization of possibilities, all in favor of the partner with whom I have entered into a long-term relationship? The ideology of growth, which is one-sidedly individual oriented, will deny this. In the last analysis, however, limitless claims to individual growth may well produce an effect that is the opposite of their intended goals. Identity—the person's sameness and selfness—means precisely that the person's growth finds and retains an internal continuity, an internal line: by defining myself, I simultaneously limit myself. Also, the demand that I live completely in the here and now may well cause me to miss the historicity of my own existence and thus to succumb to a sense of absurdity and lack of direction. Thus the ultimately relevant question is, what is growth? Do we understand it as the development of as many potential characteristics as possible, and the search for the greatest possible diversity of experiences? Or do we also understand it as self-discovery made possible by the limits set by the relational systems of which each of us is a part, as well as by partners with whom we share a history? "It is limitation that renders form possible," says Govinda (1976). Real maturity and therefore the aim of real growth are likely to lie in the ability to accept the limitation of one's own form, and to transcend it as part of a suprapersonal wholeness.

GROWING TOGETHER, NOT APART

Mutual growth in a common process compensates for the restriction of individual growth in a partnership. Two persons' potentials for development may be dissimilar. Quite often one partner runs against the other's rigid limits, and then breaks down and resigns because he or she does not succeed in stimulating any further growth in the other. In this case, the partner who is willing to grow senses a dilemma: whether to restrain his or her own development for the benefit of the partnership, or to endanger the survival of the partnership by pressing on with his or her own personal development. Many people find a compromise by supplementing the continuing, common dyadic system with individual activities and relationships in which they can develop themselves. Nonetheless, I have treated patients (frequently female, less frequently male) who fell ill with phobic neuroses because they had suppressed their personal development beyond what was conducive to their health in order to spare their partners in their limited development potentials.

Certainly, there are relational situations in which a meaningful common process is no longer possible. In heavily neurotic collusions both partners sense at times that, despite all developmental efforts, they are overtaxed by the task of trying to pull out of their difficulties together. They keep being caught in the same destructive games, and can no longer avoid constraining and hurting each other.

On the other hand, there are always some people who accept restrictions of their development, and of whom it simply is not true that personal growth and self-realization are the only crucial objectives in their lives. This can most easily be seen in a situation where one of the partners has been struck by a serious, chronic, and disabling illness. From the individualistic concept of growth it is far from evident why a healthy husband would severely restrict his personal growth because of his wife's illness, which is not his own, after all. In contrast to this, a thorough investigation by Daniel Hell (1982) of schizophrenic and (endogenetically) depressive patients' marriages concluded that stress on a marriage caused by a psychosis does not contribute toward divorce in a statistically measurable way. Although the divorce rate among schizophrenic patients is three times the average, there is no greater proportion of divorces *after* they have fallen ill than before they have fallen ill, as there presumably would be if stress caused by illness were the major cause of an increased divorce rate. Endogenetically depressed (affective psychosis) patients are divorced more frequently than average *only before* their first hospitalization. *After* they have fallen ill, their divorce rate drops significantly and corresponds to the average rate. Hell comes to the conclusion that a divorce is more likely to cause a (monopolar, endogenetic) depression than a depressive illness is likely to cause a divorce.

In concrete terms: these patients are not disabled people who must be looked after because they are bedridden, or who must be pushed around in their spare time because they are tied to a wheelchair. Rather, they are people with whom the healthy partner can no longer hold a sensible conversation once the illness has set in, with whom a personal exchange is hardly possible any longer, who spread a depressive and oppressive mood, and who also isolate their partners socially, as their fellow human beings withdraw from them. From an individual-centered perspective it can hardly be understood how people can want to take such a situation upon themselves. Many psychotherapists tend to attribute pathological motives to the healthy partner who remains in the relationship: that he or she needs a partner who is ill and dependent on him or her, that he or she tolerates the situation only for reasons of social obligation, or that the illness distracts from unresolved conflicts in the partnership. Hell has told me that partners, when questioned, replied as follows: "We have spent many nice years together; now I can't just leave him [the patient] in the lurch. Our relationship has given me a great deal for many years." Or: "It has always been difficult with her. But I did decide to get married to her and now that she is ill I can't just leave her on her own." Or: "After such a long and beautiful companionship I don't want to, and can't, start all over again." But at times we even hear: "Caring for my partner has given me a task and a purpose in life. Before I depended too much on him and let him guide me. Now his illness has proved a challenge for me to take over more responsibility myself." This creates an impression of faithfulness to a shared history that has become identical with their own. Time and again we hear the partners say: "Well, it's struck *him* now. Could as well have struck me. And then I would have been glad, too, if he had stayed with me." Here again we come across the difficult problem of what personal growth actually is.

Does personal growth imply the development of qualities such as creativity, independence, expansion of consciousness, and integral development of personality? Or does it possibly mean faithfulness to a common history that is also my own, responsiveness to what actually happens in this history, and thus also a capacity to limit my own development in favor of a meaningful participation in processes in which I am needed?

WANTING OTHER RELATIONSHIPS

Freud's observation that, with neurotics, fantasies take precedence over the demands of external realities was later one-sidedly reduced by many representatives of humanistic psychology to give the individual's demands priority over those of the environment. Those humanistic psychologists seem to assume that the highest human function is to live entirely according to our own needs and fantasies, and that no one has the right to restrict the realization of these needs. This becomes a problem particularly when love relationships are maintained parallel to a long-term relationship. The argument is that I have a right to my own emotions, about which nothing can be done anyhow. If I feel as I do, it is more honest to admit it, since it does not make much difference whether something is done in fantasy or in reality. If I fall in love with someone else, this will be noticed by my partner in any case. Thus I would like to include my partner in what is happening, so that he or she knows what I am doing. Knowing that I have fallen in love with someone else, he or she is bound to feel insulted and hurt anyway, and therefore it is a mere formality whether or not I experience this love for another person in its entirety, even physically. I want to have enough courage to stand by myself and my emotions; I do not want to avoid the experiences that impose themselves on me. I want to live them out in the open.

Thus one of Rogers's sources maintains (1977, p. 55)

> that you have the right to experience what you are experiencing, and that you don't need the permission of your partner to do it. At the same time, you care enough for your partner to stay with him while he is having his feelings, and listen to them without feeling overresponsible and letting them control your behavior. . . . I think the ideal situation is when you can tell the partner: "I need and I owe it to myself to experience this other relationship now. I'm hearing your hurt, your jealousy, your fear, your anger; I do not like to receive them, but they are a consequence of the choice I'm making, and I love you enough to want to be available to work through them with you. If I decide not to have this other experience, it is because I choose to do so, and not because I let you stop me."

The justification runs something like this: is it my fault if such needs and fantasies develop in me? What better can I do than be completely open to all experiences that impose themselves on me? Is it my fault if these are experiences that hurt my partner? If I renounced these experiences simply out of consideration for my partner, then I would have to suppress needs and repress emotions of my own. Would the damage not be even greater then? So I behave as if I were the victim of my needs, desires, and fantasies, as if I were at their mercy, without any power of choice or decision.

As a consequence of this sort of popularization of psychology, many ideas have been spread, particularly in this field, that have had a fatal impact on many relationships. Freud never thought that the choice was merely between freely realizing or repressing impulses and needs. Rather, it is the concern of psychoanalysis to admit such needs in the imagination. It is a characteristic of a strong ego that it is capable of regulating such needs according to the principles imposed on it by the external world (reality principle as opposed to pleasure principle). "The ego decides in this manner whether the attempt at satisfaction should be carried out or postponed, or whether the demand of the instinctual drive should not really be suppressed as being dangerous" (Freud 1940b, vol. 17, p. 129). These considerations are more generally accepted with regard to aggressive impulses. Everyone must learn to handle aggressive impulses in a way that is constructive and serves his or her own purposes. The fact that they are not acted on in an unbridled way does not necessarily result in the "damming up of instinctual drives." There is a critical difference between being enraged enough to kill someone in fantasy and doing so in reality. Real is what has real consequences. If someone enters into real rather than imaginary love relationships with third parties, this brings about realities for both long-term partners and the "third party" that may become independent processes over which none has control. I have already mentioned the crucial difference between dream and reality in waking life. Confusion always ensues as a result of not differentiating between a love relationship and a long-term relationship, of saying that a love relationship is equal to a long-term relationship, that the lover has the same relational claims as the long-term partner, and that it is inadmissible to break up a relationship with a lover simply because the partner is hurt.

I think that the problem of handling our needs for intimate relationships with others cannot be solved ideally. Extreme solutions are erroneous here, just as they are almost everywhere in social existence. Most long-term partners get accustomed to living according to an unspoken agreement that prescribes the observance of certain rules, but tolerates a gray area even if it does not openly declare and affirm it. Most couples experience tensions caused by problems that can never be entirely solved. The problem of openness often causes confusion. I have come across many examples, particularly in theologians' marriages, where the idealistic demand for absolute mutual openness had fatal effects. In an often positively purist, indeed loutish, fashion, people tried to detach themselves from the previously prevailing double moral standards, according to which outside relationships (formerly predominantly a male privilege) took place in stealth, while in public all feigned absolute "marital faithfulness." The double moral standards, however, were now reversed, into a morality of openness that, unfortunately, is equally mendacious and hypocritical. Openness often merely serves as a pretext for admissions that hurt the partner, make the partner insecure, or blackmail the partner into accepting the fact that other relationships are desired. If the partner reacts with jealousy, this is called an improper claim to possession, of which he or she must be cured. In any case, the buck is passed to the partner.

Openness cannot be realized unilaterally, but only interactionally. My openness in a relationship can be no more than an exact correlate of my partner's openness toward me.

Openness is a common process of opening oneself for each other, which is always subject to limitations. There is no unrestricted, absolute openness. The partner, and the limits to the partner's ability to be open, must be respected, and the partner must not be disqualified as possessive and egoistic because of these limits. My opening up is codetermined by my partner's openness. It is not always sensible to communicate incidents to a partner who experiences them in a way that differs completely from my own—who, in other words, cannot be open to the significance that a certain incident has for me. Just as I have no right to impose openness on my partner, the partner has no right to commit me to absolute openness. Openness is relevant to all that concerns the shared process, the shared relationship. Here, bilateral efforts at opening up for each other as widely as possible are important. The decisive factor, however, is not the mutual communication of facts, but rather the creation of an atmosphere, of a climate of openness. The encounter of two partners, however, always remains limited. Each has areas that are not shared with the partner, and personal aspects that are better understood by others than by the partner. The demand for unreserved openness often destroys the privacy to which everyone is entitled. This privacy is a right, a part of personal liberty. No one has the right to press the other for information unless the information directly concerns the mutual relationship.

The demand for openness often does not do justice to the person's complexity. A person's emotional life, and thus also partnerships, develop on many levels. Each person is a being full of contradictions, with light and dark sides, as Jung emphasized. The person is often at a loss to understand his or her own contradictoriness. In many respects the partners remain, and must remain, a mystery to each other. Especially in the erotic-sexual sphere, a person often experiences fantasies and desires for instinctual satisfaction that seem simultaneously fascinating and shameful, and does not want to presume upon the partner to understand them. In the erotic-sexual sphere, the person often needs to keep such fantasies secret, and may derive erotic tensions from them that in turn stimulate the partnership.

In the longer term, very few people direct their erotic aspirations exclusively toward one person. Erotic relationships with different people are various and variable, and need not reduce the erotic quality of a long-term relationship; on the contrary, they may often enhance it. The revelation and "clarification" of all secrets threaten to make life flat and one-dimensional, and to deprive it of its wealth of complexity, of the fantastic, and of the unfathomable.

Externally, the erotic relationship with the partner may remain stable, but internally it usually fluctuates between nearness and distance, turning toward and turning away, openness and secret, in the intensity and diversion of erotic aspirations toward other relationships. All these changes are part of the shared life, part of the alternation between happiness and injury. In practice, the demand for complete openness paradoxically often results in reserve, which cannot, however, be broken because of concealment and denial.

> Two parents, who had both been reared in family conditions strongly characterized by instinctual-drive suppression, resolved to be completely open toward their children as far as sexual matters were concerned. There should be no closed doors in the house; all should be open to all. But what was the result of this openness in reality? The partners had less and less sexual intercourse, which took place only late at night, with the bedroom door open but with lights off. Both performed the sexual act with bated breath so as to hear the deep, regular breathing of their children and thus to be assured of their uninterrupted deep sleep.
>
> Another couple came for sexual-medical consultation because of the wife's sexual reluctance. The husband was proud of having converted an attic in such a manner that they could live in it without doors, with constant aural

contact, and mostly with visual contact. After a prolonged argument the wife finally succeeded in having a door installed at least on the bathroom. She would often sit on the toilet for a long time in order to secure at least a little bit of privacy. The husband recorded exactly how long these sessions lasted every day. Excessive demands for openness caused the wife's sexual reserve.

An architect was proud of his own construction of a one-room or "fluid space" house. In this house, family life was supposed to take place without boundaries, in complete openness and transparency. Life in this house became sheer agony, particularly for the wife. She had to use the dishwasher in her husband's absence and plan everything so that when he was at home he was not disturbed by her noise. She was very sociable; he preferred to spend his evenings alone. She would have liked to invite friends over, but this was not possible without disturbing him. She liked to go to bed early; he liked to listen to music or watch television in the evening. Since they had no doors, neither could live as he or she wanted without disturbing, or being disturbed by, the other.

CONSTRUCTIVE AND DESTRUCTIVE DEVELOPMENT

Are there rules or conditions that promote constructive common development? Let us once more consider the yin-yang symbol: an image of the dialectical tension between the male and female principles. In this symbol, yin and yang have the same valence. Each needs the other in order to formulate its own particularity. Two principles confront each other in a relation of tension. Each must be able to withstand the other's pressure so that a balance can be maintained.

The relationship between two partners is similar. Both partners want to expand within the relational space; each offers the other resistance. There is a paradox in that, in this relation of tension, each struggles to expand, but must at the same time avoid a one-sided victory. The contest must be fought so that finally both partners retain approximately the same proportion of the relational space. This presupposes that both partners are of almost equal strength; otherwise an optimal relation of tension could not be sustained, and one would expand at the other's expense. It is perfectly possible to be victorious in this lasting contest; it is possible to use force, to blackmail and suppress the other. The victor, though, must ask himself or herself the question, at what price? *For if one expands in the relational space at the other's expense, or if the other no longer resists but yields, then the relationship as a whole degenerates, and the common process again becomes undifferentiated: in effect it is both who lose out.*

It is a dangerous aspect of ecological systems that they are often flexible and easily manipulable, and that their self-regulation can easily be stopped. The effects of this become visible only after a certain time. In those areas in which I am myself part of a common system, my suppression of the partner harms me as much as it harms my partner. My wanting only to assert myself is bound to make the relationship deteriorate.

There was a doctor who suffered from the heavy burden of having to support three women. First he was married to a wife who had three children by him. At home, he regarded it as his right to reign supreme. When the wife began to raise a little opposition, he divorced her, but continued to support her and the children financially. He married his assistant, a competent woman who, as his employee, had already been accustomed to obeying and not resisting him. She looked after him faithfully and diligently. Above and beyond this, however, no personal relationship was established. Therefore he took a mistress twenty years his junior, with whom he spent weekends and holidays, and who was supposed to exist only for his pleasure, as it were. He bought her an apartment and supported her financially. He controlled all three women and countenanced no contradiction. All three women depended entirely on him. And what did all this earn him? He was slaving away in order to support three women financially. He felt increasingly exploited, and had the impression that the three women had conspired against him and were playing a mean game with him. Who was the winner in all this? Who controlled whom?

If I strive for growth, then at the same time it is in my own interest to make sure that my partner can keep up with this process, that my partner's responsiveness grows as an opposite pole to my own. The weaker, not the stronger, determines the common pace. It is like a team race: if the fastest outruns the whole group, the other participants will hardly be stimulated. They might even be discouraged, and find it even more difficult to keep up. It is in the interest of the stronger to help the weaker along. Sometimes this can restrict one partner's development greatly.

One couple who came for sexual-medical consultation consisted of a husband who was lovable but shy and dull, and of a wife of effervescent vivacity. During sexual intercourse she worked herself into a state of ecstatic desire that so frightened the husband that he reacted with impaired potency; this frustrated his wife, which in turn increased his impotence. In therapy the wife learned that she could get more by wanting less. In the interest of the common sexual process she had to adjust her demands to the husband and renounce the absolute assertion of her own sexual needs. Thus her sexual realization within the relationship did not match that of her dreams, but because she loved her husband very much, the relationship was worth the restriction. It also proved a positive experience for her to see how she could substantially improve her husband's potency by changing her behavior. By demanding less, she, too, found more satisfaction in sexual intercourse.

When there is faulty development of a dyad, each partner must ask the question, What have I made of my partner? In therapy I have noticed that doctors in particular develop one-sidedly at their wives' expense, and that when the children detach themselves from the family, the doctors find that their wives are depressive. A husband in this situation can no longer constructively confront his wife, because she has been too long accustomed to not offering him any resistance. One doctor said that all his life he had lived according to the motto Man and Woman Are One. But It Is the Man Who Is the One. But it is not only the husband who must ask himself, What have I made of my wife? The wife must equally ask herself, What have I allowed myself to be turned into in the relationship? What were my motives for giving up our strug-gle, for demanding nothing from my husband, for no longer claiming my share of the common space, for no longer as-serting myself against him?

Bachard Wyden (1969) rightly point out that in marital strife there are neither winners nor losers. Either both lose or both win. *Each is responsible for his or her own contribution toward the development of the dyadic self. Shared growth means a constant struggle with each other, a constant mutual challenge, and reciprocal resistance. Shared growth does not mean complete surren-der to the partner or to the partnership, nor does it mean fusing with or sacrificing oneself for the partner.* Yin and yang do not fuse, but they mutually produce each other. Their shapes relate to each other and together create a whole. It is crucial that this struggle with the partner does not become an end in itself, but is focused on the fulfillment of the aims and objectives of the common process.

BOTH PARTNERS ARE RIGHT

In my previous books I have pointed out that "guilt" in marital arguments is caused in approximately equal propor-tions by both partners. This fifty-fifty rule has proved its worth in couples therapy. What has increasingly impressed me in recent years, however, is the deeper wisdom contained in the partners' mutual reproaches. Superficially they often appear to be excessive and unjustified, but they are about something of central significance almost every time. The pattern is expressed in a well-known story about a rabbi.

> A woman calls on the rabbi and complains about her husband. The rabbi listens to her and says, "You're right." The woman returns home and tells her husband, "The rabbi says I'm right." A day later the husband calls on the rabbi and complains about his wife. The rabbi listens to him and says, "You're right." The husband returns home and says to his wife, "The rabbi says I'm right." Enraged, the wife goes round to the Rabbi at once and says, "First you tell me I'm right, and then you tell my husband he's right." "You're right," says the rabbi.

As such, this fifty-fifty rule is not a surprise; after all, the partner is that human being who as a rule deals most intensively with me. From an ecological point of view, my partner's development and mine are codetermined to a great extent. No other human being is so much affected by my development as is my partner, and vice versa. In couples therapy I have almost always found that whatever the wife reproaches the husband for is precisely what I, too, would criticize him for. What she demands from his way of personal development also seems to be right from my point of view. Conversely, whatever the husband reproaches his wife for usually corresponds precisely to my own observations. Basically, each holds up a mirror image for the other, showing those aspects that he or she does not want to see.

I often feel uneasy when two partners separate in the course of therapy, because I have the impression that they are taking flight before they have really confronted both each other and themselves. External separation is an escape from a challenge that, if rightly understood, could definitely further personal growth.

Why do partners find it so difficult to listen to the truths they tell each other about each other? In part this depends on the way in which they communicate. The more one partner's demands seem like blackmail, the more defiantly the other will shut off and resist every kind of change, which in turn reinforces the partner's blackmailing behavior. Partners like these are locked in a clinch where neither may yield even a fraction of an inch, because the one who yields is defined as the loser. The therapist will then have to ask, "How can I help the partners to improve their capacity to each hear what the other wants to tell? How can I make the partners listen to what the common self, the common process, wants to reveal to them? How can I succeed in making them experience criticism not as humiliation or injury, but as a real labor of love?" After all, criticism is always a sign that one is committed to the other and wants to deal with the other constructively. If the partners succeed in improving their hearing, as it were, then each mysteriously discerns the other's voice in his or her own, and vice versa. I trigger off in the other what he or she tells me, just as it is the other who makes me speak. Whatever the other tells me corresponds to what an inner voice tells me; and I can shut my ears to that inner voice just as I can shut them to my partner's.

I do not think that a long-term relationship becomes boring because two partners have got used to each other and no longer have anything to say to each other. Usually they no longer have anything to say to each other because they are no longer *allowed* to say anything to each other. If criticism is regarded as merely a personal insult or elicits a counter-offensive, then it will be stopped. This takes the strength out of the common process, however. A relationship does not become dull because two partners get accustomed to each other. It becomes dull because both partners withdraw from each other in resignation, and do not demand anything from each other any longer.

According to the collusion concept mentioned earlier, this process can be comprehended as follows: the partners' collusion consists in the fact that each partner splits off part of the self that he or she does not want to accept and transfers it onto the partner. The progressive partner delegates weakness, anxiety, and helplessness to the regressive partner; the regressive partner delegates demand for admiration, strength, and self-confirmation to the progressive partner. This part of myself that I have split off and delegated to the partner is now expressed by the partner, just as the part transferred to me now speaks out of me to my partner.

SHARED GROWTH AS BALANCE

The art of shared growth is a question of balance. To understand that shared growth depends on balance is in itself an art. In our Western thinking we tend to suppose that if one thing is true, then the other must be false. This opinion is inconsistent with ecological thinking. What is true does not become any truer if it is made an absolute; usually it then becomes false. If justice is made into an absolute, the result is the highest injustice (*summum ius, summa iniuria*). Good, too, does not become better if it is made into an absolute; rather, it produces the bad it needs to gain shape. The strong man does not become stronger if he appropriates too much power; his power will eventually destroy him.

All this is proved by innumerable examples in world history. The turning of values into absolutes, as well as every form of extremism, is fundamentally wrong. This aggravates the presentation of psychological problems. In order to make something visible, I must exaggerate it to a certain extent, at the risk of then making it false again. In order to change values, I must turn them into absolutes in a certain sense. Extreme attitudes and revolutions are necessary to kick off social processes, although the absolute postulates are almost always false. What is true is difficult to portray in general terms. Those who are directly affected by it in a concrete situation can usually feel it very clearly if they are sensitive to it. To support the partner may be right or wrong; to limit the partner may be right or wrong; to provoke the partner may be right or wrong. Whether it is right or not cannot be judged from one side, but only from the effects, from the interaction, from the result: "You shall know them by their fruits." Certainly too much support, too much limitation, too much provocation can be harmful and effect the exact opposite of what was intended. But too little support, limitation, or provocation can be equally unpropitious. It is not the measure of happiness and harmony that is crucial, nor the measure of individual development, but the common history that is being shaped. It is of prime importance whether this history as a whole can be experienced as meaningful and fruitful despite all difficulties, despite all suffering and chaos; whether it can be experienced as the history with which I am identified, as my and our history.

Everything that has been said in this chapter about shared growth in a dyad can be projected onto any form of long-term relationship: life in the family, in the working team, in religious, political, or ideological groups. It can even be projected onto the coevolution of different nations and superpowers.

Everywhere in ecological thinking, the *what* is less important than the *how* and the *how much*. It is usually not a question of maximizing quantity, but of optimizing its interaction with all other factors.

CHAPTER 5

Marriage As a Source of Well-Being

The assumption is widespread today that marriage not only restricts growth but also has a neuroticizing influence. In fact I meet many patients whose behavior outside the marital relationship is reasonable, constructive, and adapted, but within their marital relationship they behave regressively and neurotically. There are also patients who used to be independent and self-confident as singles, but became dependent, insecure, and depressive in marriage. The therapist who concentrates on the individual often considers the success of his efforts to be prejudiced by the partner in the marriage who is not being treated. He begins to think that only a separation would clear the partner's way toward a healthier and more mature development. For this reason, divorce in the course of therapy is often judged to be a success, like the disappearance of a symptom. Separation and divorce may in fact clear the way for a positive development; they need not do so, however. In this chapter I would like to present the opposite case, and to show that partnership can substantially contribute to the recovery of a previously neurotic personality.

Many present-day epidemiological investigations agree that neurosis and the lack of a long-term relationship correlate statistically. In this context, I would like to quote the latest research work known to me, the Mannheim Cohort Project, led by Heinz Schepank (Schepank et al. 1984). His team conducted a field investigation into the incidence of psychogenetic illnesses among the general public of the German city of Mannheim, using six hundred randomized testees born in equal proportions in the years 1935, 1945, and 1955. One result of the investigation was the fact that the testees identified as psychogenetically ill were significantly more often single, separated, or divorced, whereas among the married persons, those not identified as psychogenetically ill were overrepresented. Of course this raises the question, Are married couples *statistically* healthier, or is it the firm relationship that keeps people healthy?

WHAT PSYCHOANALYSIS ASSUMES ABOUT ADULT RELATIONSHIPS

Psychoanalysis continues to assume that unless neurotic fixations and regressive tendencies are overcome by the individual, there is a neurotic compulsion that causes partners to be persistently chosen according to the same patterns, relationships to always end with the same disappointments. It is assumed that a neurotic personality in a partnership tends to act out the neurotic wishes, works himself or herself up into excessive fear of their fulfillment, and thus gets entangled in collusions. It is further assumed that attempts at self-cure through partnership are bound to fail from the start, and that a person must develop a stable identity and a mature capacity for relationships before he or she is able to have a stable, subjectively and objectively satisfactory relationship.

According to Michael Balint (1965), the ideal type of

genital or postambivalent love ought to be free of traces of ambivalence or pregenital object relation: there must be no lust, no insatiability (i.e., no oral traces), no wish to hurt or dominate the object (i.e., no sadistic traces), no wish to deprecate the partner (i.e., no anal traces), and no trace of the phallic phase or of the castration complex. The positive characteristics of genital love, according to Balint, are expressed in that fact that you love your partner because you can satisfy each other, and because together you can experience a full orgasm almost or completely simultaneously. According to Kohut (1971, p. 298), the capacity for object love is tied to a firm, cohesive, and clearly delimited self: "the more secure a person is regarding his acceptability, the more certain his sense of who he is, . . . the more self-confidently and effectively will he be able to offer his love (i.e., to extend his object-libidinal cathexes) without undue fear of rejection and humiliation."

Meissner (1978) wrote a very good account of psychodynamics in marriage from the point of view of psychoanalysis. He, too, argues that only a mature self can enter into and maintain a functional relationship. In strong identity deficiencies, the lack of identity is tantamount to an incapacity for listening to others, for paying attention to them, and for differentiating one's own point of view. Meissner writes (1978, p. 35), "One of the most important features of the functioning of the mature and individuated personality is the fact that *his emotional functioning tends to be contained within the boundaries of his own self.* He is able not only to maintain his own emotional functioning with his own boundaries, *but also to buffer himself in relation to the hurts, pain, and suffering of others around him*" (italics mine). For G. and R. Blanck (1968), one characteristic of mature love is the ability to maintain a relationship independently of the partner's physical presence,. not requiring the partner's presence for refueling.

As a precondition for starting a workable relationship, psychoanalysis postulates that a person must be self-regulating, independently of the partner, and not need the partner for purposes of self-balancing. The relationship should be based on an independent and autonomous self that puts itself into relation with another independent and autonomous self. Humanistic psychology, too, understands a comprehensive person as self-regulating and independent of actual partners.

In my writings on the collusion concept (Willi 1972, 1978, 1982a), I have shown in depth and with many practical examples how a neurotic, largely unconscious interaction can evolve between two partners. During the process of choosing a partner, similar unmastered difficulties exert a strong mutual attraction. Both partners hope to satisfy all of each other's unfulfilled childhood desires. Both hope to compensate for all the previous frustrations and injuries in such a way that each need not be afraid of the other, because each needs the other to carry out the behavior that each needs in the attempt to be cured. This seemingly ideal mutual correspondence, however, proves to be too rigid an arrangement in the long term; it may help to ward off common fears, but it does not allow for a common development process. Therefore a collusive relationship is almost certain to reach a serious crisis sooner or later; the crisis then brings about some kind of change, be it a growing out of the pathological collusion, a neutralization of insoluble conflicts by means of illness, or the dissolution of the relationship through divorce.

The opinions and attitudes of psychoanalysis served to counter an earlier tendency—also widespread among doctors —to recommend marriage as a remedy to compensate for development deficits, to stabilize the insecure, and to soothe the overwrought. If marriage did not have the hoped-for effect, the couple was advised to have a child, and if that did not work, to have more children. I do not think that nowadays many people will seriously maintain that marriage partners and children may be used for purposes of self-cure, or for any purposes at all. The failure rate of such self-cure attempts is much too high.

And yet: with increasing experience in the observation of couples dynamics, I began to doubt the general validity of these psychoanalytic hypotheses, which had never been systematically investigated. More and more frequently I encountered treated and untreated neurotic personalities who did not keep on staging the same collusive arrangement in their relationships, but were obviously capable of learning from the failure of one relationship for the benefit of the next. More and more often I saw seriously neurotic, even psychotic personalities who could maintain lasting, subjectively satisfactory, and objectively workable relationships. I also kept on meeting seriously neurotic personalities who appeared much happier and more stable in a relationship, and who did not at all support Balint's assumption that the strenuous and energy-consuming adaptation to a love object can be accomplished only by a healthy ego.

So far I have not been able to find any literature on positive corrections of neurotic behavior by marriage. As a consequence of the general tendency to pay more attention to the pathological than to what is healthy, what is pointed out is merely that neurotic personalities have a tendency to fight their conflicts through their partners.

In the following I will report on five couples, each of which consisted of two partners whose seriously neurotic personalities were clinically confirmed. I knew that each couple had been sharing an apartment for several years. I was interested in the extent to which these relationships could be described as objectively workable and subjectively satisfactory.

HEALTHY MARRIAGE, NEUROTIC PARTNERS

I have been in charge of the Psychotherapy Unit of the Psychiatric Hospital of the University of Zurich since 1967. In this unit, only seriously neurotic people receive inpatient treatment, for about three months, in a combination of individual therapy, group therapy, physical therapy, and situational therapy. Patients who join us have usually already experienced outpatient psychotherapy once or several times. As a rule, inpatient treatment is provided because outpatient psychotherapy does not appear feasible. Almost all our patients have seriously neurotic personality disorders. Admission is usually preceded by a marked reduction in the patients' fitness for work. Our patients suffer especially from serious disturbances of their ability to form relationships.

My investigation involved all those testees who had got to know each other in the Psychotherapy Unit and had entered into lasting long-term relationships with each other—in all, five married couples. Such pair formations are rare. I chose these couples because of their neurotic personality disorders, which had already been diagnosed in each person separately before they had paired off with each other. None of the ten partners had been in therapy with me personally; so I could not be suspected of acting as a matchmaker. I did not know exactly how the couples had fared after leaving the unit. After discharge from the unit, four of the ten testees underwent no further psychotherapeutic treatment (F1, F3, M3, M2); three of them completed several years of psychoanalysis (F2, F4, M1). Within the period of fifteen years that my investigation covered (1967–82), no other marriage was concluded between patients of the unit.

I conducted semistructured individual interviews with each of the ten testees. Subsequently Dr. Linde Brassel-Ammann carried out a joint Rorschach test (Willi 1973) with each of the couples and analyzed it independently of my own results. Additionally, I had detailed medical records from the time of the couples' inpatient treatment.

External Workability

At the time of this investigation the five couples had been living together for between four and sixteen years. None of the five couples ever contemplated a divorce. In the first couple, the wife had taken an apartment of her own because she could no longer tolerate her husband's compulsive rituals. She still keeps house for him, though, meets him at least every second day, and has no intention whatever of leaving him. The other four couples have externally workable marriages: both partners are capable of assuming the responsibility that their partnerships demand from them; they are able to work, are financially independent, and, externally, live well-ordered lives. Nine out of the ten have experienced substantial symptom remissions since being discharged from the unit. Couples 3 and 4 apparently have no sexual problems; in couple 5 the wife can reach orgasm only through masturbation, owing to her sadomasochist fantasies; whereas couples 2 and 1 have not had sexual intercourse for three years and seven years, respectively, after years of a functioning sexual life.

None of the ten testees was entangled in destructive interactions with his or her family of origin, which would have put pressure on marital life. Two of the five couples have children (couple 2 has two children; couple 3 has one child). Couple 2 tends to find bringing up their children rather difficult. Early-childhood brain damage was diagnosed in their first child (stagnation of physical growth in the first year of his life). The parents find it difficult to provide the boy, now age six, with limits and structures. The boy is undergoing child psychiatric treatment. The other children seem to be developing well.

In all five couples the wives appear to be healthier, better balanced, and more able to take stress. With one exception (M3), the men have not been able to make the careers for themselves that could have been expected according to their education.

Subjective Description of the Partnership for Couple 4

The wife, by now thirty-five years old, was treated as an inpatient in our unit eight years ago. At that time she had been suffering from states of exhaustion, whose commencement coincided with her father's remarriage. Her mother, who had suffered from schizophrenia, had hanged herself some months before. The patient, who had looked after her mother, reproached herself because of this. One year before admission to the unit, a serious cardiac neurosis occurred; it eventually meant that the patient no longer left her apartment by herself and spent the greater part of her days in bed. This illness prevented a planned marriage to a lawyer.

On the basis of this record and of the patient's behavior in the Psychotherapy Unit, approximately the following partnership could have been expected. The patient showed a typically phobic social behavior. Externally she was well adjusted and amiable, could stand no interpersonal tensions and conflicts, was afraid of her aggressive and sexual tendencies, and tended toward attachment and the avoidance of separations. She was unhappy in her relationship with her fiancé, whose behavior toward her was arrogant and unloving. She did not dare demand anything from him, however, but looked above all for security and support in their relationship. Finally her illness spoke for her, because she would not have dared inform her fiancé about her reservations about the marriage. At the time she had a need for a secure, reliable father, but at the same time she was afraid of being inferior to him, and of being left by him. It could have been expected that she would enter into a predominantly anal-sadistic collusion.

Present relationship and personal development. At the time of hospitalization, the patient was a student of natural science. She made progress professionally and is now a university lecturer, gives lectures, and examines students. Her relationship with her husband evinces no traits of anal-sadistic collusion. He is inwardly torn and has continuous feelings of ambivalence toward her. Because of him they were undecided for years about whether they wanted to get married, and even now they are incapable of deciding whether to have

Marriages of seriously neurotic personalities who became acquainted during hospitalization in the psychotherapy unit

| Couples | Diagnosis in Psycho-therapy Unit | Symptoms* | | Duration of rela-tionship and of living together in years |
		Manifes-tation in Unit	At the time of investiga-tion	
1. ♀ 48**	Gastric ulcer, infantile-hysterical personality	XXX>>	X	
♂ 50	Disabling compulsion illness	XXX <	XXXX	17/16
2. ♀ 36	Depression, schizoid personality	XXX>>	0	
♂ 39	Schizoid personality, problems at work, sex-ual sadomasochism, alcoholism	XXX >	XX	10/8
3. ♀ 26	Neurotic mendacity and stealing, emotional deprivation	XXX>>	0	
♂ 32	Psychosomatic gastro-intestinal disorder	XXX>>	X	8/6
4. ♀ 35	Cardiac neurosis, claus-trophobia, agoraphobia	XXXX>>	X	
♂ 34	Work problems for several years, schizoid personality	XXX >	XX	8/6
5. ♀ 30	Depression, schizoid personality, sexual sadomasochism	XXX>>	0	
♂ 34	Borderline case	XXX>>	X	5/4

*Symptoms: 0 = healthy
      X = slight neurotic disorders without restrictive influence on practical life
      XX = medium neurotic disorders with social restrictions
      XXX = serious neurotic disorders with considerable social restrictions
      XXXX = serious neurotic illness with incapacity to function socially

**Age in years at the time of the investigation*

children of their own. Within the relationship it is she who makes decisions and exercises leadership functions, whereas he provides her with emotional support and eases her anxiety and her overconscientiousness. She says about the relationship, "Mutual help is the basis of our relationship. We feel needed and important for the partner. With my previous fiancé it was a continuous to and fro. He was never able to really love me, and he gave me no security. In my present relationship I feel treated as an equal, and I am sure that my partner loves me. We're very different from each other, in many ways almost opposites. At times I'm afraid of my work, in which I must assume quite a lot of responsibility. On those occasions he is perfectly calm and tells me to phone and say I'm ill. From the way I was brought up, I would never dare do something like that. I've done it four times so far, and it has done me good. There are fewer problems at work now than before. I know my partner well. I know that even if he moans terribly today that he can't stand his work anymore, he'll be better off tomorrow than I will. Sometimes I have to take him into my arms like a mother and be very close to him. Then again he treats me like that. He strokes my head, just as my father did years ago. I like that a lot. When my father died a few years ago, I was afraid that I could not take the stress. My husband supported me while my father died in my arms. Even if my husband still has many personal difficulties and is still far from being fully efficient at work, he is way ahead of other men in other respects. He is much more spontaneous, natural, and sensitive, and above all he stays calm when I become too afraid.

The husband, who is thirty-four years old, came to the Psychotherapy Unit owing to serious work problems. He was a student at the time, had twice postponed his preliminary examinations, and had been idling for months. His grandfather and his father had had work problems before, and could not keep to deadlines; their careers developed neither according to their wishes nor, possibly, according to their capacities. This man always found it difficult to fit in anywhere. He experienced any expectation or obligation as an intolerable coercion. In the course of therapy he could not be won over to a working alliance, since he regarded painstaking, detailed work as philistine and humiliating. In his imagination, he expected some grand revelation that would launch him on a flight that would relieve him of all his difficulties.

In his case, something like the following partner relationship could have been expected. He had always had bad luck with women. He always felt that he could not conquer the women he desired but had to tolerate those who desired him because he could not defend himself against them. Before entering the unit he was living with a woman. There was a continuous tug of war until this woman got involved with another man. This threw him into utter despair and left him with the one goal of winning this woman back. He became seriously suicidal, since she had definitely turned her back on him. According to his relational history, it was questionable whether he would ever be capable of having a stable relationship, and whether a woman could tolerate him for any length of time. A narcissistic collusion would have been most likely, with a continuous closeness/distance conflict, with fantasies of grandiose fusion and simultaneous rage because of the unattainability of his desires, because of mutual injuries, and because of rejection due to fear of fusion.

Present relationship and personal development. He obtained his degree by the skin of his teeth and now works professionally in a subordinate position. At work he is slow and tends to have his head in the clouds, but can at any rate retain a job for a longer period of time. At the same time he still indulges in delusions of grandeur and dreams of performing a great feat in a surprise coup, which will bestow world fame upon him. In his relationship he is outwardly stable, although he is still inwardly torn and unable to confirm whether he really loves his wife. He is also somewhat jealous of her career, although at the same time he despises his wife because of her professional conformity. Ultimately, however, he is very pleased that his wife provides him with support and creates a fixed external framework for him. He is aware of the fact that he needs this fixed framework, although he fights it and suffers from it at the same time. He is filled with self-pity because he has not succeeded in realizing his dreams. During interviews he therefore burst into tears, which were suddenly followed by a roguish smile.

In the joint Rorschach test the husband shows a well-nigh inexhaustible store of ideas; he puts more life into the relationship than does his wife; he has a playful imagination; and he breaks the rules but also extends them. For him, life seems to be a game for the most part, a drama with unlimited possibilities. He evidently finds it difficult to commit himself to only one possibility. His will shows a marked ambivalence in practically all areas of his personality, as well as in the sexual sphere, where he wants to be man and woman at the same time.

In the joint test, the wife lays down structures and rules. She restricts, has a better relationship with reality, is highly demanding as regards achievement, and is more capable of practical realization. She also shows phobic tendencies, however, which she can confront with the help of her husband. She keeps her husband on the terra firma of reality, and gives him support and confirmation. She is fascinated by his wealth of ideas.

Together they show a strong need for affection and tenderness, which they can openly express and mutually accept. The husband expresses desires of fusion, which he simultaneously rejects, however, just as they are rejected by his wife. The administration of the test lasted three hours, which is an absolute record. (The average time is about 45 minutes.) The decision phase can be a severe confrontation for this couple, but they untiringly struggle for a good solution and do not settle for dubious compromises. They often create good integration solutions from the inkblot interpretations they proposed separately. They pay a great deal of attention to each other, and each is interested in the other's ideas. They do not give up their opinions for the partner's benefit, nor do they severely devalue each other. In this manner they find joint solutions on which they are in a high degree of accord. The intradyadic boundary is clear. Each respects the other person's opinion.

SHORT DESCRIPTION OF THE REMAINING FOUR COUPLES

Couple One

The wife. At the time of treatment, seventeen years ago, an infantile-hysterical personality was diagnosed. She had once been engaged to a con man and had later been married to another criminal for five years. She had let both men exploit her financially and humiliate her personally. She was afraid that she would not satisfy the men unless she let them exploit her in her solicitousness. In her present marriage, which has lasted sixteen years, to someone with a compulsion illness, her capacity for care is also much in demand but is highly esteemed by her husband. She has gained more self-confidence in the relationship. She knows that without her care, her husband would long since have been institutionalized. She must do without sexuality and physical tenderness in her relationship. She has gone through a great deal with him, but has never regretted being married to him. She admires her husband despite the disability caused by his compulsion illness. She has the impression that he is her intellectual superior and that she can look up to him. She says, "My two former men were totally different from him. They did nothing but exploit me. But sexually my relationship with the first man was very fascinating. My present relationship is much deeper. If my husband was not such a valuable human being, I could not tolerate his [compulsion] illness. He had no sexual experience whatever. I had to teach him everything, even how to touch his own member. He was very happy about this. There was a time when our sexual relations were completely normal. But after several years he again started to wash his member too frequently. I now think I ought to have been harder with him. Although I miss sex a lot, I don't regret having married him. This relationship has improved my mind. I can admire my husband even though he's ill. He's read much more than I have, and he knows a lot. He also knows how to give me more self-confidence when I suffer from feelings of inferiority at work."

The husband. At the time of in-patient treatment, seventeen years ago, he already suffered from a serious compulsion illness, with ablutions lasting hours, which had made him unfit for work for three years; indeed, he hardly ever left his bed. During treatment and particularly in the course of his seventeen-year relationship with his wife, there was first an amazing recovery. He was again fit to work and suffered from his compulsions only subjectively. During the last seven years, however, his compulsion illness has again got worse, so that he is now completely unfit to earn a living and can leave the house only occasionally to go shopping. His washing compulsions made living with him too stressful for his wife, who therefore lives in an apartment of her own nearby. They see each other daily, however. She continues to look after him. She has never thought of divorcing him. He had previously never had a relationship with a woman. He was himself surprised that he was able to maintain sexual relations for many years without increased compulsions. "After we were married I was better than ever. My wife told me how to wash. That helped a lot. But after seven years the difficulties started again. It was a mistake not to obey my wife but to give in to my fears."

Couple Two

The wife. Twenty-six years old at the time, she was admitted because of depressive and contact disorders with seriously narcissistic personality disorders. She was barely fit for work, had recurrent "depressive holes" during which she experienced a kind of inner collapse, could not be active in any way, and could only retreat into bed. She tolerated the fixed external framework of the unit with great difficulty, and felt all the rules as violations. She had many failed relationships behind her. She repeatedly tended to adore and idolize a partner, and to completely give herself up personally. She would have been expected to look for a narcissistic partner, in relation to whom she could have been a complementary narcissist (Willi 1982). It is amazing that she refrained from choosing a narcissistic partner, and instead selected a man whom she cannot idealize but who demands from her a down-to-earth relationship. She says, "My husband is often so utterly without hope. I love him very much and want to spend my whole life with him. I hope we can also cope with our sexual crisis. I have never admired and idealized my husband in the way I did in former relationships. The good thing was that like this there was never such a gap between us. Of course I still tend to idolize men. That brightens me up, but that is all it means to me now." She experiences her greatest difficulty at present in her relationship with her children, against whom she finds it hard to maintain personal boundaries. She is too understanding, tries to pay attention to everything, and can therefore provide her children with little structure and support.

The husband. A twenty-nine-year-old student at the time, he was unfit to work because of depressive crises and alcoholism as well as general contact disorders. He regarded himself as unable to have relationships with women, owing to fear of sexual failure. He was also burdened by masochistic desires. In order to avoid women, he took refuge in alcohol. In the Psychotherapy Unit he showed a tendency to humiliate himself in public. Previously he had never had contact with a woman for any length of time. If anything, he would have been likely to look for a mother figure by whom he could have let himself be humiliated.

Since leaving the unit, he has obtained his degree, but he has not had a successful career. He is dissatisfied with himself and with the world. Nonetheless he has ceased to consume alcohol in the course of his marriage. Sexual relations with his wife were problem-free at first. Gradually his masochistic desires became so insistent that for the last three years he has not been able to have sexual intercourse with his wife. He says: "Without my relationship with my wife I would have been dead long ago. Marriage gives me a framework that demands things from me and supports me. External normality gives me support rather than appearing to be a coercion. At times I feel overtaxed by my wife and would like to let myself go and break out of everything. But I know this would lead to nothing. It is a general observation that in life, fantasies loom larger than realities.

"I have a particularly intense relationship with my son. I have the feeling that he is the human being who needs me most and to whom I can also give a great deal; so he is a counterbalance to all those people who demand too much from me. Since being treated in the Psychotherapy Unit I have found a certain discipline. Perhaps I pay for this external normality with a certain feeling of illness. But if I let myself go I would lose all support. My wife understands all this."

Couple Three

The wife. When she was undergoing treatment in our unit eight years ago, she was only eighteen years of age. She was an illegitimate child and had been in the position of a scape-goat all her life. Her mother continually devalued and humiliated her. She was admitted because of neurotic lying and stealing, emotional deprivation, and a conflict situation in the family. She says about her marriage, "We could not live without each other. When I was in the hospital with a miscarriage, my husband panicked and thought I could die. My mother-in-law also confirms that my husband would not have done so well without our relationship. She thinks I look after him well. It is simply quite important for me that I'm needed. My mother always used to tell me I'd never be able to keep house. Now I wanted to prove to myself and to her that I could. Of course I was often annoyed at first when my husband was full of his own pomposity. Now I am more able to make fun of it. His behavior is not as arrogant as it used to be by far, though. He used to be so tough when there was a conflict at work. Now he tends to withdraw and says he needs time to calm down. He emerges again only when he has got himself under control. You must know how to take him. I feel family life is a continuous challenge." In the husband's judgment, the wife is rather pedantic in her housekeeping. She herself has the impression that she is scrupulous in bringing up her boy, particularly when, on occasion, he does not tell the truth.

The husband. At the time of his inpatient treatment, he was suffering from a functional gastrointestinal disorder. He regurgitated almost all his food, especially if it had not been prepared by his mother. This infantile mother fixation resulted in overcompensation in his other behavior. Particularly at work he showed an arrogant, tough façade. In the Psychotherapy Unit he was given the nickname Pasha because he enjoyed being served by women and showed a passive-aggressive attitude. He had had many disappointing experiences with women. He would have been expected to enter into an oral collusion with a woman who would look after him and mother him, and whom he would try to humiliate at the same time. His relationship with his then (female) therapist had developed along exactly those lines.

During marriage he has put on twenty-nine pounds, so that his weight has returned to normal. His bulimia has completely disappeared. He is domestic, appears less arrogant, and is more open to criticism than he was at the time of his treatment. He says, "My wife knows how to take me when I react in such an oversensitive way. Marriage has done me good. It gives me a stable framework."

Couple Five

The wife. She was treated in our Psychotherapy Unit five years ago because of a serious depressive-neurotic development with work problems and contact phobia. In the unit she was hardly able to express herself, mostly sat around intimidated and as if in a daze, and provoked the desire in others to badger and provoke her in order to sound her out. Previously she had never had a relationship with a man. She was seized with strong sadomasochist fantasies, however, particularly desires to be raped. She would have been expected to enter into a sadomasochist collusion. Since her stay in the unit, her development has been amazingly favorable. She is self-employed and appears substantially more open-minded and self-confident. She says, "I used to be so preoccupied with myself that I could not spare any energy for a relationship. In our relationship I find it very important that we can understand and help each other. Difficulties weld us together. When he is in a bad way, I become strong. I have found that you always get the strength you need. When he is depressed, I listen to him and give him closeness and physical contact. After all, I have known such depressive disorders myself. On the other hand, when I am nervous, he knows how to calm me down. As to my sadomasochist fantasies, I want to satisfy them only in my imagination—that is, with masturbation. I could not ask him to act out these fantasies. But I don't think I would want to act them out myself, either. It would probably end as it did with my horse. I once urgently wanted a horse of my own. When my parents bought me one, I didn't dare tell them that I had wanted it only in my imagination. The horse and I did not like each other, and I ended up making the horse completely neurotic. Sometimes it's better if desires are not fulfilled."

The husband. Twenty-nine years old at that time, he was admitted to the unit because of serious thoughts of suicide. He showed a schizoid personality with a tendency to have depersonalization experiences and with a serious contact disability, particularly toward girls. Even during his stay in the unit he appeared highly vulnerable and sensitive to criticism. He had been acquainted with many women, but none of these acquaintances had resulted in a long-lasting relationship. He had lived in complete isolation and without social contacts. He says, "At times I find it difficult to believe in myself. I'm afraid then of getting too dependent on my wife. It is good for me to feel that I, too, can guide and support her. I always used to think that when I'm going through a crisis, I'd become too much of a strain on my partner and that she would withdraw from me. So I just put on an outward show and played the part of the tough guy, or else simply retreated. I used to be a loner and had no friends. Now I do have them. I always used to say, 'Don't show any weaknesses, avoid all conflicts, try to be on the safe side.' In this relationship I am confident that you can always find a common way again. It is a great help to me that we can mean so much to each other. My wife often tells me that if I were always that strong I couldn't stand by her. Strangely enough, we never have a crisis together. If one drops into a crisis, the other gets stronger. When my wife has a crisis, this strengthens my self-confidence, because I can support her."

ARE THESE COUPLES TYPICAL?

Because of their small number, the couples described are not representative of marriages between neurotic personalities. I wanted to investigate couples in which serious neurotic personality disorders had been diagnosed in both partners before they entered into the relationship. There were thus special conditions, in that the couples came to know each other as patients and as members of an inpatient therapy group, which may have diminished projective tendencies from the start and encouraged perceptions more in line with reality. As I mentioned, however, I am rather more concerned with examining some basic assumptions of psychoanalysis about couples dynamics. In this respect, the results from studying these five couples may be significant despite the small number of testees. Moreover, they coincide with experiences related to me by many therapists about marriages between participants in therapy groups.

WHAT THE RESULTS MEAN

The couples' objective ability to function may be described as good to very good in two cases, as good in another two cases, and as satisfactory in one case. During the partnership, the neurotic symptoms (neurotic personality disorders, as described) have been almost cured in four of the five women, and have improved or substantially improved in four of the five men. Sexual relations are good for three of the couples, and were stopped some years ago by two couples after they had been functioning well for years. This summary does not seem to touch the intensity of the relationships, however. Subjectively, all interviewees describe their partnerships as central in their lives. They feel personally challenged by the dyadic relationship; they feel needed because of their partners' difficulties. They value their partners' understanding and tolerance. All of them emphasize that they still have great personal difficulties, but that their partners are a substantial help to them in coping with these difficulties.

The Structural Features

The five couples under investigation make clear the significance of the three functional principles I described in my book *Couples in Collusion*:

The boundary principle. The partners show clear, unequivocal, but transparent boundaries toward each other in the relationship. Projective tendencies are barely noticeable. Neither attacks the other because of personal difficulties, but neither feels overresponsible for the other's difficulties, either. The two partners perceive each other in their difficulties in a realistic manner. There are also clear boundaries between these partners and their families of origin, without conflictlike involvements and intrigues. Boundaries with friends are equally clear (four of the five couples have both individual and mutual friends).

The balance of self-esteem. All ten interviewees emphasized that it was just as important for them to be needed and challenged as it was for them to need and challenge their partners. The sense of equality gives them confidence and security. The experience of being able to help the other efficiently strengthens self-confidence.

Progressive/regressive balance. Each of the partners indicates regressive crises, in which he or she feels weak and small, and is in need of the partner's help. Nonetheless, there is no unilateral polarization in any of the couples; in no case does only one partner assume the regressive role, while the other assumes only the progressive role (helper, leader, strong person). In temporal succession and in various relational areas, progressive and regressive relational patterns are ultimately balanced out for all interviewees. There is a division of functions in most of the relationships, a symbiosis in the biological sense of the word—that is, a symbiosis for mutual benefit. A fusion does not take place.

Joint Coping, Not Collusion

As I mentioned, psychoanalysis assumes that a strong and healthy ego is a prerequisite for the maintenance of healthy partnerships. The ten testees examined still show neurotic personality structures and relational dispositions. Very likely, psychotherapy taught them to deal with their neurotic relational tendencies in a way that prevented destructive consequences. They chose partners with whom they could regulate their regressive and progressive needs enough to be neither excessively stimulated nor excessively frustrated. The neurotic wishes still exist, but need not be overtly repelled, because the partner knows how to stand up to these wishes, and how to accept the person with these wishes. There was no collusion in any of the five couples. The partners show no specific responsiveness to neurotic desires. The partner is neither specifically fascinated nor specifically threatened or frightened by the neurotic desires. It might well be decisive for the success of the partnership that partners are chosen and accepted who are indeed not particularly suited to satisfying the neurotic wishes, and whose restricted relational capacity makes it clear that in such a relationship these needs cannot be fully satisfied. These partners help each other handle the frustration resulting from the nonsatisfaction of needs.

One of the men and one of the women had distinct sadomasochistic desires, which their partners tolerated but did not respond to. A woman with a tendency toward narcissistic idealization occasionally succumbed to these tendencies by being infatuated with other men; for marriage and starting a family, however, she chose a partner whom she could not idealize and who in this way did not let the relationship become dangerous, either. A woman who had previously tended to let herself be exploited and humiliated by the men in her life married someone whose compulsion illness was threatening to disable him. This woman in particular stressed how the relationships with the earlier men had been substantially more exciting and fascinating, but had also regularly failed. Two of the men with borderline disorders suffer from a profound ambivalence toward steady ties and partnership obligations, although they sense that without these relationships they would lose all support and structure. Their wives tolerate this ambivalence without being overly offended or hurt, without overrating their husbands' self-pitying moaning, but also without harshly rejecting it. Rather, they remain calm in their realistic certainty that these men remain stable despite all their instability, and that they themselves mean a great deal to their husbands in achieving this stability. In contrast to Balint's definition of genital love, according to which you love a partner because you can satisfy each other, I would say that you love a partner because he or she helps you to cope with the frustration resulting from unsatisfied desires.

Presumably it was less because of any adult capacity for mature relationships that the ten testees were capable of having functioning relationships than because they chose partners who enabled them to regulate their neurotic dispositions. No dream partners were chosen, and there were hardly any idealized expectations of a life full of happiness and bliss. I think that both the ego-psychology and the object-relation theories of psychoanalysis need to be supplemented here. It is assumed that the developing human being's first early childhood experiences with other persons provide the lifelong pattern for relationships with his or her own self and with other people. According to M. S. Mahler (1968) the infant is in an autistic phase during the first three months of its life; in this phase, it perceives neither its own self nor other persons. The gradually dawning perception that needs are satisfied from the outside leads the infant into the next phase, that of symbiosis.

During this symbiotic phase the infant takes its—at first only vaguely perceived—mother as part of its own self. Once phase-specific needs for closeness are satisfied, the infant may reach the next phase, that of separation and individuation. It must be put down to satisfying experiences during the separation/individuation phase that the infant emerges from the "symbiotic membrane" and gradually achieves the identity of an individual separated from the mother. Now, the assumption is this: if fixations with irreversible regressions to this early development phase continue later in life, then this will result in pathological partnerships: "the spouse who experiences the self as part of the marital partner is in a pathological condition and does not have the separate identity that is the normal consequence of adequate transition from symbiosis through separation–individuation" (Blanck and Blanck 1968, p. 50).

I think that there is an alternative to symbiosis and individuation, a form of relationship characterized by division of function and interdependent autonomy, which may well be the most important relational form in partnerships. The partners perceive each other as two separate centers of consciousness, responsibility, activity, and development, but they simultaneously experience themselves as related to each other and as mutually evoked and shaped. They use their partners for purposes of self-regulation and self-stabilization, just as they let themselves be used by their partners in turn. Using the partner and being used by the partner result in a circular regulation through function divisions that complement and, in sum, offset each other, and that, in a favorable case, have a beneficial effect on both partners by strengthening the ego, reducing fear, regulating needs, and encouraging development.

Perhaps one of the most important working principles of psychotherapy is that a man in therapy should learn in his relationship with the therapist to create environmental conditions for himself that enable him to check his neurotic dispositions and to regulate them so that he will not get involved in destructive escalations. It is not so much a question of his needing to learn to solve conflicts independently of other people and the environment as it is of his learning to use his environment constructively in order to avoid or minimize conflict. Healthy people may be defined as those neurotics who have succeeded in constellating their environment in such a way that the environment keeps them in good health.

König and Tischkau-Schröter (1982) remark that there is self-cure potential in partnership. They say that the strength of being different enables the partner to communicate new experiences that help the other to overcome memories of earlier, less-healthy relationships. These new experiences will help stabilize and be integrated into the ongoing interaction with the partner. In our five cases, inpatient psychotherapy has surely contributed substantially toward the renunciation of the mutual projection of unhealthy and idealized objects, and toward recovery in a real relationship.

Many neurotic dispositions probably turn into abnormal behavior only when they find an environment responsive to them. Such corresponding responsiveness occurs with collusions, where, instead of looking for a partner who can help them regulate their own pathological dispositions, people look for a partner who can satisfy their regressive tendencies (by spoiling, protection, security, social status, or fusion), who promises narcissistic gain, or who enables them to confirm themselves progressively as superior, strong, helpful, a leader, or a splendid status symbol. The temptation of this collusive fulfillment of wishes is particularly strong for neurotic dispositions, which feel a need to make up for lost time or a need for continual self-confirmation, or which make unrealistic claims to fabulous happiness.

A human being with neurotic relational difficulties is not, however, simply at the mercy of all this. Such people can still decide, at least to a certain extent, what they want to make out of a relationship: whether it should satisfy collusive needs, or whether it should serve a shared purposive process that demands growth, and therefore frustration and continual challenge.

IMPLICATIONS

According to the results of this investigation, human beings with neurotic difficulties in making social contacts are not incapable of a long-term relationship from the start. It does not seem generally valid to say that someone must first achieve a high degree of personal maturity, ego strength, and self-consistency in order to be capable of mature love. The results reveal that partnerships can also be successful attempts at self-cure. Neurotic personalities are not destined to end up in collusions. What is crucial is the attitude toward the relationship. Despite continuing relational difficulties, the couples described were motivated to refrain from satisfying regressive relational desires and from overcompensatory defense formation. Although mutual aid had a very high value in the relationships, there were no actual help collusions. None of the couples gave the impression that their progressive help functions were being misused for purposes of self-stabilization—for example, one trying to "fix" the other in a codependent manner. None of the partners tended to manipulate the other by taking advantage of the other's weakness and helplessness. The result was that the relationships made recovery possible.

The relational difficulties of neurotic personalities are not, however, fundamentally different from those of everyone else; at most they are more marked. So-called healthy people, too, are inclined to expect their partnership to be a paradise, or to satisfy their regressive desires to be spoiled, looked after, and admired. They may also hope, in a relationship with a certain partner, to be spared the fear of being left, betrayed, oppressed, or exploited. A crisis in a partnership is generally, and too quickly, traced back to neurotic or mistaken partner choice. A long-term relationship is a shared developmental process. Growth results from going through, and coping with, crises. Most long-term relationships go through a phase of disillusionment. Partners *can* change, can learn to retract their original claim to the mutual satisfaction of needs, can learn to concentrate on the mutual encouragement of each other's development, can learn to cope jointly with the tasks and difficulties of life in a constructive manner. The motivation for effecting this change, which is imposed on most long-term relationships, is nowadays weakened by paradigms that focus too strongly on the satisfaction of needs and on the actualization of the individual. In brief, it is not that we must first be mature in order to marry successfully. Rather, it is precisely the process of succeeding in marriage that enables us to mature, that *is* maturity.

Aren't the observations described here rather sobering? Wouldn't, in the light of this description, a "marriage of convenience" be the only sensible partnership? Should not any form of being in love be avoided if possible? It is not an accident that the state of being in love is also experienced as craziness or as mental illness. Being in love transforms a person; the shell of character is broken, releasing a multitude of feelings and fantasies that up to now had to be suppressed and warded off, or could be admitted only in the imagination. Being in love permits certain tendencies that were prevented from being realized before; the locked gates are opened; the ego spends less energy on fending off tendencies; the idea that so many unfulfilled possibilities may be realized in the partnership is tremendously stimulating. The person feels revived and rejuvenated, and often also appears outwardly changed—more beautiful, more graceful, stronger, more energetic. The relationship starts as a shared game with mutual challenges. The inspiring initial experiences lay the foundations for a joint history. Gradually, however, the persons must learn to differentiate between possibilities that can be actualized in their relationship, and those that must be relegated to the imagination. *The intensity of the original feelings of love contains a strong maturing power, which maintains the motivation for this process of differentiation.*

Less easy to bear is the disillusionment through which mutual idealization loses its magic, and with which a natural ambivalence toward each other enters the relationship, though without it no relationship could last for a long time. The dream image each has created of the partner is being corrected. Each observes that he or she can influence the partner's emotions and behavior only to a limited extent. This return to earth after the fanciful flight of being in love can be an important process of maturing and mourning. Criticism is often directed not only at the partner but also at oneself. Each realizes that all the beautiful and ideal feelings that were so stimulating when the couple was first in love cannot be maintained in their original form in a long-term relationship, and this causes disappointment and frustration. The extent to which each devalues the partner is equal to the extent to which each devalues his or her own emotions toward the partner. In a rage each realizes that he or she has not been worth loving. The woman who confronts this criticism, however, will be able to look more deeply into herself, and deal more effectively with her affective life, to the same degree that her understanding of her own desires and limits is improved. Lemaire has provided a very detailed description of this maturing process.

CHAPTER 6

How Family Concepts Evolve

A s I mentioned in chapter 3, the person can be described as an autopoietic system that continuously exchanges matter, energy, and information—or, rather, ideas—with the environment. Now, the nature of the ideas that a person receives, stores, processes, and produces does not depend on chance. Rather, a person is part of suprapersonal systems, and so each person's ideas substantially coincide with the ideas of those systems of which that person is a part. One of the most important of these systems is the family. This chapter will describe how a person coevolves not only synchronically with his partners but also diachronically with his ancestors and offspring.

EVOLUTION OF THE FAMILY STOCK OF IDEAS

Grandparents, parents, and children participate in a common history. Their efforts are normally directed at the optimal encouragement of the children's growth. On the part of the parents, these efforts are neither purely egoistic nor purely altruistic. But the children, too, avail themselves of parental encouragement in a manner that is neither purely egoistic nor purely altruistic. Parents endeavor to ensure the best possible development and expansion of what they pass on to their children. That which is developed by the children has its roots in a mental-ideational inheritance handed down to them by parents and family. What has been handed down links the members of a family both diachronically and synchronically, and evolves as the family's stock of ideas. The individual member's endeavor to develop as fully as possible is part of, and serves, the family endeavor to develop this stock of ideas further.

The boy's development is determined by the development of his family history, and continues to be related to the family even if he detaches himself from the family. Of course, there are other influences that work on him: peer group, school, working environment, social trends and fashions. Nonetheless, what the individual member hopes to make of his life remains related to the history of his family, even when his code of values is opposed to that of his parents. The members of a family are more or less, positively or negatively, interlinked by family ideas. They develop and modify these over the generations, in interaction with the cultural environment. In the family, cultural values, norms, and ideas are articulated and communicated. Politicians and religious leaders have always been aware of this and have, depending on their intentions, either supported the influence of the family or tried to detach young people from the familial relational history.

In tradition-conscious families the family stock of ideas, the consciousness of familial belonging and identity, contains a sense of "who we are," "where we have come from," and "where we are going." It contains attitudes and views, values, convictions, principles and norms, habits and prejudices, familial ideas and images that are all peculiar to one family.

Are there any such tradition-conscious families left? Are they not merely relics of the social upper class, where the bequest of family property or of the family company creates a family history evolving down through generations? Today, when so many families are broken up by divorce, and when a high degree of alienation has arisen between the generations, the family of origin has less effect on values, attitudes, and objectives. And yet: the reappraisal of relational experiences within the family of origin, particularly with the parents, has continued to be a central topic of psychoanalytic treatment, which usually lasts for many years. Today as before, conflict-oriented family therapy observes that children's and young adults' growth and development are blocked by parental influences. It also observes, again and again, the strong influence of family members who are already dead, as well as the need to mourn their loss in order to further develop one's own life. The relational networks of families are more complex today, and less clear. Relationships with family members, however, are still of central significance for the young person in creating his or her own life process, or in discovering his or her own identity. These relationships have become more individual-centered; the development of a self-contained family dynamic, family history, or family identity is less distinct. Nonetheless, even today family members are conscious of a history influenced by their mutual relationships, and they derive the objectives of their own lives from this same history. Family ideas are effective even when the family is split by arguments or outwardly dissolved, even if the family members are estranged from each other in many respects, even for a young woman who does her very best to detach herself from the family and to become her parents' opposite in every respect. The ideational world developed by the individual members will always contribute toward the development of the other family members' ideational worlds. All family members share in common the effort to continue the best possible development of their mental heritage—that is, of what the family has handed down to them—according to their own experience and responsibility, and to continue the evolution of family tradition.

The concept of the family stock of ideas should not be unfamiliar to psychoanalytic thinking, since it approximates many of Freud's formulations about the creation of the superego. According to Freud (1940c, p. 73), "when bringing up their child, parents follow . . . the directions of their own superegos. . . . Thus the child's superego is *created not in his parents' image, but [in the image] of his parents' superegos*; it is filled with the same content, it becomes a *vehicle of tradition*, of timeless evaluations, which have been transmitted like this over generations."

Thus Freud views the superego as a *vehicle of the family's cultural stock*, of its traditions and values, *which bridges generations*. Parents bring up children not so much on the basis of their own ideas, needs, and judgments, but guided by, and referring to, a family perspective that transcends their personal lives.

The superego—the internalized laws, rules, prohibitions, and restrictions, as well as the ego-ideal as an example toward which identification with parents is oriented—could therefore be described as *an authority transcending the parent/child relationship, to which parents and children refer in an equal manner, and for which they feel equally responsible*.

What I mean by the family's stock of ideas is also close to the psychoanalytic concept of *inner objects*. Inner objects are likenesses of external objects, such as the parents, within the psyche. These internalized representatives of the parents serve as signposts: they direct, control, and fix targets. They are an important prerequisite for giving direction, aim, and sense to progress in the development of life. According to

Stierlin (1975b, p. 103) they determine the course of life like a gyroscope, which keeps a ship on course and counteracts driftage. The inner objects play an important part in the formation of the superego. Psychoanalysis regards the correction of negative inner objects as one of its tasks. If we start with the fact that the behavior of the parents themselves was heavily influenced and set on course by their inner objects—that is, the representatives of their own parents—then it becomes evident that the parents' representatives also contain those of the grandparents, their ancestors, and the whole family history. The inner objects thus become the signposts for the development of a familial potential. The inner objects render an individual relatively independent of the real presence of external objects. It may be assumed that the "loss" of real parents during adolescence is partly compensated for by the inner representatives of parents and family.

When bringing up children, parents strive to encourage them to develop as best they can the family potential they themselves have received from their own families. According to Boszormenyi-Nagy and Spark (1973), the most estimable and most logical way to become free from obligations toward your parents is to become a parent yourself. What parents owe their own parents is dynamically offset against the affection that they show toward their own children. Young adults are at pains to assimilate what they have "inherited" from their parents, and to develop and differentiate it further in their lives—at work, in personal relationships, in their social and political commitment. This endeavor encompasses passing on what they have received and processed to a next generation, and of thus stimulating its development.

Parents and children may cause each other to feel guilty in relation to the family heritage. Parents may exploit the child's preparedness to take in "ideas," and use the child for their own needs instead of *serving the development of the family's heritage of ideas.* Children may reject the demands that development of the family heritage imposes upon them by exploiting the parents' needs to continue to look after them, and to retain close ties with them.

ARE ALL PARENTAL EXPECTATIONS HARMFUL?

One of the most negative effects of the present-day small or very small family is the fact that the individual child is often an only child, or an isolated child, exposed to parental, and particularly maternal, influences much more intensely than was the case in the extended family, where within the kinship group far more relational correction by other members of the family used to come into play. This may be a reason why nowadays parents are frequently too child oriented.

Psychoanalytically oriented individual and family therapy points out the pathogenic influences of neurotic partners upon their children. Such parents do not love their children as they are, but accept them only insofar as they can fulfil the expectations placed on them, and insofar as they are prepared to exercise certain functions toward their parents. Parents may use their children to fulfill their narcissistic needs—for the execution of assignments and missions, for example—which restricts the children's genuine self-development. Recently, the harmful effect of parental expectations has been especially well dealt with by the psychoanalyst Alice Miller. In her book *The Drama of the Gifted Child*, she writes, as an analyst, about what she was told by (mostly female) analysands. She discovered that analysands have false selves, because as children they never had the opportunity to develop true selves. They felt pressed to be there for their mothers, to look after them—indeed, to mother them or to fulfill their expectations and to appreciate them narcissistically. If a mother is emotionally insecure, and if she depends on the child to behave in a way that keeps a narcissistic balance, then the child develops an amazing ability to respond to this need in the mother. For the child, this function ensures the parents' love or, rather, their narcissistic attention. The child senses that he or she is needed, and this gives existential security. Such children become their mothers' mothers. They develop a special sensitivity to the unconscious signals of others' needs. Miller assumes that the child is completely at the mother's mercy:

> A child is available. A child cannot run away as her own mother once could. A child can be brought up to become what she would like him to be. A child can provide respect and can be expected to tolerate her own emotions; she can be reflected in his love and admiration; she can feel strong beside him; she can leave him in the care of others if he gets too much of a burden; at last she is the center of attention, because a child's eyes follow the mother wherever she goes. . . . It is one of the turning points in analysis when patients with narcissistic disorders arrive at the emotional realization that all the love they conquered with so much effort and self-sacrifice was not meant for the persons they really were; that the admiration was meant for beauty and achievement and not actually for the child as it was. Behind the achievement, the small, lonely child wakes up during analysis and asks, 'What if I had stood before you, scowling, ugly, furious, jealous, lazy, dirty, and stinking? Where would your love have been then? And I really was all that, too. Does that mean that it was not I who was loved but what I pretended to be?' [Miller 1981, pp. 27, 33.]

H. E. Richter, W. Wirschung, and Helm Stierlin (Richter 1976, 1970; Wirschung and Stierlin 1982) deal with parental expectations of the child in a family-oriented way. Parents often give their children assignments and missions to carry out, and send them out as their delegates. These tasks may serve one parent's affective needs. Parents who are in danger of stagnating in their standardized bourgeois way of life may give the child the unconscious order to supply them with reports about sex orgies, drug parties, and criminal adventures in which the child has taken part; thus the child makes possible the parents' vicarious satisfaction in spheres of life otherwise closed to them. The child may receive orders to support the parents' ego strength by protecting the parents from greater conflicts, and also by fighting conflicts as a parent's delegate. However, the child can also take on tasks that serve a parent's ego ideal by fulfilling the parents' unfulfilled tendencies and hopes. This child is under an obligation to the parents that is based on an invisible loyalty. The concept of delegation, now so often used by family-dynamics-oriented therapists, may involve the risk that a picture is painted of a linear process, as if parents were orderers, as if the child were sent out by them as their delegate to carry out a mission. This approach may tempt therapists to make the parents responsible for the genesis of an infantile neurosis or disorder.

The question as to how much parents can influence the child's development has aroused great controversy among psychotherapists and psychological researchers. The child is not like a blank page, not malleable like clay in the parents' hands. Rather, a child has its own center of activity from birth, and its stubborn resistance and obstinacy can drive many parents to despair even in the first months or years of life. Many children successfully resist their parents' narcissistic manipulations and expectations without being neuroticized. Many narcissistic mothers undergo a curative learning process because of their child's resistance. Even so, it is conceivable that there are subtle strategies to manipulate the child's fear of losing love or of being left, and the child's desire for confirmation and parental affection, in such a manner that the child can be harmed. I maintain that the parents', and particularly the mothers', opportunities to influence the child are seen too one-sidedly, and are also often overestimated.

The mode of delegation should be extended by a circular

perspective, indications for which can be found in the latest description of the Heidelberg Family Therapeutical Concept (Wirschung and Stierlin 1982, pp. 97, 115). The child's being tied to the mother can also be understood as a collusion, that the delegate assumes not only duties but also a claim to having these achievements be recognized by the family. I think children are not sufficiently seen as sharing the responsibility for what happens. In observing many more than one hundred families with crises during the detachment phase, I noticed time and again that there is a pattern regarding which of the children ends up being the delegate. Unless they were arrested in an age-related dependence on their parents and thus restricted in their growth, the delegates were frequently children who had stood in their siblings' shadow from birth. In comparison with their siblings, they were less energetic, less successful, and less assertive, and found it difficult to keep pace with their peers and to cope with age-related development demands. During adolescence these children are particularly afraid of detaching themselves from their families and of standing on their own two feet. If such children discern an opportunity of making themselves indispensable to their parents by assuming one particular function, they may tend to concentrate all their powers on fulfilling these tasks, and at the same time excuse themselves from development demands among peers. A boy may offer his services to his parents to, say, mediate in marital tension, support one parent's weak self-esteem, protect one parent against the other. A girl may offer her parents a sensible task by producing symptoms and thus distracting them from marital difficulties. If we observe all this in terms of exploitation, it is not only the parents who exploit the children's dependence needs but also the children who exploit the needs of parents threatened by the "empty nest."

How often children actively participate in the maintenance of a delegation arrangement comes to light in family therapy: the children frequently resist a therapeutic change much more obstinately than the parents, although it should be expected that the children would feel relieved when released from a certain task.

Parents and children should be seen in their circular relatedness. Parents can assign tasks only if a potential addressee takes them on and identifies with their execution. The Oedipus complex may be offered as the most common example of this interaction. In order to cope with it, the mother must withstand her son's offers of love without either stimulating them excessively or frustrating them excessively. If the mother's relationship with the father is unhappy, she may be particularly responsive to her son's offers of love. On the other hand, the mother's frustrating situation may stimulate the son to outrival his father as a lover. The son will ward off his mother's offers of love, however, if he perceives sufficient opportunities to have age-related relationships with girls. An insoluble Oedipal situation will result if mother and son, joined together against the father, are in an equal sense responsive to their mutual relational offers.

In every family, parents and children expect a great deal from each other. They try to assign verbal or nonverbal tasks to each other. In healthy families, the children limit their parents' expectations, and vice versa, insofar as they sense that their fulfillment will give rise to destructive developments. A destructive, development-hindering delegation process is usually possible only with a *bilateral and equal responsiveness of both parents and children, which possesses all the qualities of a collusion.* My colleagues Barbara and Claus Buddeberg (1982) have described such family collusions.

I think that the difference here is the same as between collusion in partnership and coping in partnership. Expectations have pathogenic effects if they serve the joint defense against parents' and children's existential fears or the satisfaction of regressive needs. In such a case, the family relationships contain their own purpose in themselves. Through and with each other, parents and child would like to satisfy their regressive needs: their need to be spoiled, protected, entertained, and screened against the outside world, their need to have their self-esteem increased, and so on. If the satisfaction of such needs becomes the central concern of a relationship, the relationship amounts to rejecting the demands of a natural familial process of evolution. Healthy familial evolution is a growth process shared by two or three generations, in which each developmental step is correlated with complementary developmental steps of the other generation. If this familial evolutionary process constitutes a comprehensive perspective, then the parents will be proud when their growing children detach themselves from the family in order to take their fate into their own hands and assume responsibility for it. They will be disquieted if their children still stick to them once they have come of age. The children's detachment from their parents, however, is also the parents' detachment from their children. For the parents, too, a new phase of life begins at this juncture, in which they again have more time for developments of their own. Delegations can, but need not in any way, have pathological effects. Many famous people were their parents' delegates. Quite likely a child cannot develop at all without parental expectations.

There are family histories in which children take on assignments in order to eradicate family insults, to repair or compensate for familial damage, or to support the parents actively. In many cases such tasks provide both aim and purpose in life. They may strengthen an individual's ego, encourage his or her identity, and constitute a successful attempt at coping and repair for the family. This is one way in which families as autopoietic systems continue to regulate themselves.

I would like to adduce the example of Henrik Ibsen, who was born into an affluent merchant family in the Norwegian maritime trading town of Skien in 1828. When he was six, the family's circumstances changed abruptly. His father had taken on too much financially. The family lost its stately home and had to move into the country. This downgrading must have left emotional scars on young Henrik that never completely healed. Thus he devoted his life's work to exposing the hypocrisy of society. On November 18, 1877, after his father's death, he wrote to his uncle, Christian:

> Ever since my fourteenth year I have had to look after myself; I have fought often and long in order to assert myself and to arrive where I am now. The reason why, during all these years of struggle, I wrote home so rarely was mainly because I could be of no help and support to my parents. Writing seemed pointless to me where I could not act; I always hoped that my circumstances would improve, but that came only very late and is still not far behind me. It was thus a great solace to me to know that my parents, and now at the end my old father, were surrounded by loving relations. My thanks, sent to all who extended a helping hand to the deceased, are therefore also meant for the help and the relief that this was for my own path through life. Yes, dear Uncle, let yourself be told, and tell the other relations: what you all have lovingly taken over of my duty and obligation has *substantially supported me in my reflections and aspirations, and has helped to encourage what I have achieved in this world* [my italics]. [Rieger 1981, p. 7.]

With the help of his work, Henrik Ibsen repaired the familial humiliation. This, however, demanded a supreme effort from him. According to his own words this was possible for him only because his relatives took on the task of looking after his parents at the same time. Familial coping results from the interaction of different roles.

Children often want to help their parents even though no expectations have been placed on them, even though they have been assigned no tasks. The following example may show how grown-up children can devote their entire lives to helping their parents, and how they defy any therapeutic attempts to stop them from doing so. The therapy results in a change only when the suffering child realizes that he or she can help the parents more effectively by means of healthy behavior.

Heidi, a twenty-two-year-old patient, was admitted to our Psychotherapy Unit because of paroxysmal hyperventilation. In these fits she let herself fall to the ground; her breathing was loud, panting, and accelerated; she seemed unconscious; she rolled her eyes. On her own (unconscious) initiative she worked herself up into states that appeared highly alarming to those around her. She had been in psychotherapy for years, but it had been impossible to reduce the frequency of these fits. As a personality she gave the impression of stunted development. From early childhood she had been shy and had always been tormented by jealousy of her younger, energetic, and successful brother. She hardly ever played with her peers and always timidly withdrew. She had to attend remedial school. She was generally considered silly and dumb, although tests had proved that her intelligence was normal. From childhood on she kept developing neurotic symptoms, such as enuresis, scotophobia, and agoraphobia, that ensured that she was allowed to sleep in her parents' bedroom. Later she suffered from psychogenic vomiting, until the respiratory paroxysms occurred for which she was now being treated in therapy. It was particularly familial stress situations that triggered these fits.

Circumstances at home were utterly depressing. The father is an alcoholic. When Heidi was two years old, he fractured his skull and was in a coma for a long time. Subsequently his affect remained labile, and he became violent, particularly under the influence of alcohol, smashed furniture, and beat the mother. The mother is a careworn silent sufferer. She suffered the father's physical violence, allegedly for the sake of the children. A classic alcoholic marriage evolved, in which the husband feels humiliated by the wife's tolerance, and so gives in repeatedly to destructive tendencies and physical violence. The father's behavior also became unacceptable at work, and he has difficulty now in finding a job at all. Heidi was the only person with whom the father could talk things out. Sexual relations occurred between the father and Heidi, which presumably provided the father with the feeling of being loved by at least one person; on the other hand, he also felt guilty, which further undermined his self-esteem.

The mother, who in recent years had been caring for and supervising the suffering Heidi, was very worried about her daughter's hospitalization. She was highly frustrated that Heidi did not tell her about the therapeutic conversations in great detail. She continually accused the nursing staff of not supervising her daughter closely, and worked herself up into claiming that in our unit Heidi had lost all sexual restraint, which, considering Heidi's extreme contact inhibitions, seemed grotesque. She interrupted her furious reproaches by saying that no one was taking any notice of what happened to her, that she could be beaten to death at home by her husband without anybody knowing anything about it. When she burst into tears, we tried to show her that we felt compassion for all she had to bear on account of her husband and her sick daughter. The mother, however, vehemently parried any suggestion that she was in need of help. She hinted that she had always been very deeply disappointed whenever she had accepted someone's affection.

We then conducted several family discussions, which kept on degenerating into chaotic destructivity. The pattern of the discussions remained mostly the same: father, mother, and brother would attack Heidi, block her with contradictory reproaches, and then get into a rage when she did not answer despite all attempted pressure. She was continually told to own up at last and say what she did not like about the family, but whenever she began to speak she was cut short. The father, who looked like a down-at-heel tramp whose character had been changed by excessive drinking, was evidently full of fear that his incestuous relationship with his daughter might be raised in conversation. Taking the bull by the horns, he challenged Heidi to tell the whole truth at last, regardless. What was communicated to her all the time, however, was, "Speak, for heaven's sake, but don't you dare say anything!"

What most impressed me were Heidi's tireless efforts to turn the family discussion into constructive conversation in spite of all their sabotage. Here, she emphasized, a conversation should for once take place in which everybody could participate; no one needed to be excluded or destroyed. All members of the family hinted that they understood Heidi's concern and basically agreed with her. The father once hinted that he thought the mother and both children were ganging up on him. After walking out of a session in a rage, the mother returned in tears some time later. She then confirmed Heidi's statement that all four of them had much to suffer together, that all four of them were concerned and needed help. The strongest resistance was put up by the brother, who was hostile and cynical toward us therapists, and who admitted only when he was feeling subdued after intense confrontation that he had many unsolved problems himself but could not bring himself to speak about them. All these rays of hope were mere glimpses, retracted as soon as we wanted to pay them more detailed attention. Again and again the situation deteriorated into destructive chaos. Hints also made clear how important Heidi was for the family to be able to function. The mother once said between sessions that when the father had to be hospitalized because of his agitation, Heidi had been the only one who in that turbulent situation had kept calm and stressed that the family would have to stick together. At that time Heidi had proved the strongest person in the family.

Finally there was a session that ended in utter chaos. The father exclaimed that he would never again appear for a family discussion; the mother agreed with him, supported by the brother. After this last family session, I told Heidi that she could no longer afford to keep on falling ill. Her family needed her as a healthy person who could use her energies for their benefit and who could show them the way. Heidi expressed the fear that if she were no longer ill, all the others would attack the father and that he would go downhill all the way. I again emphasized that it was not a question of diminishing her commitment to the family; on the contrary, she would have to acquire the competence to be of real help to them. To my own astonishment her hyperventilation attacks disappeared after that. Heidi took an apartment of her own and became substantially more independent. In consequence, the other family members felt they had to depend on themselves more. The mother, in particular, began to establish contact with women of her own age, whom she met occasionally and went out with. She was generally substantially better. The father continued to drink, but was only rarely involved in violent scenes with the mother.

Heidi had tried to protect the father from being expelled from the family by offering herself as a patient, by attracting the parents' attention by means of her dramatic hyperventilation attacks, and by thus keeping attention away from the father. In this way, however, she had had to neglect part of her personal development. She had tended to excuse herself from developmental demands ever since childhood. One may also argue that she had been the family's victim and had been made ill by them.

What impresses me is the natural loyalty that Heidi felt for her family, a loyalty that had defied all therapeutic attempts to encourage Heidi's autonomy and to detach her from the family. In such a case, encouraging the patient to become independent would not be a reasonable goal for therapy. On the contrary, the therapeutic objective, which must also be agreed to by the patient, is to become more competent to help the family. This, however, presupposes a therapeutic paradigm according to which participation in, and joint re-

sponsibility for, the suprapersonal familial process of evolution is something original and authentic, and not something
that must be eradicated by means of therapy.

Parents naturally try to instill their family "inheritance"
in their children as effectively as possible. If parents expect
their children to develop much of what they themselves were
not permitted to develop, this need not indicate a narcissistic
disorder. Rather, these expectations could serve the best possible further development of the family's heritage. Thus the
parent generation of the boom postwar years, for instance,
was able to create social and economic conditions that provided its children with access to better education and training
than the parents themselves had been able to enjoy. The creation of such conditions imbued the parents' activities with
sense and direction. The services that the parents thus rendered to their family in turn exposed the children to expectations that they would themselves serve the development of
the family heritage. In fulfilling their own parents' expectations, the parents performed well in academic life and were
successful in business. At the same time they reared children
who questioned their achievements and put quality of life
before achievement, ecological thinking before consumerism,
and social commitment before individual assertion. I think
that this transgenerational family dynamic is not based only
on obligation and guilt (Boszormenyi-Nagy and Spank 1973,
Boszormenyi-Nagy 1975). Rather, *each child endeavors to develop the parental heritage in his or her own interest; in doing so,
the child ultimately always also acts in loyalty and relation to the
family and ancestors, and not only out of egoism.*

CORRECTING A FAMILY HERITAGE

Independently of parental expectations, the family heritage
becomes an integral part of an adolescent's person. With this
stock of ideas he or she must meet the challenge of life. In
the face of this challenge to assume the responsibility for his

or her own life, *the young person must, with the help of this internalized stock of ideas, be able to cope with reality.* In order to do this he or she must, as a first step, question it fundamentally; indeed, he or she may have to oppose it, in order to examine the ideas taken over, gradually and without external pressure on the part of the parents, and begin to own them as part of his or her own experience.

In this process the young person must often break out of the family, go off on travels, go to far continents, join the alternative scene, in order to gain distance from his or her parents. The adolescent examines, experiences, and appropriates things not merely as an individual, but also as a member of a family. He or she tests the parents' stock of ideas for its usefulness, weighs and evaluates it. The adolescent's examination of the family stock of ideas often hurts the parents. The adolescent judges them relentlessly, and shows a tendency toward excessive criticism. He or she will question many problematic attitudes that the parents have failed to modify out of habit or resignation.

Many individual-centered therapists create an *unnecessary contrast between the adolescent's claim to self-development and the parents' demands for family loyalty.* Viewed from the perspective of need satisfaction, it is clear that not all the adolescent's needs can coincide with those of the parents. But we need not assume that the adolescent has internalized only negative, destructive, and development-obstructing aspects of the parents; rather, his or her substance, and potential as a whole, has been fundamentally formed by parents' and siblings' influence; so his or her self-development will always also involve the further development of the family's stock of ideas.

If the parson's son becomes an atheist Marxist, this can be the son's correction of a poorly developed religiosity on the part of his father. The enthusiasm of the son's social commitment cannot, however, be understood as detached from his conflict with his father. If the daughter becomes a fanatical fighter for women's liberation in sharp contrast with her bourgeois, middle-class mother, her fanaticism cannot be understood without the family's history. If a banking executive's son breaks out and joins the alternative scene, rejecting any thought of profit as exploitation, his development, too, cannot be understood without his father's materialistic attitude. Or if in a family of successful academics a child shows no readiness whatever to attend school and work diligently, this is in contrast to family ideology, with the child correcting a one-sidedly developed family potential. Again, if adolescents from deprived families form extremely authoritarian street gangs, they are creating a corrective social structure. *With their renunciation of their parents' developmental course, adolescents execute a corrective movement, which in the last analysis serves not only themselves personally but also the family as a whole.*

It frequently happens, however, that adolescents are overtaxed by trying to keep this correction within reasonable bounds. At least at the beginning, they are often spellbound by another extreme, such as political radicalism, rejection of society, drug taking, or religious fanaticism. That radicalism with which they break with their parents assumes a placatory dimension if, no matter how deep the rift, connecting links can still be shown. The radicalism with which adolescents and young adults oppose their parents often shows the immense effort that such a correction of the internal heritage demands. There is often an almost magical fear: "In spite of all my efforts, I may ultimately fall victim to the same fate as my parents." Quite frequently, family transgressions and catastrophes have become so grave that it will take several generations to correct them. One generation's extreme development will call for the next generation's counterextreme, and thus it will be only the third generation that can find a more relaxed middle way. Such three-generation developments can frequently be seen in Germany—for example, in the attempt to come to terms with the transgressions of the Nazi era (Sperling et al. 1982).

MODIFYING THE PARENTS' ERRORS

The adolescent not only deals critically with the family heritage and tries to correct the family's history but also at the same time usually assumes an intensely critical stance toward the parents, in an attempt to change their lives. The adolescent's "disturbances" often particularly disturb family members—which, of course, is part of the reason for them. As a rule the adolescent wants not merely to feed the parents with excitement and sensations to serve their elementary and affective needs in this manner but also to shake the parents out of their entrenched attitudes by means of shocking behavior, in order to get them to reflect on, and change, their ways. The intensity with which parents respond to such provoking behavior indicates that their rigid façades often conceal a longing for another way of life. Almost like a therapist, many an adolescent would like to activate the parents' hidden responsiveness, to help it break through, and to show the parents a way toward a new life. In doing so, however, the adolescent finds that the parents' life can be modified only within narrow limits; so he or she must embody the change that is secretly or openly desired by the parents. In spite of expulsion by, and breaks with, the parents, such an adolescent may well be more loyal to the parents than are siblings whose lives conform to the parental façade.

For example, a high-ranking police officer has been sent to me because of multiple psychosomatic complaints, his family background being chaotic. He suffers from gastric disorders, insomnia, tremors, general nervousness, depressive disorders, and exhaustion. His marital relationship is extremely strained. His wife keeps on lapsing into trancelike states in which she rages and lashes out. The chief topic of arguments is the bringing up of their three children.

The eldest of these, a twenty-two-year-old daughter, finished her vocational training but then became addicted to
heroin and is now about five thousand dollars in debt. She
lives on her own. The twenty-one-year-old son, Bruno, finished his training as a mechanic and then dropped out. He
now works on paper rounds; he does not earn much money,
but feels free and independent. He lives with his nineteen-
year-old girlfriend, a former drug addict who has recovered
with the help of his strong commitment. Seven months ago
she bore him a child. The youngest, seventeen-year-old Peter,
is the only one still living at home. He has just been dismissed
from his apprenticeship because of repeated absenteeism.

Even externally, the father looks as if he came from a
different world. He wears the clothes a police officer is expected to wear when not in uniform: slightly casual and
sporty, clean and neat, but not in any way obtrusive. The
two sons are the opposite: punk hairstyles, headbands, and
mountaineering boots make them look like bogeymen of
the middle classes. Only the two parents and Bruno participate in the first discussion. The problem appears to be
that the father feels isolated in, and excluded from, the family because the three children and the mother have formed
an alliance against him. His professional commitment is excessive; but within his family he would like to be respected
as an authority, and would like his children to give him a
token of appreciation for his achievements. The children,
however, fundamentally reject his worldview, which is based
on achievement, ideology, conformity, and law and order.

In the course of the family discussions, it is a new experience for the father to be able to express his personal views
openly. He, too, is permitted to say for once, "It's all a load
of crap. I'd like to chuck in my job and lead a different kind
of life." The family begins to understand the father's situation. He recounts that he comes from a drinking family, that
in his youth he was happy-go-lucky himself, that he was
summarily dismissed from his apprenticeship, and that for a

time he was considered unfit for national service. His mother-in-law regarded him as unfit to cope with life. Wherever he was, he was in a low position and suffered from deep feelings of inferiority. With an iron will he worked his way up and had a successful career. Although he suffers from the police-force pressure to conform, he also finds support and firm guidelines in it. He wanted to do his best to spur his children on to high achievements, both at school and at work, in order to give them a chance to rise socially.

For me as a therapist, but also for the family, it is astonishing how very similar to his children the father was in his own adolescence. Yet this is precisely why the father is afraid of again losing his hold, and why he adheres so rigidly to conventions. He is ashamed of his children. Once, from a streetcar, he noticed his youngest son standing in the street dressed in punk gear; people next to him pointed at this young man with disgust. He was only too pleased that no one recognized him as that young man's father. He also suffers from the fact that his professional ambition has not been adopted by his children, but instead rejected. This makes him feel that all his efforts have been in vain. The open discussions between father and family help to relax the family atmosphere. The wife and the three children are very committed and warm-hearted people who, in their opposition to the father, have come to be his extreme opposite. In the course of the therapy, the daughter overcame her addiction under her own steam, and largely paid off her debts. In a tough discussion between mother, Bruno, and daughter, the latter was told that it was pointless for her to struggle internally against the father's mentality because basically she was as ambitious and achievement-conscious as he was, even if she did not want to admit this. Ever since, the daughter has become more balanced and has learned to stand by herself to a greater extent. Bruno has also undergone a change, in that he says he wants to reenter society and build up something that makes sense. He says that he has lost many years because of his "foolishness," but does not regret this, because he has also experienced and learned a great deal. He has emigrated to Australia in order to build up his own business with a friend who is already there. His girlfriend and their child have followed him. The relationship between the father and the mother has also improved. The mother no longer suffers from her previous emotional disorders. The two of them go hiking together in the mountains, and have made progress in talking to each other. Only the youngest son remains a worry for the time being.

This family's development could be interpreted as follows. In his forced efforts for achievement and conformity, the father delegates his unconscious desires for freedom, nonconformity, and alternative life to his children, who live out these aspects for him and provide him with the opportunity to be disgusted by this as well as to participate in it. I doubt that such an interpretation, even if it existed only in the farthest recesses of a therapist's brain, could contribute anything substantial toward a constructive therapeutic atmosphere.

Alternatively, the family's development could be interpreted in this manner. Frustrated by excessive work demands on her husband and by his striving for achievement, the mother seeks vicarious emotional satisfaction in the children and unconsciously instigates their opposition to the father, whom they fight as her substitutes. What remains questionable to me in this interpretation is whether the children's loyalty to their mother is so intense that they stake their whole existence on supporting her in her fight against the father. I am also reluctant to attribute to the parents an unconscious diabolical intent to use their children as allies to such an extent that it will destroy them.

In my opinion, the children's abnormal attitudes resulted not from their being their mother's or father's delegates, nor from any attempt to distract their parents' attention from their marital conflict, but rather from the father's extreme behaviors, with which he tried to correct his own parents' abnormal attitudes, and which provoked abnormal attitudes of the opposite extreme in his children. The children attempted to correct the father's misdirected development; this came out clearly in therapy. Combined with this, however, was the attempt, in their very own interest, to correct what they had adopted from their father. The mother encouraged the children's extreme development by putting up no determined resistance, because she, too, revolted against her husband's extreme attitudes. Therapy helped all parties to approach each other on a middle ground, which allowed subsequent constructive development for everyone concerned.

As a second example, consider the following. A family made an appointment for therapy after the younger child, Andreas, a young man of twenty, had made a serious suicide attempt. Before the first family discussion the father wanted to have a conversation with me alone in order to test me. He was afraid that I might identify myself with his son's reproaches against him. The son reproached him for being too authoritarian, and for averting all personal critical discussions with the aid of rational argument. Out of a feeling of powerlessness the son used to react highly emotionally, lose control, and behave completely irrationally. It was in connection with such a conflict that the son had tried to commit suicide. The father now feared that family discussions could harm the family.

The father had come to Switzerland as a refugee from Hungary at the time of the 1956 revolution. Working very hard, he had built up his own business together with his wife. Andreas's sister, Beata, who is two years his senior, is very successful at the university. She is highly conformist and does not cause her parents much worry. Andreas, on the other hand, was the only one in the family who was always very impulsive. The mother tries to mediate between father and son. As for the rest, she completely subordinates herself to her husband, has no demands of her own to speak of, and seems very much disquieted on account of the tensions in the family.

What astonished me in the course of the first family discussion was the extent to which the children are still tied to the family. Although the parents have allegedly released the children or even encouraged them to go out, they both, at twenty-two and twenty years of age, still spend their spare time with the family and have practically no contact with peers.

In the course of the third and last family discussion, an impressive conversation took place. Andreas was moaning at great length about the family, where each felt lonely and not understood, where there was no warmth, and where everything was desolate. The father was very much hurt by his son's reproaches. He thought they were neither justified nor just, since he had always done his best for the children. When Andreas had had difficulties at school, he had offered him every possibility for coaching and tutoring; he had even attended Andreas's lessons at school in order to understand his son's difficulties better. Evidently he had always arranged everything with great conscientiousness, and had given his children a great deal of support. In the course of the therapy session, the father remarked, without being prompted, that the prevailing atmosphere in the family was neither relaxed nor cheerful. I asked him how he could endure this. He parried at once by saying it did not matter to him, that he had lived through things a thousand times worse. When I inquired, he replied that he had held a Swiss passport for more than ten years, but did not feel Swiss and was not accepted as a local by the Swiss themselves, either. In his heart he had remained Hungarian. His heart would not take root elsewhere. You could not have two hearts. He said that he liked visiting Hungary, and going to the theater there, and that he enjoyed the Hungarian language, which his children did not understand; so he usually visited his home country by himself. I asked the father about his loneliness in Switzerland and in the family. He excused his wife and children by saying that it was not their fault that he had not been able to put down new roots.

I now asked Andreas whether he was able to empathize with his father. He replied that it weighed upon him that his father had not digested his past, but he did not want to admit it. Next I asked Beata about her experience of the situation. She had just realized that, basically, she, too, was Swiss intellectually but not emotionally. It was like heredity, she said. You are always a bit like your parents, but that is not the parents' fault. I replied: "No, but it's the children who take over certain problems from the parents, so as to solve them in their own lives." Beata then mentioned her fantasies about emigrating to South America, where there was more real feeling.

In this session the family first spoke about a topic that had previously been repressed by all of them. It was as if something had opened up. The father showed his own emotional situation for the first time. He then canceled the next session. It was only about two months later that Andreas came to see me to report progress. After that meeting he had contacted a church youth group, where he spent one evening a week. There he had found a relationship with a girl for the first time. My impression was that with that session the family's evolutionary process, which had been blocked for a long time, had started to flow again. Andreas had always attacked his father in order to provoke him into more emotion. What he did had invariably had the opposite effect: the father entrenched himself even more in rational arguments. Instead of trying to change his parents, Andreas now concentrated on coping, in his own life, with the problems he had taken over from his parents.

SCAPEGOAT AND BLACK SHEEP

In the literature about family dynamics, the scapegoat plays an important part. The scapegoat is a person who can be loaded with the guilt for family misfortune and whose punishment exonerates everyone else's from guilt feelings. If an exacting system of values and norms is prevalent in a family, and if all family members cannot live up to it, then the family may create a scapegoat onto whom they can discharge the disappointment about their failure to satisfy the norms. According to Richter (1976), a general tendency toward narcissistic relational forms is a prerequisite for the creation of a scapegoat. That is, scapegoating is a tactic of parents who predominantly experience the child as an extension of their own selves. Often the child is first cast in the role of prodigy, of the ideal child who can compensate for the parents' own shortcomings; once the child refuses to fulfill these expectations, he or she is thrust into the role of the scapegoat, and punished. Often parents conjure up the disasters they allegedly intend to ward off. If, for instance, they warn a child, excessively and in a stereotyped manner, not to give in to certain dangerous urges, they directly seduce the child into the behavior they apparently want to avert. Thus parents' exaggerated drive suppression may provoke a child into uninhibited sexuality, or their exaggerated achievement ideology may make the child a failure at school. The vehicle of negative family identity then offers the other family members an opportunity to participate in the child's escapades, and simultaneously to feel confirmed in their way of life whenever those fail.

As a matter of fact, I have often had patients who play the part of a scapegoat. Contradictory expectations on the part of the parents, who seduce the child into doing something for which he or she is subsequently punished, have a neuroticizing influence on the child. And yet scapegoats often not only do not feel like victims or failures in their families, but retain a feeling of superiority over the family. If a child fails to meet exaggerated parental requirements for achievement, or violently breaks unreasonable moral rules, all this is not simply happening to the child as a passive victim, since he or she is defiantly trying to correct parental exaggeration into its opposite.

Even if adolescents fail in their adventurous escape from the family—say, if young runaways promptly cause an accident with their stolen car, or show a particular talent for being arrested by the police for possession of drugs—this failure may not result from guilt feelings, self-punishment tendencies, or an urge to embody the parents' negated, bad impulses in order to accept punishment deserved by the parents. It appears to be more natural to say that leaving the parents' world causes fear and uncertainty in a child. In his escape, the adolescent is walking on thin ice, in an area with which he or she is not familiar, and there is no member of the family on whom the adolescent can model the behavior required in this area. Given this isolation, the failure predicted by the family will soon return him or her to the safe care of the parents.

Often the adolescent embodies the parents' "negative identity" (Richter 1976) not as a scapegoat, but as a *black sheep*. The black sheep is a member of the family who does not conform to family norms and who, as a kind of "mutant" or variant, cannot be integrated into the ranks of the siblings. The concept of the black sheep differs in nuances from that of the scapegoat. It often seems to me to describe a role better than the concept of the scapegoat does, because it contains a valuation that is ambivalent rather than negative. The black sheep is the child who arouses half aversion and horror, half fascination and admiration, in the family. It is black sheep who are often particularly loved, as can be seen in the parable of the Prodigal Son. It is often also black sheep who pursue new and creative ways. Many famous men and women were the black sheep of their families. There is a similarity to genetics, in that black sheep may be considered to be mutants who are particularly suited to initiating a new development, but who also run the risk of failure. Black sheep intensify the family dynamic. Often the siblings form an alliance against the black sheep, move closer toward their parents, and show a tendency to expel the black sheep. This pattern need not depend on the family's casting of the black sheep in a particular role. Rather, it is sufficient that the black sheep voluntarily dares something that the others anxiously reject. The alliance against the black sheep protects the others from the temptation to emulate him or her and thus to expose the family to even greater danger.

Most authors dealing with the sociology of the outsider agree with Emile Dürkheim that the outsider's main function within the group is the encouragement of solidarity and the stressing of rules and norms. The same has been noticed in group dynamics. The outsider reinforces the group members' self-confidence and enables them to express feelings, fear, and hostility. Thus the scapegoat is expected to preserve a system that is no longer functioning. This view strikes me as very one-sided.

Outsiders, black sheep, and scapegoats do not only reinforce the existing structures of a group and the solidarity of its members. On the contrary: they often cause a fundamental restructuring and evolution of an existing ideational system. Thus the fool becomes a genius, the black sheep a saint, the boaster a scientific authority. One and the same person may be a scapegoat for one group and a hero for another. Black sheep often prove to be the most loyal members of the family, because they renounce popularity and security for the benefit of the family evolutionary process. They must often tolerate the fact, however, that their parents and siblings describe them as disloyal. The consciousness of doing the right thing frequently provides them with the strength to follow the path they feel is right in spite of all hostility.

For example, a family was referred to me after the eighteen-year-old daughter, Ursula, had been hospitalized in a psychiatric clinic because of suicidal tendencies. She had been undergoing outpatient individual therapy for six months, and suffered from atypical anorexia nervosa consisting of daily bouts of bulimia, spontaneous or finger-induced vomiting, absence of menstruation, depressive irritability, and idleness at school. Her highly unstable weight was kept, more or less, within a normal range.

The autocratic father was making so much money in business that the family thought they were going to drown in it. He put all his energy into his work and returned home completely exhausted, wanting to be looked after and spoiled. He did not concern himself very much with bringing up the children, but left this responsibility to his wife, who felt that she was treated like a maidservant. She came from an ordinary background. She thought she was barely tolerated by the family. The father was closely tied to his mother, who in turn rejected her daughter-in-law. He often made chauvinistic remarks to his wife—for instance, that women had to be trained, otherwise they could not function. The wife was a discriminating, intelligent, and sensitive woman who hoped to acquire her reason for living by having her children be brilliant at school. The eldest, Thomas, developed into a proper family star by effortlessly attaining the highest achievements at school, by generally behaving like a paragon, and by never causing his parents the slightest worry. He completely overshadowed Ursula, and also treated her with contempt and arrogance. In the family sessions it became clear that the family consisted of two subgroups—namely, a clan of men on the one hand, and on the other hand the women, who were regarded as naturally inferior and were treated disparagingly.

Ursula's disturbing behavior was the focal point of the therapy at first. She greatly upset her surroundings by continually involving herself in dramatic fights with her mother, and by putting a knife to her throat and saying she was going to kill herself. She kept tormenting her mother with maneuvers of defiance and blackmail, or else shocked her family by not wiping up what she had vomited. After she had changed schools several times, it became the family's great concern that she should pass her graduation exams. In this respect, too, she behaved irresponsibly; her mother had to urge her to do her homework, and supervise her when she was doing it; and she had to be driven to school in the morning because otherwise she would be late.

The first therapeutic measure I carried through was that she should behave like someone of her age, and we discussed a definite plan as to how she herself would from now on assume responsibility for educational matters. She would do her homework by herself, and have it checked not by her mother but by her father, so that the latter could improve his contact with the children. She herself would have to be responsible for arriving punctually at school, keep a checklist regarding this, and submit this list to me at each session. Within a very short time, Ursula's behavior became more responsible and mature, and she got out of the impasse with her mother. Ursula no longer seemed depressive, but was more open-minded. During sessions we also discussed how she could assume responsibility for the organization of her leisure time, particularly for her returning home late at night and forming friendships with young men. Up to then she had been worrying her parents by going dancing and romping around madly with friends. Furthermore, the men with whom she preferred to enter into relationships were social deviants, drug addicts, and misfits, all of whom she had meant to help.

As Ursula's condition improved, her mother's became proportionally worse. She became increasingly depressive, pale, and weak. She devalued Ursula's progress, and evidently felt no longer needed in the family. Although she began to intensify her professional activities outside the family, she did this without any enthusiasm, and obviously blamed the family. After six sessions, an important change occurred. Ursula had chosen to move in with another family, where she felt better. The bouts of bulimia had ceased, the atmosphere brightened up, and she felt very well. This independent initiative taken by Ursula caused an amazing change in her mother, who said that Ursula had not had enough room in the family to develop her good qualities. These qualities were more on the emotional side, for which Ursula would need different surroundings. The father surprised me even more when he said that he was not worried about his daughter, that she would find her own way in any case, but that the elder son's development worried him much more. The son, he said, was too close to the mother, had never had a girlfriend yet, and lived in isolation from his peers.

The fact that his sister had moved out evidently made the brother, Thomas, move also. He was doing his national service at the time and, in a surprise announcement, said that afterward he would not return to the family, but would move into a three-room apartment with friends. Suddenly, Ursula was no longer the black sheep but the family idol, embodying spontaneous emotions, zest for life, carefreeness, and openness—a paradigm of a life beyond achievement and conformity. There were astonishing conversations between mother and daughter, in which the mother said without my prompting that Ursula had changed *her* life, too, that she had shown her how she did not assert herself in the family on account of her depressive, martyred attitude, and that she never said what she actually wanted. The mother modeled herself on the daughter and became substantially more emotional and more aggressive, particularly toward her husband. This behavior resulted in a marked improvement in her morale. She also blossomed physically and began to look like her pretty daughter.

The daughter gave up school and moved abroad in order to attend an art college. During one of her visits home, she phoned me because she was worried about her mother's condition. She asked me to keep a watchful eye on her mother during her absence, and to look after her when she was ill. I had the impression that Ursula wanted to transfer to me a function that she had herself fulfilled up to that time. I assured her that I would do everything possible. It became more and

more evident that Ursula's development was stagnating because she felt responsible for her mother and father, and
thought that she should not leave her parents to themselves.
The feeling that the parents could get support from me in
therapy gave her more freedom to devote herself to her own
development.

Thomas had changed his relationship to Ursula. He wrote
to her from the army that he would have to learn a great deal
from her. He seriously discussed with her his relationships
with women, and his coping with emotional, personal development. For the first time, too, he had a girlfriend.

In therapy, the mother now began to be concerned with
her own development, not only for her own sake but also in
order to enable the children to detach themselves. She had a
particularly intense relationship with Thomas. Partially, she
regarded him as a surrogate husband because her husband
gave her so little. Thomas had always been strongly oriented
toward her and had tried to fulfil her expectations. Within
only very few therapy sessions, the mother made astonishing
progress. She reported on dreams that illustrated her situation. She kept on having dreams in which her throat was
filled with a glutinous mass that she could not remove and
that nearly choked her. She would pull at this chewing-gum-
like mass, would panic more and more, would remove more
and more of this stuff, which also included physical organs,
but there would always be some left. Now she had had this
dream again, but this time a man had been beside her who
wore the same shoes that I did. This time, many physical
organs came out with this stuff, and she showed them to this
man, who said, "That's not all, that's only the liver; you
must get the heart out, too." She had the impression that in
these dreams she pulled out of her everything that she had
suppressed in more than twenty years of marriage. Everything, even her heart, the central organ, was infected.

Another dream that impressed her was this: she would
see a coffin in the cemetery at the crematorium. An attendant

was there. She could not see his face, but his hair was like mine; so she suspected that it was me. The attendant opened the coffin. It was empty, however, and this frightened her. Now she could see a child sitting on the ground a little distance away from her. Looking more closely, she recognized in this child her daughter Ursula as she had been in the first years of her life. Suddenly Ursula stood up and grew and grew. The attendant said, "Now she's too tall to be put into this coffin." The mother interpreted the dream as a therapeutic instruction not to lock her daughter into a coffin anymore, but to let her live. At the outset, the mother's striving for emancipation was still strongly in opposition to the family; now her emancipation was increasing for her own sake. She was no longer depressive but considerably more energetic and cheerful, and she accepted the compromises that life demanded from her. Her relationship with her husband, however, remained a sore point.

In the meantime, her husband had become increasingly depressive, and the wife had serious misgivings, thinking he might break down. He was by no means as strong and balanced as he would have others believe. When, two years before, the wife had to be hospitalized because of illness and an operation, she had had to return early from the hospital because the father had fallen prey to a serious depression that had to be treated psychiatrically. His wife's hospitalization had made him lose his footing completely. He went to church every day, donated money there, cried, and was utterly helpless. It was also revealed how much the father had been dissatisfied with the family's development in the previous few years. In his view it was his function to ensure his family's material security, as he had learned in his family of origin. He sensed, however, that the material security or, rather, the material abundance that he provided for his family did not earn him any recognition. The only member of the family who offered him understanding and emotional warmth was Ursula.

There was a phase in which he apparently became even more obsessed with the idea that material affluence would bring him happiness and satisfaction. He built up a valuable collection, for whose safeguard he had a security wing built into the house, from which the rest of the family was excluded. He purchased a car for more than forty thousand dollars; it was so precious that he did not dare drive it around for fear that it could be damaged. He thought he did not have the time for therapy, but was worried that his wife continued the therapy on her own. "That's how I'm paying for my own funeral," he remarked in jest. Almost defiantly he became even more obsessed with his work, and seemed to be trying to work himself to death. I ordered him to attend a session despite his lack of time, calmly listened to his excuses, and then said, casually, "It's clear to me that you can't handle your situation by yourself." And after an interval, "Let's wait until a heart attack comes to your aid. You'll have time then." This now made him more accessible, too. He said how deeply it hurt him that no one in the family appreciated his commitment to work, and no one valued his devotion to family duty.

Gradually he also found his regressive aspects more accessible. He had had an open discussion with Ursula, who had told him how she felt about him. Ursula had recognized the soft core behind the tough exterior. Fundamentally, he longed to be understood better by his wife. Although outwardly he had treated his wife disparagingly, he had always put her on a pedestal, as being unattainable and intelligent in the highest degree, but he had missed emotional warmth in the relationship. Ursula had uttered precisely what he felt himself—namely, that she had received no love at home. Achievements had been expected all the time, but there had been no warmth.

The daughter's illness had brought the family into therapy. The daughter had tried, according to her parents' wishes, to finish school, and she had also carried out the hidden task of conveying to her parents, by means of her illness, the emotional satisfaction and warmth that they could not find in their own relationship. She embodied the family's negative identity as a woman, as a failure, as an emotionally uninhibited and instinctual person. During therapy, the daughter's position shifted completely. When she left the family, it suddenly struck the family members that she, who was ill and suffered from behavioral disorders, was in fact the healthiest and strongest person in the family—indeed, the actual model whom brother, mother, and father were now trying to emulate. Thus the daughter, by expressing her authentic feelings, not only corrected the potential she had received from her parents but also corrected the development of the family and its members. The failure changed into a model; contempt for her changed into admiration; the patient became a "therapist."

HOW FAMILY CRISES REPAIR FAMILY FLAWS

Adolescence can be viewed as that phase of life in which a human being, in order to survive in the real world, must learn to own what his or her ancestors have handed down. The adolescent endeavors to develop the potential he has been given in a changing world. Two important decisions that he or she must make as a young adult may fix such corrective efforts in reality: choice of occupation and choice of partner. Just as bisexual reproduction, in joining together the genetic makeups of two gene carriers, can improve the adaptability and the reproduction success of species (relative to unisexual reproduction), marriage can (expressed in ethological terms) increase the behavioral variability of the family members, their adaptability, and, as it were, their "reproductive success." Marital partnership is possibly the most intense stimulus for a personal correction of the family stock of ideas in adulthood. This is the second time the family stock of ideas is intensely tested. Views, attitudes, values, norms, habits, and stereotypes peculiar to both partners' families must be adjusted to each other, so that they are reasonably compatible. The history of one family connects up with that of the other in the persons of the two partners. Both families' stocks of ideas are woven into the history of a new family.

If a member of one family corrects that family's ideas with the marital partner's support, then the partner is often turned into a scapegoat by that family. Each change of the now-married child is ascribed to the partner's bad influence, and the offended family awaits the failure of the marriage so that the ideational correction linked with it can be canceled and the member of its family won back. The clash of the worldviews of the two families within marriage may result in continuous tensions and arguments. It may, however, give rise to new "ideas," in the sense of creative solutions. A major differences between a marriage and a nonlegalized long-term relationship is that a wedding ceremony unites not only two persons but two families. It integrates the couple into the system of the extended family, with the advantage of wider-spread relatedness and the disadvantage of more meddling by relatives.

The following example shows how a married couple can gradually try to correct certain family "ideas," and how these attempts at correction are often difficult and may partially fail.

A married couple, both members of the legal profession and about fifty-five years of age, made an appointment for treatment, after the husband had for two years had an extra-marital relationship with an ex-domestic thirty years his junior. For a long time the wife had not been aware of this. Finally the husband confessed the relationship to her at his girlfriend's instigation. The wife was most deeply hurt about it. She could not understand why her husband could get involved with such a primitive "tart." She was also profoundly disappointed because she herself had taken this ex-domestic, then unmarried and pregnant, into the household and had done a great deal for her. The girl's family background had been difficult, and she acted the part of an enfant terrible in the family. She used her employer's cosmetics without the least inhibition, and dressed up in her evening dresses when she went dancing. The patient and the family were horrified by this incredible impudence and arrogance, and yet they tolerated it because, despite all upsets, this girl brought a certain amount of warmth into the family, and they had all grown fond of her.

The transgenerational history of the wife's family was as follows. Her grandfather, a businessman, had been a real moralizer. Her father majored in law, and tried to distance himself from his father's influence by marrying a woman from the French-speaking part of Switzerland. This woman was full of life and had, apparently, lived it up a bit in former years. At any rate, her father-in-law rejected her all his life, calling her a common hussy. In the course of marriage, her husband also developed into a strict moral Catholic with a Jesuit cast of mind. She adjusted herself without having any great influence on the "ideas" of the family. They had four children, the lawyer in question being the youngest daughter. The two elder sisters fell out with their puritan father, and moved to other parts of the country as soon as they came of age. The only son also became a lawyer, but later became addicted to morphine and lost his license because of delinquency. The father felt isolated in the family. His only ray of hope was the present patient, who even as a girl endeavored to fulfill his expectations. She was his favorite child. She was educated in a strict Catholic boarding school, where she also learned how to behave like a lady of taste, with flawless manners. She rejected anything sexual as animal and suppressed all sexual fantasies. She developed into a sporty and attractive woman. While studying law at the university she was always besieged by many men, which rather pleased her. She had no close relationship with any of them, however.

Her present husband, who had studied law with her, had

been one of her many suitors before they got married. He is a very pleasant, sociable man with a good sense of humor. He came from a less sophisticated family background, and had placed all his ambition into conquering this woman. His father-in-law did not find him suitable, however, since he thought that his favorite daughter should either marry a king or remain single and run a legal practice. The husband had to fight for his in-laws' goodwill for as long as they were alive. Thus he did a great deal of work for his father-in-law and helped him in every respect. In order to prove himself socially, he also pursued a military career and was a member of various prestigious clubs. Nonetheless, his in-laws continued to let him feel that he came from too primitive a home. The husband tried with great patience to develop his wife sexually. He was successful only within limits.

The wife had retained her deep-seated revulsion against everything sexual. In her younger years she had temporarily suffered from anorexia, and for several years during her marriage she could not conceive or else had spontaneous abortions and miscarriages. Finally, she gave birth to two children. Her life was very strained and hectic because, besides bringing up her children, she still ran her legal practice part-time. She would never have let her husband embrace her in front of the children. When the husband returned from work in the evening and wanted to kiss her, she at once withdrew from him, saying that she would have to go and cook. Although the wife basically hoped that in her relationship with the husband she would achieve a correction of her father's strict moral ideas, the paternal puritanism again became prevalent in this family. She kept house tastefully and perfectly, and she set great store by always having the table laid in an elegant manner, and by having the whole family appear impeccably dressed.

Five years previous to the present treatment, the patient submitted herself to psychoanalysis. After her father's death she had fallen prey to depression. In analysis she was greatly occupied with her hostile attitude toward the physical, which she had taken over from her family of origin; she thought that she had become substantially more open-minded and more positive about sexuality. She could therefore understand even less why her husband had started an extramarital relationship with this girl now, when she herself thought she had become more sexually liberated.

In therapy we asked whether the wife was running the risk of keeping her husband away from her through her continual accusations and suspicions; there was, conversely, a chance of integrating into their own relationship what the husband had found in the other woman. The wife proved very responsive to this, and they enjoyed better sexual relations than ever before. The extramarital relationship had the effect of a catalyst, and reactivated a stagnant marital evolution.

The two adolescent children were another problem. They often annoyed the patient by refusing to be as well mannered and tidy as she wanted them to be. The children's rooms were in such a mess that the patient could no longer ask the cleaning women to enter them. She was furious about this. Her husband laughingly remarked that he could see a time when the future daughters-in-law would ask their husbands' mother whether she had not been able to bring them up to be tidy. One of the boys bought a set of percussion instruments with which he created an earsplitting din and thus brought more emotionality into the household. The husband attempted to mediate in the quarrels between mother and children, but it was evident that he did not consider the children's opposition to be all that inconvenient. Within certain limits, the wife learned to tolerate the children's differing attitudes, and even to laugh at them. Whether in the long term the puritanical ideas of the family history can be corrected in the children remains an open question for the time being.

★ ★ ★

If marriage cannot sufficiently redirect a family's misdirected stock of ideas, then the young adults have an additional chance to do so when bringing up children of their own. They can try to bring up their children completely differently from the way in which they themselves were reared; they can instill in their children different values and norms, different views and attitudes, different habits and stereotypes. At least the burdens that have been handed down from the families of origin should not be passed on to yet another generation. Parents often attempt to achieve in their children those corrections of the family's ideational development that they have been unable to effect in their own lives. Extreme attitudes in bringing up children are often based on the parents' fear of repeating their own parents' mistakes. Tragically, going to the other extreme frequently has an identical result. Emotional deprivation and inability to tolerate frustration may be caused by overspoiling as well as by the withdrawal of love; the development of a healthy self-confidence may be impaired by an overly permissive as well as by an overly authoritarian upbringing; sexual inhibition hay be caused by forced sexual permissiveness as well as by exaggerated sexual tabooing.

And thus, as it has been said, the more things change, the more they stay the same. Often it seems that a family has been burdened by a curse for generations. As therapists, however, we see only the cases where such attempts at correction have failed; they are likely to be successful far more frequently than we think. Attempts to correct ideas through bringing up children often manifest themselves, in therapy, as the parents' pathogenic expectations of the children.

A further chance to correct the family history occurs with the death of a family member. The loss of one part of the system causes a reorganization of this system, and it is difficult to predict which direction such a change will take. As

I mentioned in the preceding examples, the death of a puritan moralizer may enable his or her children to lead a more liberated life. Equally, they may accept the puritanism of the deceased as an inheritance that must be carried on even more strictly.

SOCIAL COMMITMENT AS COMPENSATION

Suffering because of the family, and correcting the family history, can also express themselves in a commitment to other human beings or to a social idea. In such activities, I might like to work off much of what has become a thorn in my flesh, and to create new, better realities. I would like to punctuate my history and mark my trail. Protagonists of ideologies and social movements often derive their commitment and their energy from the attempt to cope with traumatizations by their own families in this manner. In recent decades this has been seen in the sexual-liberation movement, in the women's movement, and, in the last few years particularly, in the peace movement and in new religious communities. The personal experience of hostility toward the sexual drive in the family, the patriarchal, authoritarian, and personally unapproachable attitude of many fathers, a parental attitude to life that is determined purely by consumerism and exploitation—these are among the motives that caused many young people to commit themselves to changing the social conditions and thus their parents' attitudes. Certainly there is the occasional risk that a person will become a fanatic about an ideological movement, and lack detachment, because of not being able to cope with his or her own experiences. I observed, for example, how the woman in charge of a home for battered women persisted for years in identifying with the battered wives against the husbands. She denied the husbands any contact with the wives who sought refuge with her. The practical experience of working with these women gradually made it clear to her that her radical attitude did not actually aid her cause, since it helped neither the women nor their children to solve their problems. Thus she increasingly began to deal with couples dynamics and family dynamics.

Another woman, who has rendered outstanding services to women's groups, traces her motivation back to the suicide of her mother, who died when she herself was six years old. She is convinced that her mother had been destroyed by patriarchal conditions. She now wants to spare herself and other women the injustice done to her mother. She has the feeling that her mother is with her in all that she does, and that she is engaged in a continual dialogue with her. When she speaks to other women, it is really her mother who is speaking to them.

Work in a social profession or for an ideology often becomes an inner coping with unfinished aspects of our family history. Such work makes it possible for us to know the success of our personal correction by its fruits.

PART III

The Reality
of the
Suprapersonal

CHAPTER 7

How Relationships Begin

The preceding chapters have mentioned the person as a vehicle for ideas, as an organism capable of selecting, receiving, storing, processing, and disseminating ideas. In chapter 6 this view was illustrated in terms of the family, whose history can be represented as the evolution of a family stock of ideas, whose development joins a person's own development. In this chapter, the perspective of the person will again be extended: the person will be seen as a vehicle for, and an embodiment of, suprapersonal ideational processes. We will ask how such processes organize themselves and develop.

Suprapersonal as a term must be distinguished from *transpersonal*. The Latin prefix *trans-* means "beyond," in the sense of "on the other side, across." So-called transpersonal psychology (Tart 1975) was developed in the United States in the 1960s; its concern is to interrelate insights of psychology, the humanities, and religion. It investigates experiences during which consciousness is extended beyond the usual ego limits and beyond the limits of space and time. Among such altered states of consciousness are borderline experiences, particularly of a mystical and spiritual kind.

The term *suprapersonal* should be understood as systemic. It concerns processes that are larger than the person as an individual, and that interact with other persons' processes. The person is part of these processes. These processes are more than, and different from, the sum of the participants' personal shares in them. Suprapersonal processes are processes that integrate persons into a superordinate whole.

How does a suprapersonal process form? Or, in easier terms: how does an interpersonal relationship begin? For each relationship consists of at least one, but usually many, suprapersonal processes. A fictitious example will show how such processes are formed.

WHAT ALLOWS A RELATIONSHIP TO FORM

Let us assume that I get on a train for Berne in the Zurich railway station. I ask a woman who is sitting on her own in a compartment whether there is a vacant seat. She replies in the affirmative; I sit down, begin to thumb through a magazine, and every now and then casually look at the woman opposite. After a certain time she consults her watch, looks somewhat baffled, and compares her time with that on the station clock. Consulting my watch as well, I notice that the train should have departed two minutes ago, which is highly unusual in Switzerland.

I: It's late today.

SHE: Yes, I've just noticed that, too.

I: Last week I was only thirty seconds late, and the train was gone. Highly inconvenient for me. And all because

the streetcar had been held up by some demonstration
or other.

Here, the ensuing conversation may take completely different
courses.

Variant A

SHE: Do you go to Berne regularly?

I: Well, not really. I've only got to go another couple of
times. I have a cycle of lectures there on Tuesdays.

SHE: Oh, you lecture, do you?

I: I do, but this is more on the side, really, a course for
psychotherapists on the psychology of partnerships;
that's my field, you see.

SHE: Oh, well, that's an important thing, isn't it, if you
think of all those divorce cases; but does it work at all?

I: Well, yes, you may ask yourself that—I do, anyhow;
I'm interested in this question.

SHE: Well, everyone has their problems. My sister, too.
She's separated after being married for ten years.

The woman gives me sufficient leeway to describe myself as
a lecturer on partnership psychology, and describes herself
as someone who is prepared to go into my professional interests, and to base on them a subject matter we share in
common. She indicates that everyone—including herself—
has problems in this respect, and she sounds out my competence and my responsiveness by mentioning her sister's

marital difficulties. The conversation develops personally, while as a therapist I am in a position to pass on some of my professional ideas to her.

Variant B

SHE: Oh yes, more of those demonstrations again. Aren't they pointless?

I: Perhaps they're important all the same.

SHE: Do you think so?

I: All these initiatives always start up good things, too.

SHE: I don't believe it anymore. I was in the '68 movement. I also had the impression then that you could change society. I've given that up now. I'm living in the country.

I: Do you farm there?

SHE: Nothing big, only vegetables—organic—chickens, two goats, and two children.

I: Well, that's always been one of my dreams, too. But how can you live off it?

Here the conversation takes a different course. I am not granted the opportunity to describe myself as a professional and as an expert. Instead, the woman, by indicating her alternative lifestyle, appeals to some of my deeper personal longings, and this establishes a common topic. She has obviously had many experiences in which I am interested. She talks to me about her philosophy of life and about her experiences, and finds in me fertile soil for her ideas.

Variant C

SHE: It's always annoying to miss a train.

I: It is, but it doesn't usually happen to me.

SHE: One Sunday two years ago I wanted to go skiing with a friend in Davos. She first said, "Let's go by car." I said, "No, it's much more comfortable by train, no problems with traffic jams and parking." She agreed, and so we said we'd meet at the station at half past six. I was two minutes late, and the train had left. Of course she was mad at me.

I: But you still went skiing, I suppose?

SHE: Well, we went to Engelberg instead. There was trouble again, though, because an avalanche had come down across the track just in front of the train, so we lost two hours waiting to be picked up by a bus.

I: Well, we all get into a spot of trouble once in a while. The worst that ever happened to me was in Tunisia, ten years ago, when there were tremendous winds and rainfalls, and all the bridges had been washed away. We were really there with a tourist party, but we were completely cut off from everything and hardly knew how to get to the airport . . ."

Here, the conversation does not go beyond the relatively impersonal recounting of anecdotes. Both interlocutors describe themselves as people who go in for activities despite the trouble they may have to accept. Up to this point, however, no basis for a personal encounter has been established.

Variant D

SHE: Always those demonstrations. Why can't the police stop them, I wonder. One should be much firmer, and bring them to an end.

I: Do you think bringing in the police would solve the problems?

SHE: Those people should stick to the proper legal means when they express their problems.

I: How do you mean?

SHE: They can start a petition, collect signatures, then there'll be a vote, and you know where you are.

I: And to all intents and purposes they'd lose that vote.

SHE: Well, of course, because the majority happens to have a different view. After all, this is a democracy, right?

I: But it's happened to me, more than once, that I've only noticed problems because of these demonstrations.

SHE: Same here, but in a negative sense. If someone wants to impose something on me, I'm against it from the start, no matter what it is.

Here, the woman is very resolute and has precise attitudes to life, about which nothing is uncertain. I have two alternatives: either I break the conversation off by stating that there is no common basis, no topic about which we could have a mutual exchange of ideas, or I end up in a clinch with her because each of us finds the other representing that aspect of the topic that we are vehemently fighting. To her, I am an opportunist who encourages the demonstrators' attitudes by means of his overtolerant views; to me, she is the self-righteous citizen who shows no readiness at all to deal critically with a changing world. Neither offers any fertile soil for the other's ideas. At most, each expects the other to confirm his or her own views. No common process ensues.

How can these four possible variant courses of a conversation be understood? According to the transmitter/receiver model, it is a matter of sending a message from a source with a transmitter to a destination with a receiver. I send a message to the woman, which she receives and processes; she in turn replies by sending me a new message; and this to-and-fro of transmitting and receiving then develops into a communicative process. This is still a very superficial description, however.

Phenomenologically, it was crucial that the woman and I were in the same external situation, which is what enabled me to speak to her. After intruding into her territory, the railroad compartment, I withdrew for a time and leafed through the magazine so as not to look obtrusive. I spoke to her in German, assuming this was her language, too. In the common discovery that the train had not departed on time, we had a common concern that provided the first immediate cause for interactions. The peripheral mention of the fact that the previous week a train had left right in front of my nose offered a wide range of possible courses the conversation could take. Each individual course contains a thematic possibility that is available in myself, that gets entangled with the interlocutor's thematic possibility, and that thus creates a common process into which each interlocutor can feed more or less of his or her potential. Each can participate in this process only to the extent allowed by the other. Variants A and B would allow creation of an ideational process that could outlast this encounter situation.

The following general conditions and requirements play a part in the formation of a relational process.

- There must be temporal and spatial conditions in which a conversation can take place.
- There must be a mutual responsiveness between the people involved that makes the start of a relationship possible.
- The people must be able to communicate through a common language.
- They must be able to establish a common topic.
- The topic must be suited to dialectical differentiation.

A Common Situation

The first requirement for the formation of a relationship or of a common process is a common situation (temporal and spatial conditions). In a sense, this requirement assures an environment that makes interactions possible. The fact that the woman and I were in the same railroad compartment, and knew that we could be together for more than an hour, and that most likely no one else would join us, created an important, interaction-favoring situation. If another person had joined us, I might not have started the conversation, or else it would have taken a fundamentally different course. If we had been sitting in a streetcar or in a café, opposite each other and at the same distance, I would not have started the conversation, either, because on the one hand there would not have been sufficient time, and on the other hand it is less customary in Switzerland to speak to someone in a café than in a railroad compartment. The fact that we were in the same external situation, which was not disturbed by any outside influence, was an important prerequisite for the beginning of our conversation. The knowledge, too, that our conversation need have no consequences, and that no one else was involved in it, favored a rapid, mutual process of personal opening up. On the other hand, the limitation of the common situation also limits the objectives that a common process might aim for.

Mutual Responsiveness

The second requirement is mutual responsiveness to a common topic. Prior to verbal interaction, a nonverbal sounding out about fundamental readiness to talk took place. When I stopped in front of the compartment and looked in, the woman briefly looked up and drew her handbag a bit closer toward her, which I intuitively interpreted as meaning that she expected someone to join her in the compartment. After my inquiry about whether the seats were free, we glanced at each other for a moment and thus signaled to each other a fundamental readiness to talk. What really triggered off the conversation, however, was a common concern. As such, this common concern, the slight delay of the train, was trivial. Most conversations start with such a trivial common concern, however. It can be a discussion of the weather, which affects most people in roughly the same way. Or one person may ask the other, "Going to Berne, too, are you?" or "So you've caught this train as well, then?" These remarks sound ridiculous, but they have the function of signaling a common situation. Literature and films abound with examples where precisely a common concern on a trip may give rise to dramatic stories, be it a murder on the Orient Express or spending the night in the waiting-room of a Siberian railroad station. This common concern due to an accident or a crime causes complete strangers suddenly to enter into intense relationships with one another. The prerequisite for this is the common responsiveness of all concerned.

The psychological space in which an encounter can take place is limited by a mutual responsiveness to a topic or topics—by an *affinity of spirit*, as it were. If the topic of concern in the situation is important, as in a motoring accident, the mutual responsiveness may be quite comprehensive. If, however, the concern is practically meaningless, as in this fictitious example, it only assists in the search for mutual responsiveness. Even in this search, potential partners exchange I/You definitions, sound each other out, and search with tactfully veiled curiosity for interest and attitudes, but also for information on social status, marital status, and occupation.

A Common Language

Without this, an exchange of ideas and a differentiated encounter would not be possible. I will deal with this problem later on.

A Common Topic

Depending on the extent to which the previous three requirements have been met, the establishing of a common topic will come into play. Two strangers will often spend a long time looking for a common topic. There are commonplaces, such as football and cars for men, or possibly illnesses for elderly people; looking for, and finding, a common enemy is particularly popular, as such a figure makes people vent their anger and brings a certain degree of affect into the conversation (examples would be demonstrations, as mentioned above, complaints about the state, traffic conditions, or damage to the environment). The conversation will always be restricted to those areas where a common responsiveness has been found. The Greek philosopher Pythagoras (ca. 580–500 B.C.) formulated the theorem "Only the similar can understand the similar." The more spiritually related to us the recipient of our message is, the more easily we can convey to that person what moves us most deeply or disquiets us, what we want to formulate and to pass on. Once it is possible to establish a more comprehensive topic on the basis of mutual responsiveness, there is the possibility of a differentiated common process.

Development of the Discussion of the Topic Can Become More Detailed and Elaborate

As a rule, a relevant interaction will become possible only after establishing a common topic. Bin Kimura says: "In every real conversation . . . a 'horizon' must first be discovered, in which the participants share an 'atmosphere' in common, which in turn renders possible an interpersonal/ intersubjective encounter." He also writes (1974): "A presence . . . must take his own self out of this original mutuality and make it his very own. The taking out of the self, however, necessarily entails the emphasis of what is not part of the self—i.e., of the other in the same mutuality with oneself. . . . One and the same act, by means of which I take my self out of the original mutuality of potential I and potential You, and by means of which I come to myself, also emphasizes You, the other, encountering me here and now, in the same mutuality."

The Japanese have a particular sensorium for this common ground or horizon. According to Ueda (1982), the deep mutual bow of the Japanese welcoming ceremony signifies more than mere politeness. In fact, it helps each person to turn himself into a "nothing" before the other; and both thus acknowledge their readiness to descend to a depth where there is neither I nor You. The aim is the comprehension of the original "nothing," in which and out of which alone the duality of the encounter is possible. Only then, after straightening up again, arising from nothing, do the two partners in conversation turn toward each other as I and You, but in a manner which is at once "neither I nor You" (Grassi and Schmale 1982, pp. 49ff.). Between the self and the other, something new occurs, which cannot be traced back to one or the other partner in conversation, nor yet to both of them. In the Japanese greeting ceremony, neither person enters immediately into an I/You relationship; both first lose themselves in an in between, so as then to arise face-to-face. It is the atmosphere that makes us speak. It is the topic linking us that makes us appear as I myself and You yourself. In this way, a conversation may become an encounter, or it may lead to a dispute, a thematic differentiation.

Another precondition for interactions is a tension between the two interaction partners, such as a difference between levels of information (i.e., one knows what the other desires to know) or a "trial-and-error situation" (one tries something to which the other responds) or a dialectical situation (the one's thesis and the other's antithesis strive for a synthesis). Once the tension is neutralized, interaction dies; if the relationship is to continue, a new topic must be found.

A conversation and a relationship do not consist only of a mutual exchange of message between two or several persons. Rather, they first and foremost consist of the establishing of a common topic, which then expresses itself apparently independently in the interlocutors, and develops into a process. It is as if the topic used the interlocutors in order to express itself. Whereas the topic is the basis, the ideational process is a whole that derives from it and is both purposive and self-organizing, and both transcends and includes persons.

At the beginning of a relationship, there is a common resonance of those strings that have the same vibration and whose sounds now start to reinforce one another. We are warming up to a state in which "we think our own 'thoughts' as well as the 'thoughts' of others, can feel our own feelings as well as those of others (in compassion). . . . At first there is merely a stream of experiences, which is indifferent to the distinction between I and You, and which contains what is factually its own and factually foreign to it in an undifferentiated mixture. Only gradually are more distinctly visible eddies formed in this stream, which slowly involve more and more of the stream's elements, and which can only very gradually be attributed to different individuals in this process" (Scheler 1948, pp. 264–66).

A relationship between people may therefore also be seen as a suprapersonal ideational process: two or more persons are linked on the common ground of a topic and arrange themselves to create a purposive ideational process. The ideational process is like a third party in whose creation I and You manifest ourselves, a third party that—now viewed from the other side—itself assumes shape and expresses itself in Me and You.

Let's apply all this to the examples at the beginning of this chapter. In Variant A, the topic "couples therapy" will express itself as well and as extensively as my traveling companion will permit me to express it, or as I will make her respond to my messages. In Variant B, "alternative lifestyle," the same is true, but the roles are reversed. In Variants C and D, only few strings are plucked, as it were, and even those will not produce their full sound.

LANGUAGE AND IDEAS

Language is both a vehicle and substance of suprapersonal ideational processes. Languages are phenomena that characterize common consciousness and ideas. Language makes the formulation of common consciousness possible. The area of expansion of a language is the area of expansion of common consciousness.

Thoughts, and thus ideas, need language. Extralinguistic thinking, and thus extralinguistic production of ideas, is not really possible. Insights are largely bound to linguistic expression. Thoughts can be shaped and formulated only as language. As I mentioned earlier, a thought, an idea, needs language in order to be thought. Language is the creative organ of the idea. I can comprehend the idea only in its linguistic formulation.

There are two fundamentally different forms of human

communication (Watzlawick, Beavin, and Jackson 1967), digital and analog. In digital language, information to be transmitted is provided with names or signs that are as unequivocal and unmistakable as digits. The word is the vehicle of fixed denotations; language is the tool of nomenclature. Most scientific, technological, and economic achievements would be inconceivable without the development of digital communication. Technical data, plans of machines and buildings, chemical and physical instructions, financial transactions, even the playing of pieces of music according to musical notation can, in the appropriate digital language, be transmitted so precisely that the recipient can reproduce them in the same way as the transmitter; no explanations are necessary.

Analog communication is of equal significance for human beings, however. A man who receives analog information decodes what has been communicated, and draws an analogy between this message and a previous experience of his own that strikes him as similar and whose significance he is able to interpret. Forms of analog communication arise in the area of relationships. As a way of expression, they are much more original than the digital ones. Exclamations, gestures, and mood signals are forms of analog communication also used and understood by animals; these forms of communication signal relationships with others rather than referring to objects and abstracts. Wherever a relationship becomes the central topic of communication, digital communication proves unclear and insufficient, as in love relationships, in hostile relationships, in care, and so on. Analog language has undertones of the expression of moods, of onomatopoeia, of invocation, and of evocation. Analog language is the language of poetry, literature, and song.

The process that complements speaking is listening. The recipient of digital communication must be able to decode the signs and names into their exact meanings, which is possible only if he knows the code, if he has learned the meanings of the signs. Digital language interconnects the initiates in a cognitive manner. It makes the exchange of scientific information possible and is a prerequisite for scientific progress. Just as in analog communication, the word is not merely the vehicle for finished thoughts but also that which makes thought possible. Listening does not amount to mere digital retranslation. Rather, it is the listener who gathers the thoughts from the words and gives them meaning. Thus communication work develops between the interlocutors. "There is therefore something like taking over another's thoughts in the passage through the word . . . a capacity for following the other's thoughts . . . " (Merleau-Ponty 1966). "For the word . . . is not an imprint of the thing as such, but the image created by it in the soul" (Humboldt 1968).

In analog language, listening is never mere reproduction but a work of interpretation, a creative act, an innovation that reaches as far as the listener's responsiveness and concern can reach. Thus thought may become clear as a result of joint communicative work. The discovery that an addressee may be approached far more personally, emotionally, and deeply by means of analog language is now being applied methodically in psychotherapy through body language, metaphors, fairy tales, and psycholinguistic techniques. It is no coincidence that the language of analogy, the language of relationship, has particularly been used in hypnotic techniques, where the therapist uses suggestions to put a patient into a state of responsiveness. Moreover, analog language is consciously used in advertizing, in rhetoric, and in public speaking.

The common topic, which formulates itself as an idea between two or several persons, is situated somewhere in the field between digital and analog language, depending on whether it is of a more cognitive, abstract, and rational nature, or whether it is more emotional and relationship-creating. Language is the medium for the dissemination of cognitive ideas. Language also expresses conditions and moods that people have in common.

Language and Responsiveness

Language is the medium that provides, and makes available, the basis for mutual responsiveness. Language is the product of an immeasurable wealth of spiritual experiences throughout human history, the expression of a common culture, of common historical roots and ideas about the nature and meaning of the world, of life, and of humanity. Language provides the form with which such experiences can be exchanged. It joins insiders and separates them from outsiders. Language establishes boundaries against strangers. Language's ability to express experiences is limited, however. For example, Swiss German is an archaic analog language with a high degree of onomatopoeic expression but with a primitive grammar. Swiss German has only two tenses, the present and the perfect. If a German-speaking Swiss wants to express something with scientific precision, or if he wants to add weight to something, he uses the High German standard language. On the other hand, English as a scientific language challenges the native German speaker to formulate more clearly, more exactly, and more simply. As a rule the English translation of a German text is at least a quarter shorter than the original. On the other hand, when an Italian or French song is translated into German, it becomes so guttural that it loses its grace. When the French films of the 1950s and 1960s are dubbed into German, they lose their atmosphere. The common consciousness thus assumes shape in language and gives shape to this consciousness.

Language Arises from Common Consciousness

Language is neither fixed nor immutable, but is continuously being created and creatively modified. Languages have their lineages and different historical developments. Thus the original Indo-European language developed into the Italo-Celtic,

Greek, and Germanic trees. Of the Germanic tree, the Gothic and Vandal branches became extinct. North Germanic developed into Icelandic, Danish, and Swedish; West Germanic into German, Dutch, and English. There are languages that are becoming extinct, and others that are being newly created. All this expresses a common human consciousness that has its creation, its development, and its death (Wickler and Seibt 1977, pp. 351ff.).

The area of expansion of a language signals the area of common ideas. Each family has its own language, as has each working team, each occupation, each people, each social stratum, each nation. Men have their languages, women theirs; the young have their languages, the old theirs; each era has its own language. Language is the expression of common ideas, of a common identity.

The development of any given language may be observed at close quarters in the evolution of slang expressions during two or three decades. What was the rage in the fifties was old-fashioned in the sixties; what was fashionable in the seventies sounds dated now. Additionally, there is the geographical factor: an expression fashionable in one city may never be heard in another, or terms prevalent in urban areas may never be used in rural districts. Gender, too, has an influence: men's slang differs from women's; it is often rougher. Then, of course, language is a social classifier: upper-class slang is far different from working-class slang. But who invents slang? Who decides which linguistic grouping uses what type of slang? There are no pertinent prescriptions, no laws, no formal agreements; and yet population groups develop both a spontaneous common consciousness of norms and a common responsiveness to the modification of these norms, without ever formulating this in any detail.

It is also interesting to note that some words never spread beyond narrow regional limits, although their expressive, descriptive, or onomatopoeic power exceeds that of other words that mean the same and are used in neighboring regions. Why is it that words like this cannot spread geographically, but other words may eliminate competitors for no apparent reason? Humboldt (1903) said: "Language as understood in its real nature is continuously and in every instant transitional. . . . Itself, language is not an act (*ergon*) but an activity (*energeia*). . . . It is the eternally recurring activity of the mind to enable the articulated sound to express thought. . . . In the true and most essential sense, language can only be considered the totality of such speech, as it were."

A group's linguistic peculiarities particularly strike the noninitiate, the one who approaches from the outside. I gave courses in couples therapy to a circle of Berlin psychoanalysts at two-year intervals. When I was there the first time, I noticed that the participants kept using the expression "up to a point." "This disorder may up to a point have been caused by . . . ," "Up to a point, therapy could help to . . . ," "I'm of the opinion, at least up to a point . . ." Two years later it seemed impossible to discuss therapy without using the expression, "with much, much love." Another two years later, love had faded, and the term *to delegate* was in vogue: whatever anybody thought and felt and wanted was delegated to, or taken over as a delegation from, someone else. Such formulations express the group members' common consciousness and ideas as well as their continuous change.

A language not only indicates an identification with the same culture and ideas, and thus characterizes a common identity, but also reveals an openness toward foreign influences and foreign ideas. This can be measured by the yardstick of formulations and words borrowed from foreign languages, which characterize the acknowledgment of a cultural lead in general or in specific areas. The spreading and acceptance of foreign words or even foreign languages thus point toward an expansion of cultural influences and power. At the moment, the German-speaking area of the West is accepting many American words, particularly among youngsters in pop and rock culture, and generally in economic life, in technology, and in the sciences—as in medicine, where Latin used to be the insider's hallmark. The French, who particularly suffer from the worldwide diminution of their influence, recognized this early on. In Quebec and in other countries they try to maintain their francophone spheres of influence, but sadly, their prospects of success are slight.

Switzerland, split up into many small valleys, has to this day retained distinct regional dialects. This was favored by the fact that Switzerland was never the center of a culture with a far-reaching influence, and therefore never had to agree on a national language of its own. In the German-speaking areas, the spoken language is the Swiss dialects, but the written language is standard German, which has to be learned at school like a foreign language. On the other hand, the fact that Switzerland was hardly a significant center with its own cultural ideas made it highly accessible to outside influences. A. Berner-Hürbin (1974) has described how Romance paronyms were adopted in the Swiss German of the fifteenth and sixteenth centuries. The problem was the same then as now: a tension between the will to assert oneself and to preserve one's own values, and the will to keep pace with the Romance-speaking peoples (who are considered superior) by opening oneself to them. The Bernese responded to French culture, whereas the Zurichers and the Eastern Swiss were more strongly influenced by Italy.

The expansion of a language indicates the expansion of cultural ideas, and simultaneously creates the bases for the expansion of a culture's power and influence. In the natural sciences, in medicine, and in psychology, it is less and less possible nowadays to gain international recognition when writing in German. One is forced to publish in English. The reason given for this is that a lingua franca, as Latin used to be, would facilitate international exchange. It is obvious that someone for whom English is a foreign language will not experience this facilitation in quite the same way as a native speaker of English.

The acceptance of a foreign language is a problem that particularly concerns legal aliens. There are Italian families in Switzerland in which the women have learned no German in more than twenty years. They move almost exclusively in their own circles, and assimilate themselves to German-Swiss culture as little as possible. The same can be observed in the middle and upper classes: French-speaking Swiss women who ended up in the German-speaking part of Switzerland because of marriage will often refuse to speak German even after decades. The refusal to adapt linguistically reveals a refusal to adopt to another culture and its ideas. People who refuse to adapt are frequently very isolated and unhappy, and therapy's first task is to deal with this linguistic assimilation.

A PERSON HAS MANY LANGUAGES

One and the same person employs different languages, depending on whether he or she is speaking to children, animals, deaf people, members of the upper class, or members of a lower social stratum. This is particularly clear in the sphere of psychiatry. Psychiatrists use distinctly different languages when speaking to a depressive, or to an alcoholic, or to an emotionally deprived person. This is a particularly good example of the fact that a person is not a self-contained individual, but in part a manifestation of the relational field. The clearest examples are the linguistic creations used by people in love. Every pair of lovers have a language of their own and thus create for themselves their own identity, a common self. In sexual therapy this is used consciously on occasion: partners who suffer from sexual inhibitions toward each other may be asked to invent names for each other's sexual organs, so that they are able to speak about them, and indeed even *to* them.

Linguistic innovations are largely achieved unconsciously. They arise from common ideational processes. They have no spiritual begetters, no leaders, usually no known inventors. They occur because something is in the air, because individuals vibrate on the same frequency or suffer from, are disquieted by, or search for similar things.

The expansion of language as a wealth of ideas takes place in accordance with laws that are basically similar to those that Darwin discovered for the evolution of the species. The ideas that survive are those that do best at producing and maintaining a common consciousness between people, and that are best suited for the creation of, and adaptation to, the "environment." Those ideas that are no longer part of the common consciousness are dropped and replaced by others. In this sense there is also a spiritual and linguistic evolutionary process.

CHAPTER 8

How People Embody
Ideas

I deas evolve by expressing themselves in their protagonists. An ideational process is not only the sum total of
the ideas of its carriers; it has a structure of its own. The
carriers of ideas take up different positions within the ideational space. Frequently, ideas are grouped around certain
protagonists, who embody an idea. The more an idea is connected with a worldview or a religion, the more it needs
protagonists in order to be idealized and embodied. The protagonist personifies the idea; his life consists of a succession
of stories and anecdotes that represent the translation of the
idea into daily life; the protagonist fights for the idea, suffers
for it, possibly even dies for it. The protagonist presents
himself as a figure to be identified with—as a guru, leader,
hero, or martyr. As a role model, he or she must offer those
who follow him or her a substantial narcissistic gain, such as
being among the pioneers of a new era, healing or saving the
world, or standing out from the mass of ordinary people.
This attraction is reinforced by threatening and frightening

all those who fight the protagonist or who do not want to declare their support.

World history, cultural history, art history, literary history, and scientific history are largely described in terms of their protagonists. There is a recurring tendency to represent these protagonists as persons who, lonely and unrecognized in their own time, created something by their own inspired efforts. Hans Joachim Störig (1954, p. 30), for instance, thinks that "the great ones in the sphere of the mind [create] on their own and largely independently of external and social circumstances, indeed often even against those." Society may poison Socrates, crucify Jesus, burn Jeanne d'Arc, or guillotine Lavoisier, but it cannot prevent such people from being born, or prescribe their functions for them. If we observe only the individual fates of certain explorers, inventors, and spiritual leaders, this view may be convincing; it is less so, however, if the personal histories are placed in a broader cultural context. For example, the universal phenomenon of simultaneous invention (that is, the fact that many important discoveries have been made by two or more persons independently and at the same time) demonstrates that history does not depend on unique individuals. This viewpoint might create the impression that it is time or culture that brings forth the carriers of certain ideas, in order to express itself in them. Doubtless, particularly sensitive and responsive individuals may be ahead of the great mass, and may realize much earlier than others what is inevitably emerging in contemporary history. They may remain unrecognized and not understood by their contemporaries for a long time. In a way it is like spring, when individual tulips appear somewhat earlier and thus announce tulip time, exposing themselves to a higher risk of freezing in the process. However, tulip time will arrive anyway, sometimes a bit earlier, sometimes a bit later. In the same way, pioneering work in world history is a manifestation of the spirit of the times.

Hegel paid particular attention to this aspect of history.

According to Hegel it is not the individual who acts alone; rather, world spirit or historical necessity acts through the individual, using him or her like a tool. What makes historical personalities great is not such personal qualities as energy, passion, foresight, or intelligence, for the world spirit often avails itself of undignified and weak individuals for its own purposes. "The world spirit acts through the individual against his personal intentions and purposes. The active individual may think that he serves particular, purely personal purposes, such as the expansion of his personal power" (Störig 1969, vol. 2, p. 132). According to Hegel, great men merely seem to set the course of a historical process. It is not their subjective planning and volition that make them great, however, but historical necessity, as whose tools they act. Such people create what is timely, what is necessary. They draw from the as-yet subterranean, from what is as-yet unreal but striving to be realized. Hegel's ideas of the historically necessary that wants to happen to a people were sadly perverted by the Nazis for their own purposes, so that Germans today tend to deal with Hegel cautiously, if at all.

Jung voiced his own view of the problem. According to Jung, the collective unconscious may be affected by social, political, and religious influences. Suppressed opinions accumulate in the collective unconscious and activate it. "In most cases it will be one or several individuals of particularly keen intuition who apprehend the changes in the collective unconscious and translate them into immediate ideas. These ideas then spread more or less rapidly because, simultaneously, changes have occurred in other people's unconscious. Therefore a general readiness to accept the new ideas is prevalent, although on the other hand there is also vehement resistance to them" (Jung 1960b).

As a rule, historiography characterizes a transition from one epoch to another, or the spirit of one particular epoch, in terms of specific personalities who had a crucial influence on politics, culture, art, and science. Historians tend to credit these people with revolutionizing the world, and with setting it on a new course. I think that the appearance of these people can be viewed in a different light. It is difficult to describe historical development in terms of social and economic forces; it is a great deal easier to use people as examples of how a specific epoch assumes a concrete shape.

"Epoch-making" personalities symbolize a certain period of time as living illustrations of it. Yet they did not create their works all by themselves. Their extraordinariness usually consisted in their capacity to sense what was "in the air"; they "had a nose" for this; they could process what they sensed, and create what society lacked; they were steadfast in defending the consequences resulting from their works, and in asserting themselves against the resisting forces. In spite of all such personal merit, these influential personalities were children of their times. It was not only that they contributed toward the change in their times; the changing times also used them to assume visible shape. In such personalities a message was being formulated, which then started up a historical ideational process.

Claude Lévi-Strauss, the well-known French ethnologist, has expressed very neatly how he always forgets everything he has written

> because I do not feel that I have written my books myself. I have rather the feeling that I am a transit point for my books; as soon as they have gone through me, I feel empty, and nothing remains. . . . My work is thought in myself without me knowing anything about it. I have never had a feeling of a personal identity, not even now. I feel like a place where something happens but where there is no I. Every one of us is a kind of crossroads where various things happen. The crossroads itself is completely passive; things happen on it. Something else, equally valid, happens somewhere else. There is no choice; it's simply coincidence. [Lévi-Strauss 1980.]

The observation that time gives birth to its representatives and not vice versa seems to contradict the observation that many important explorers and researchers were introverted loners who apparently hardly noticed their environment and other intellectual trends, because they lived only for their research. Some of their discoveries even came to them in dreams. The German chemist August Kekulé von Stradonitz (1829–1896) discovered the atomic chain as well as the benzene ring in a kind of vision. He recounts how, when he was dozing in front of the fireplace, long rows of atoms formed into snakelike shapes in his mind: "One of the snakes bit its own tail, and mockingly the thing was spinning in front of my eyes. I awoke as if struck by lightning" (Störig 1954, p. 442). Many researchers were not understood, were even expelled, persecuted, and excommunicated. Many of them lived alone and in poverty, were unrecognized, were possibly "discovered" only posthumously.

All this does not contradict the thesis that they are part of a suprapersonal consciousness. Precisely because their concentration was neither disturbed nor distracted by anything, these researchers could sense what strained to become conscious, possibly far earlier than all those who remained caught up in traditions and norms and wasted their energy on sociability, so that they could not muster enough openness and responsiveness to allow what strained to become conscious. The world history of science appears as if a consistent yarn of increasing consciousness is being spun. Viewed from the angle of world history, it is irrelevant whether certain researchers' discoveries were not acknowledged by society for decades, or possibly for centuries.

Religious and political leaders, too, often withdrew from their public activities into solitude. Such a retirement, however, would be not only a retreat into oneself but also a withdrawal from daily entanglements in order to become open to what time wanted to give birth to.

The history of science abounds with evidence of the fact that important discoveries were made simultaneously in completely different places on this planet, by researchers who could not have influenced each other directly. Some examples will suffice. Descartes is held to be the inventor of analytic geometry. However, a compatriot and contemporary of his, Pierre de Fermat, who occupied himself with mathematics only in his leisure time, also found the bases of analytic geometry, independently of Descartes. His writings, however, were published only after his death. Since Descartes published his results earlier, he was accorded the laurels. Sir Isaac Newton discovered the differential calculus in the years 1665 and 1666, but published his work only in 1704. Meanwhile, Gottfried Wilhelm von Leibniz made the same discovery in Hannover, and published it much earlier than Newton. This set off one of the most bitter priority arguments in the history of science. Interestingly enough, both Newton's and Leibniz's evidence were false; yet both of them reached the right conclusions. Instinct and intuition often make use of what is correct, even if strict, logical proof does not yet exist.

Or consider the idea of universal gravity: that the orbital movement of the planets results from the fact that the sun attracts a planet with precisely the same force with which the planet, by dint of its own centrifugal movement, is trying to move away from the sun. This idea was described in 1666—independently of each other—by the Italian Giovanni Alfonso Porelli and by the Englishman Robert Hooke, at the same time that Newton was also examining this question. The German Karl Friedrich Gauss, the Russian Nikolai Ivanovitch Lobatchevski, and the Hungarian János Bolyai discovered non-Euclidian geometry in 1826, approximately at the same time, and again independently of each other. As many as four researchers reached the same conclusions, at the same time, about the transformation of heat into mechanical work: the German Robert Mayer in 1842, the Dane August Colding in 1843, the Englishman James Joule in 1847, and the German Hermann von Helmholtz, also in 1847. The introduction of ether into medicine was a discovery that led to bitter priority quarrels among four Americans, Crawford Williamson Long, William Thomas Green Morton, Charles Thomas Jackson, and Horace Wells. In fact, it was Long who had discovered ether, but he was not granted his fame because he published his discovery three years after the others. The bitter fights about fame and the patents resulted in one of the researchers going mad, another becoming destitute, and a third committing suicide.

It is also possible for discoveries to be premature, made before society is mature enough to understand them. A hundred years before Gregor Mendel, one Baron von Pernau traced, with the help of back-crossing, the succession of "mendeling" individual characteristics in successive generations. The same results, found by Mendel in a substantially more favorable time, led to his being considered the father of genetics. By the same token, an individual's great hour may come late in his life, as it did for Pope John XXIII, for Konrad Adenauer and Charles de Gaulle, and also (from our point of view, a negative example) for Ayatollah Khomeini. These men were ready to perform extraordinary deeds, but they had to await the call of the hour before they could do so.

RESPONSIVENESS AND VOCATION

Many famous personalities were inspired by ideas for which they were not prepared. Something was revealed to them whose meaning they apprehended only after the event. "I cannot rid myself of the spirits that I called," says the sorcerer's apprentice of Goethe's ballad. Many were seized with fear and retired from research. Others grew with the mission that was connected with the idea. Objectively speaking, many were hardly suited to disseminating an idea, and were not ideal for carrying out the assignment. The Bible is full of examples of God calling persons who felt, and indeed were, overtaxed by this call. The merit of persons such as Abraham, the prophet Jeremiah, the Virgin Mary, and the Apostles derives from their readiness to respond to the impossible, to obey the call without being intimidated by the fear it provoked. The term *vocation* (from the Latin *vocatio*) originally meant an instruction to do something specific. It was only after Luther that this term was applied to secular work, since Luther attributed to work the dignity of a divine command. The German noun denoting "job, occupation" is *Beruf*, literally, "calling." Unlike the word *job*, *Beruf* does not describe purely purposive activity: since it is closely linked with the German expression for "vocation," *Berufung*, it implies a suprapersonal relatedness of being called and of being responsive.

You Need Not Be Perfect in Order to Create a Perfect Work

As I mentioned in chapter 2, a person need not be perfect in order to create perfect works. Indeed, someone's inability may lend intensity and tension to his or her action. If someone suffers from imperfection, this may provide motivation to create works that embody that which he or she desires but cannot personally achieve.

There is a strong tendency in both historiography and daily life to identify work and creator, and to assume that behind an ideal work there must be an ideal person. This is not usually true, precisely because it is insufficiency, imperfection, and imbalance that are the thorn in the flesh and the driving motivation to create. Personal encounters with creators of great works are frequently disappointing, because these creators display such absolutely mundane characteristics as ambition, craving for admiration, dogmatism, and hypersensitivity.

In 1962, at the beginning of my psychiatric training, I had the opportunity to visit Ernst Kretschmer, the creator of the constitution theory, in Tübingen, Germany. He had just become an emeritus professor (that is, retired), but still had a study in the university's psychiatric clinic. When he received me there, he remained seated and left me standing in front of him. I ascribed such behavior to the absentmindedness of his advanced age and looked around his study. In the farthest corner I spotted a chair, which I carried to the desk in order to sit down. Kretschmer seemed to me to be annoyed and insensitive. He used the conversation almost exclusively to disparage me by enumerating to me all that he had achieved and published at my age. I was somewhat confused, but when I related all this to my Tübingen colleagues, they roared with laughter. Apparently, Kretschmer had the military habit of letting inferiors stand up during conversations. My nonobservance of this ritual had obviously thrown him completely off balance. I was scandalized by this weakness in such a famous man. Nonetheless, I remained affected in a positive manner by Kretschmer's writings.

In the field of psychotherapy, where we would most expect outstanding personalities and superior models of self-realization, the discrepancy between work and person is often particularly great. If these persons fall disappointingly short of their own ideals, we may be tempted to consider their work valueless, too. In the fields of psychotherapy, philosophy, and religion, writings often express the author's unrealized longing. We would be less inclined to measure the value of a work against its creator's behavior if we started from the fact that basically, the author is only the carrier and point of crystallization of suprapersonal ideational processes. I think that a work should be measured by its fruits—by the stimulation and effects that it has.

Sadly, however, creators of works sometimes tend to identify themselves with the idealized images that others may have of them. Many famous scientists and artists become ridiculous and trite once they believe that they can expostulate about God, the world, and everything else outside their fields with the same competence as they can when discussing their own defined area of competence, on which they have concentrated all their energies for decades. One-sided concentration on a certain topic often results in one-sided and restricted personal development, and this often leaves famous people less competent regarding questions of daily life than anyone who has developed more integrally without any claim to specialization.

IDEAS DEVELOP AS RELATIONSHIPS

Many, possibly all, ideas develop and are manifested not in one single person, but in the interaction of several persons: to be precise, ideas in their principles are to be ascribed to the relationship from which they have resulted rather than to one particular person. Let us consider an example from the time of the birth of psychoanalysis. Fundamental ideas of psychoanalysis resulted from the relationships between Anna O., Joseph Breuer, and Sigmund Freud: the principle of catharsis of bottled-up and repressed affect (abreacting); the tracing back of psychoneurotic symptoms to certain traumatizing situations; the observation that such symptoms can be neutralized in a therapeutic session by being recalled; as well as starting points for the concepts of transference, countertransference, and the sexual nature of psychoneuroses.

Freud and Breuer

Freud received decisive impulses for the development of psychoanalysis from his relationship with Joseph Breuer, a specialist in internal medicine and a family doctor highly esteemed in Vienna, who was fourteen years his senior. When Freud was a student and a young doctor, they struck up an intense friendship and scientific exchange. On occasion Freud would name Breuer as the founder of psychoanalysis; at other times, however, he would call himself the only begetter of psychoanalysis (Freud 1946b, pp. 44–45).

In 1880, when he was about forty years old, Breuer was treating Anna O. (Bertha Pappenheim), just over twenty at that time and a classic case of hysteria. Through her, Breuer discovered and developed the concept and method of catharsis. Anna O. described to him the first occurrence of a certain symptom in all its details, and to Breuer's great astonishment the symptom disappeared completely. The patient recognized the value of this procedure, and continued to describe to Breuer one symptom after another. Freud's biographer, Ernest Jones, in fact named Anna O. as the actual discoverer of the cathartic method, which she herself described as "the talking cure" or "chimney sweeping." Evidently Breuer had developed a strong countertransference for this patient. According to Freud, he no longer spoke about anything but Anna O., which made his wife jealous and in consequence increasingly morose and irritable. When Breuer guessed the reason for his wife's emotional state, he reacted vehemently and decided to discontinue the treatment, for which he had sacrificed several hours every day for more than a year. Anna O., who had already become much better, then entered a state of extreme agitation and produced the symptoms of contractions in a hysterical birth. Breuer "managed to calm her down by hypnotizing her, and then fled the house in a cold sweat. Next day he and his wife left for Venice to spend a second honeymoon" (Jones 1956, pp. 246–47). Freud related this incident to his then fiancée, Martha Bernays. She immediately identified herself with Breuer's wife and expressed her hope that nothing similar would ever happen to her.

For Breuer, this incident obviously meant a trauma with long-term effects. But Anna O., too, was in a bad state for years, and even had to be hospitalized. At the age of thirty, however, she began to work as a "mother" in an orphanage, an event linked by Jones with her earlier "phantom pregnancy." She became a pioneer in the field of social work. She founded training institutes for social work. She devoted herself to the emancipation of women and the salvation of children. She did not get married. Her intense experience with Breuer had possibly provoked an ideational process in her, which assumed a concrete shape in her social commitment.

It was only reluctantly and gradually that Breuer initiated Freud into the hypnotic treatment of Anna O., and in the process he left much in the dark. Freud was immensely fascinated by it, and could not understand why Breuer "had kept his inestimable discovery a secret for such a long time, instead of enriching science with it" (Freud 1940b, vol. 14, p. 45). The results discovered by Breuer seemed to Freud to be of so fundamental a nature that he asked whether they could be proved generally valid, and thus also detected in his own patients. For several years Freud experienced confirmations of these discoveries, and eventually he suggested a joint publication to Breuer, who at first violently resisted this. But 1895 saw the publication of *Studies on Hysteria*, jointly written by Breuer and Freud. In this book they described discoveries that contained essential foundations for the development of psychoanalysis.

Until that time, hysteria had been viewed as either a simulation or an illusion on which no doctor proposed to waste any time, or as a strange illness of the womb. It was to the great merit of Jean-Martin Charcot, an outstanding professor of neurology at the Salpêtrière in Paris, that he declared hysteria to be an acknowledged illness of the nervous system, which, although it was caused by congenital degeneration of the brain, could nonetheless be the subject of serious study (Jones 1956, p. 249). Charcot proved that he could use hypnosis to induce in suitable persons hysterical symptoms, such as paralyses, tremors, and insensitivity, which were identical, in the last detail, to the spontaneous hysteria shown by his other patients, and which were the type of symptoms associated in the Middle Ages with possession by demons. This proved that the symptoms themselves could be induced and removed through pure mental forces, and that they were therefore of psychological origin. Medicine now had a medical reason for dealing with patients' psyches. Freud had gone to Paris to see Charcot in order to discuss with him the case of Anna O. Although the Frenchman was not very interested in it, Freud was enthusiastic about Charcot's descriptions, and continued to devote himself, together with Breuer, to working on *Studies on Hysteria*. This book examined the genesis of the hysterical symptoms, emphasized "the significance of affective life, the importance of distinguishing between unconscious and conscious mental acts, introduced a dynamic factor by letting the systems come into existence through blocking an affect, and a homeostatic one by regarding the same symptom as the result of converting energy that would otherwise have been used differently" (Freud 1940b, vol. 14, p. 46). Breuer called the therapeutic procedure "cathartic." "Its declared therapeutic intention was to channel the affect used to preserve the symptom back from a wrong track, where it had got stuck, as it were, to a right track, whence it could depart [abreaction]." These studies pointed out that the hysterics' symptoms depend on impressive but forgotten scenes of their lives (traumas), and that the therapy consisted of having these experiences recalled and reproduced in hypnosis. Freud and Breuer tried to direct the patient's attention directly to the traumatic scene in which the symptom had originated; they tried to guess at the psychological conflict in this scene and to release the suppressed affect. In doing so, they discovered the psychological development characteristic of mental processes in neuroses, later on to be termed *regression* by Freud. The patient's associations went back from the scene that was to be clarified to earlier experiences, and thus forced analysis, which should correct the present, to deal with the past (Freud 1946b, p. 47).

The breach between Freud and Breuer was a result of their differing ways of handling their discoveries. Breuer would have preferred to forget his experiences with Anna O.

altogether, or at least to hush them up. They obviously embarrassed him. Possibly he felt guilty because he had enticed
Anna O. into harboring feelings of love, or at least because
he had not prevented her from having them. He seemed
positively relieved when Freud told him that one of his own
patients had once embraced him in a sudden surge of tenderness. Freud explained to him why, in his opinion, such
unwelcome incidents had to be understood as transference
phenomena characteristic of certain types of hysteria (Jones
1956, pp. 266–67). These remarks of Freud's appeared to
make a profound impression on Breuer. When working on
Studies on Hysteria, Breuer said that he thought that transference was the most important discovery that together they
had to communicate to the world. Although Freud and his
successors managed to cope fairly well with the intense love
emotions that often develop in a therapeutic relationship by
reducing them to transference and countertransference phenomena, Breuer did not dare continue to elaborate such ideas,
perhaps also out of consideration for his wife.

The conflict between the hesitant, timid Breuer and the
revolutionary, impetuous Freud further worsened as they
dealt with the significance of sexuality for the formation of
neuroses. Basically they had both recognized that the driving
forces of the neurosis derive from sexual life. Whereas Breuer
was embarrassed and closed his mind to this discovery, Freud
saw in it the scientifically most interesting problem. (Because
Freud also wanted to see behind the mask of hypnotism, he
abandoned Breuer's cathartic method and turned to the psychoanalytic instead, with its treatment of resistance and transference by means of free association.) The separation between
Breuer and Freud occurred in 1894, because Breuer refused
to follow Freud in the conclusions he had drawn from his
research into sexual life. Breuer could not endorse the opinion
that disorders of the sexual life could play such a crucial part
in the formation of neuroses. From our perspective now, it
seems that Breuer was probably right; yet the development

of psychology in general needed Freud's unwavering, courageous consistency and exaggeration, which shook Victorian morality and opened new fields for medicine. Freud was now approaching forty, and full of pugnacity; he saw himself as a revolutionary against traditional views in medicine, and wanted to do battle with his older colleagues in Vienna. Freud sought defiant rebellion, and felt Breuer's anxious and reluctant behavior to be increasingly disabling and enervating. Freud once said that he always needed an intimate friend and a hated enemy.

Who, then, must be credited with the discovery of psychoanalysis? Breuer? Freud? Or the patient, Anna O.? The series of events between 1880 and 1896 resulted not from the doings of any one of the three alone, but from the process that developed between them. No Joseph Breuer without Anna O., no Sigmund Freud without Joseph Breuer. Without the intense relationship between Anna O. and Breuer, the incidents would not have occurred that highly embarrassed Breuer, but that were the starting point for Freud's transference/countertransference concept. Both Freud and Breuer took pains to label each other's intellectual property in a highly correct manner. In *Studies on Hysteria* Breuer put Freud's name in brackets behind the term *conversion*; Freud on his part describes *Studies on Hysteria*, because of its "material content, as Breuer's intellectual property" (Freud 1940b, vol. 14, p. 46). Elsewhere he says that after Breuer's resignation from the team, he had to administer Breuer's legacy on his own. Freud also remarks that most of their thoughts occurred to them together and at the same time. Freud does not even ascribe to himself the idea of the sexual etiology of neuroses; instead, he ascribes it to the influence of three important persons.

> The idea, for which I have been made responsible, was not my own at all. It had been conveyed to me by three persons, whose opinions could count on my deepest respect

—namely, by Breuer himself, by Charcot, and by the gynecologist of our university, Chrobak, possibly the most outstanding of our Viennese doctors. All three men had *passed on to me an insight which, strictly speaking, they themselves did not possess.* Two of them disowned their communications when I later reminded them; the third (Dr. Charcot) would probably have done likewise, had I been granted the privilege of seeing him again. These identical communications, however, which I had taken in without comprehension, slumbered within me for years until one day they woke as a seemingly original discovery. [Freud 1946b, p. 50.]

If the production of ideas at that time was not done by Freud alone, but resulted from an interactional process with Breuer in particular, then it is certainly thanks to Freud that these ideas were put into words, and asserted against an environment that resisted the revolution they represented. In his struggle for these ideas, Freud was largely on his own, particularly opposed by the medical establishment. In his own words, he was the only one to deal with psychoanalysis for more than ten years, and all the displeasure his new theory caused to his contemporaries was heaped on his head as criticism. Breuer escaped from this criticism by retiring from any further research into neuroses. Freud rightly remarked: "I know, of course, that it is one thing to pronounce an idea once or a few times in the shape of a brief epigram, and another to take it seriously, take it literally, guide it through all resisting details, and conquer a position for it among the acknowledged truths. It is the difference between a light flirtation and a respectable marriage with all its duties and difficulties" (Freud 1946b, pp. 44, 53).

Thus Breuer dropped out of a joint ideational process because he no longer wanted to be the soil in which these ideas could grow; whereas in Freud these ideas developed in all the multilayered interactional processes of his life.

CHAPTER 9

The Ecology of Ideas

I n biology an ecosystem denotes a network of symbionts in their characteristic habitat. I will treat the ecosystem of ideas as analogous to the biological ecosystem. Ideas—that is, the contents of consciousness—are to be treated as if they were living creatures with a tendency to grow, to expand, to strive for success, and to reproduce.

Intellectual history gives us the impression that ideas employ certain protagonists to express themselves. Plato spoke of a world soul, Hegel of a world spirit; the Buddhists, in speaking of a universal consciousness, presumably mean the totality of ideas, which strive to be expressed in words and which form an immense comprehensive evolutionary process of individual ideas that penetrate, link up with, evoke, repress, and reshape one another. Retrospectively, this immense evolutionary process can be recognized in the history of Western culture as well as in the history of humanity as a whole. Nonetheless, the future development of this process can hardly be foretold, because it depends on a dynamic interpenetration of ideational processes whose course also depends on many contingencies, even if the overall line as seen in long periods of time may appear to be consistent and straight.

Plato believed that there was a world of ideas, and that ideas—everlasting and in themselves static—actualized themselves in individual things and particular forms. He regarded the objects of nature as reflections or manifestations of these ideas. In later years Plato assumed that there was a world soul mediating between these ideas as static prototypes and their reflections in matter (Störig 1969, vol. 1). Hegel considered the entire world-historical process to be a self-development of the spirit, which develops dialectically in thesis and antithesis, and which in the present resolves the contradiction that occurred earlier in philosophy into a higher unity, the synthesis. The English mathematician and philosopher Alfred North Whitehead (1933) assumed that general ideas, existing in an underlying reality, can in their generality be apprehended by only a few human beings, and then only tentatively and briefly. Whether or not an idea reaches convincing expression depends on the attributes of the genius who perceives it. According to Whitehead, an idea is often expressed only in small steps, is for a long time concealed just below the surface of consciousness, and will then manifest itself in various forms. It is a hidden driving force secretly moving mankind. Whitehead considers the history of ideas to be a history of mistakes. When great ideas enter reality, they do so in the company of evil followers and repulsive allies. The history of ideas is a history of crimes, misunderstandings, and profanation.

I do not assume a world of ideas as static prototypes, although my expositions do not contradict such an assumption. I maintain that ideas originate in the human mind. Ideas produced by people, however, often, develop a dynamic that creates the impression that it is not people who create ideas suited to themselves, but ideas that make use of human beings suited to them.

Buddhism, according to Govinda (1976), understands the world as the phenomenon of a universal consciousness. Whereas Western thinking has been inclined to regard spirit as a human prerogative, the East perceives the entire cosmos as being penetrated by spirit and does not fundamentally distinguish between spirit and matter, humanity and nature.

It is in accordance with this Buddhist way of thinking to conceive of the world of ideas as having the same structure as the material-biological world. The ecosystem of ideas has the same principles as living ecosystems in general. Of course, ecosystems can use self-regulation in order to maintain an approximately balanced state, whereas ideational ecosystems in evolving cultures are continuously changing.

The ecosystem of an idea resembles a biological ecosystem in that it is an open system, which is engaged in a constant process of exchange with its "ideational environment" and which, like every ecosystem, consists of a network of symbionts (a community of ideas) and living space (culture). The totality of all natural ecosystems constitutes the biosphere; the totality of all ideas in the universe could be called the *ideosphere*. The ideosphere consists of many interconnected ideational systems. As open systems, ecosystems are engaged in a continuous exchange with their environment. Materials (or contents of ideas) are being supplied and drawn off all the time: this is called fluid equilibrium.

If, for instance, a pond is supplied with more foodstuffs from the outside, this allows increased growth of vegetable organisms, which means that more animals can subsist in the pond. The increase in the number of animals, however, will cause a decrease in nutritious plants, which in turn will decrease the number of animals. Within a certain scope, then, the pond can regulate itself: the number and kind of its organisms remain almost the same. This system's capacity for self-regulation is not limitless, however. A heavy supply of nutrients, such as the introduction of feces, will result in increased and continuous growth of vegetable matter, and the original equilibrium can no longer be recovered. Unstable transitional phases occur, which then settle down into a new, stable state, a new homeostasis. This transition from one stable state into another often occurs not gradually but suddenly. Ecosystems change when external influences change. Ideational systems also show a certain self-regulating capacity for perseverance against external influences, with a tendency to suddenly transform into a new system once the self-regulatory power of the prevailing form of organization has been overtaxed.

As an example, let us consider the *emancipation of women*: this idea can already be surveyed as a historical process; yet it has lost little of its topicality. In dealing with it, I would like to point out only a few aspects of temporal and spatial coherence: I would like to show how ideas develop in a suitable biotope (culture) by interacting with other neighboring and related ideas.

THE EMANCIPATION OF WOMEN

According to Kate Millet (1969), the Western world has experienced several immense revolutions since the Enlightenment. Civil rights were extended, the equality and liberty of all men was postulated, democracy was developed in the eighteenth and nineteenth centuries, and a fairer distribution of wealth was sought in the sense of socialism. Ever since the French Revolution, a government has been expected to be based on the assent of those governed in order to be legitimate, and to respect inalienable human rights. Nonetheless, the position of women remained unaffected by these changes until about 1830. Traditional English and American common law ensured that, with the marriage contract, the wife became the husband's chattel. She could not control her income but had to hand her wages over to her husband, who alone decided how to spend them; she could not administer her property, could not sign a document, and could not give evidence. As the head of the family, the husband was the sole proprietor of wife and children. When he divorced her or left her, the husband had the power to deprive the mother of her children, because they were his legal property.

Interestingly enough, the actual women's movement began not with the struggle for their own liberation, but in the American women's fight to abolish official slavery. The abolitionist movement provided American women with their first opportunity for political action and organization. Slavery was so unjust that even women could dare to be provoked by it. As long as it was slavery they fought, they were allowed to break the taboo of what was fitting for a woman. They fought for the release of the slaves, thus had their first political experiences, and developed methods they would later apply in practically all their propaganda campaigns until the end of the century: petition and agitation intended to instruct the public. In the abolitionist movement, women learned to organize, to hold public meetings, to launch petition campaigns. As representatives of abolitionism they gained the right to speak in public and to develop a philosophy of their role in society and of their basic rights. While fighting for the liberation of the slaves—displacing their own concerns in the process—they also learned to fight for their own liberation; indeed, they had already initiated the first concrete changes toward their own liberation. Their own ideas began to form only in the fight for other ideas—which, however, were closely related to their own.

In the United States, the women's liberation movement officially started at the meeting at Seneca Falls, New York, on July 19 and 20, 1848. This meeting grew out of abolitionism, since two of the leading women—Lucretia Coffin Mott and Elizabeth Cady-Stanton—had been excluded from negotiations at the world congress against slavery in London in 1840, because they had been refused acknowledgment as persons. This incident united the women. The declaration of fundamental attitudes written at Seneca Falls began with a paraphrase of the American Declaration of Independence; seventy-five years after the American Revolution the women dared to apply this document to themselves, and extended its prerequisite, the basic condition of inalienable human rights, to their own concerns. They demanded control of their own income, the right to have property, the right to education, to divorce, to the guardianship of their children, and to suffrage.

A long period of fighting for suffrage ensued, with efforts to inform and educate the public. The government hid behind delaying tactics and insincere attitudes. The futility of quiet patience called for methods that would cause more of a stir, such as mass demonstration and strikes. It evidently took militant methods for the objectives to be kept alive over such a long and discouraging period of time. Apart from outbreaks of rage, with violence and damage to property, the English and American suffragettes also developed nonviolent tactics that might well have served as models to leaders of mass movements, such as Gandhi, to trade-union movements, and to fighters for civil rights. The fight for suffrage in particular provoked opposition and attracted a great deal of attention. It lasted for more than seventy years. And when suffrage was won, the women's movement collapsed with exhaustion. Evidently, the goal had been reached for the time being, and there was a lack of new impetus. The United States and Europe were affected by economic crisis and the unemployment of the years after World War I. Wherever possible, women were again pushed out of working life. In 1920 the organized women's movement collapsed. The conviction had been reached that patriarchy was necessary for the family system, that the structure of the nuclear family—as the place where human emotions and a sense of community could be cultivated in an economic world of tough and aggressive competition—was immutable.

The German women's movement had begun around the turn of the century. In the Weimar Republic, women had the vote and won seats in the parliament, the Reichstag. When the Nazis came to power, the women were dismissed from public office. Women's organizations were in any case a thorn in the Nazis' side, because they were committed not only to feminism but also to pacifist, international, and socialist causes. In *Mein Kampf* (p. 460), Hitler declared that "the aim of all female upbringing and education must absolutely be the future mother." There was a mystical idealization of sacred motherhood. Sexuality was again linked with reproduction; contraceptives and abortions were illegal. The leader of the Nazi women's organization, Frau Scholtz-Klink, maintained that the German woman's sole function was to serve the German man, to keep house for him, to look after him body, mind, and soul, continuously, from the first instant of his life to the last. Thus a virility cult developed in Nazi Germany, with an emphasis on leadership and male community.

This is not the place to deal with the women's movement that developed in Russia after 1917 as a consequence of Lenin and the Bolshevik Revolution. In the 1950s a strong conservatism was predominant both in Europe and the United States. It was only in the course of the 1960s that the women's movement revived, again not as an isolated ideational movement, but interconnected with other, similarly oriented movements as well as with the preparation of a suitable ecological niche. One essential factor in creating this niche was a technological-scientific step forward, namely the "pill." Its invention largely transferred decision-making powers about pregnancy from men to women. Previously, the most frequently used methods of contraception (coitus interruptus, condoms) had been controlled by men. With the pill, the woman could now largely decide for herself if and when she wanted to have children. At the same time, sexuality was being liberalized. It was detached from church and state morality, and the decision-making powers were placed in the hands of the individual. Sexuality was disconnected from marriage and reproduction. At the same time, however, women were being liberated psychologically as well as sexually. Up to then, the psychoanalysts' opinion that a woman incapable of so-called vaginal orgasm had stopped at the stage of penis envy and castration complex had been the common wisdom; now, however, the findings of Masters and Johnson in 1961 helped prove that the distinction between vaginal and clitoral orgasm was based on an error, and that each form of orgasm was adequate for the woman, provided it gave her satisfaction.

Simultaneously, an aversion to affluence began to spread. The authoritarian and hierarchical structure, which had made the economic boom of the postwar years possible, was increasingly called into question. There were antiauthoritarian movements and student rebellions, but also the propagation of antiauthoritarian education, and the demand for self-administration and self-determination, which reached its peak in Europe in 1968, particularly in West Germany and in France. Again, these movements inspired the women's movement.

On the one hand, the women's movement profited from "related" movements; on the other hand, it also stimulated many other current ideational processes. Women have had a decisive influence on the development of the peace movement and the movement for the protection of the environment. Feminism stopped merely struggling for equality with men, and became aware of having to save the world, because the world can no longer be left to men without being destroyed by wars or economic exploitation. What in times of male predominance had been dismissed as female weakness was now increasingly considered a goal of personal development: access to one's own emotions, the courage to have one's own weaknesses, to be affected, to mourn, and to be afraid, a caring and motherly attitude toward nature, gentle technology, gentle medical care, holistic views in ecology and the health sector, rejection of the glorification of heroism and the defense of one's honor, stronger emphasis on the quality of life as opposed to striving for career, property, and professional status. Especially the peace movement and environmentalism, including antinuclear initiatives, are clear examples of how feminist thinking spreads in ideational movements that had been nonfeminist, and how it can affect men, too, particularly those who sympathize with the women's movement.

The example of female emancipation illustrates that the historical development of a certain idea is not straight and continual, but may be interrupted again and again, by revolutions and catastrophes, and may then stagnate, partially to stabilize and integrate whatever has been gained, but partially also to lose it again. If, however, the movement is embedded in the evolutionary movement of universal consciousness, if it is interconnected with a global community of ideas, then setbacks may temporarily slow the process without, however, endangering the idea as such. The idea of the emancipation of women also shows how much the dissemination of an idea depends on there being an ecological niche for it. The women's liberation movement could not have developed in an earlier century in our culture. Among the important preconditions for it was the Industrial Revolution, because of which individuals came to depend less on the patriarchal system, on the extended family, and later on the nuclear family, and more on their own labor. The introduction of accident, life, and disability insurance and old-age pensions also made individuals less dependent on material support from the rest of their families. Further, working conditions changed. As machines reduced the amount of heavy physical work done by humans, there were increasingly fewer spheres where women could not work as efficiently as men. Additionally, housework became increasingly mechanized and lost its prestige in the same proportion. The mentality fostered by consumerism and throwaway goods made the mending of clothes and the repair of household appliances far less necessary; new canning methods made the keeping, storing, and preserving of fruit and vegetables superfluous; daily shopping was dropped as soon as it became possible to buy everything necessary once a week in the supermarket. There were fewer and fewer rational reasons why women should not enjoy real equal status with men in all areas of life. Another crucial point was effective birth control and the subsequent liberalization of abortion. Female emancipation in its present form would be inconceivable without these technological, medical, and economic developments.

It is interesting to ask whether present-day unemployment, like the recession of the 1920s and 1930s, will restore the traditional division of roles between man and woman. This is often feared by women; there may even be actual signs of it. All in all, however, a completely different development has been emerging, at least up to now, which even favors the women's movement: unemployment is being fought not by excluding women from the working world, but rather by generally reducing working hours, which could allow a real solution, in partnership, for the main problem so far unsolved by the women's movement—the bringing up of children. If working time could be reduced to approximately thirty hours a week, then husband and wife could easily work in equivalent jobs and simultaneously bring up their children together, with sufficient financial and temporal flexibility that children would not seem an intolerable burden. Thus similar initial conditions (unemployment) can either restrict or encourage the development of an idea (female emancipation), depending on the context.

All these ideational processes begin as utopian schemes that demand something that is regarded as impossible. In a painstaking process of manifestation, an idea differentiates itself into small steps and creates a world of increasing complexity, greater consciousness, greater self-responsibility and codetermination of the person. The same principle applies here as in the development of the person: an idea develops by means of the resistance it encounters. It creates its reality, its realization, in a conflict with its adversaries. Without resistance and adversaries, there is no differentiation. This conflict with the adversaries takes place in two fundamentally different forms: in revolutionary, often chaotic, and often excessively emotional and aggressive mass movements on the one hand; on the other hand, in institutionalized, organized movements concentrating on detailed work and on actualizing the idea. The former create changes in consciousness, in ideas; the latter create changes in social realities and systemic organization, in the cultural environment. Both forms are necessary for the evolution and the establishment of an idea.

There is another analogy to natural ecosystems in the evolution of ideas: the more strata an ideational system consists of, the better its chances of survival. If the subsystems of these ideas stagnate or are dissolved, the idea will not be completely destroyed in consequence; at most, its evolution is temporarily checked. Every idea is a subsystem and a component of a higher ideational process, and itself divides into subsystems. A specific idea manifests not only its specific qualities but also the qualities of the superordinate whole. Thus an idea can be understood as part of an all-pervasive, universal evolution.

HOW IDEAS ORGANIZE THEMSELVES

An idea can be actualized only in and through persons who are capable of responding to it. It usually shapes the carriers' lives, and urges them on to create for it a suitable environment for further growth.

Prevailing suffering and misery, humiliation and uneasiness motivate potential idea carriers to respond to an idea that promises a change for the better in the long term. People are also willing, however, to make great sacrifices and to accept suffering and stress in the struggle for the realization of an idea. What is decisive is the prospect of the idea's ultimate success, or at least the certainty among those who are fighting that the struggle is for a just, true, and valuable cause, and that they can experience themselves as part of a meaningful purposive process. Human beings can be won over relatively easily to identifying themselves with an idea so strongly that their desires for happiness, well-being, and health are completely pushed into the background.

In this sense the economic laws for communal psychology, propounded by the English philosopher and economist John Stewart Mill (1806–1873), are of strictly limited validity. The first law, also called the hedonistic principle, says that every person strives for a maximum of goods, happiness, and wealth with a minimum of work and sacrifice. The role that this law has played in Anglo-Saxon psychology, particularly in early behaviorism but also in industrial psychology, has been considerable and often fatal. It was believed that a human being could be manipulated in any way at all by means of reward and punishment. And yet the history of all times and cultures throughout the world records millions upon millions of people who enthusiastically accepted the hardest strains, indeed even death, for some idea or other, often even an absurd one. People may be enthusiastic about wars; they may be willing to spend their lives in prison for political or religious ideas; they may let themselves be subjected to torture. Christianity, Islam, and Shintoism abound with examples of believers whose most profound desire was to suffer for their creed and die as martyrs. Human beings like to be inspired (from the Latin *inspiro*, literally "to fill with breath, to fill with spirit"); they are inclined toward enthusiasm (from the Greek *entheos*, "being in God") and toward fanaticism (*fanaticus* was a sacred word in Latin, meaning "seized by the godhead," and was related to *fanum*, "a place dedicated to the godhead, a temple"). Collective insults, tensions, and emergencies make entire peoples sensitive to certain ideas and their representatives who promise grace, honor, deliverance, or salvation. Fanaticism then often knows no limits.

Many ideas, however, do not develop through fanaticism and revolutionary chaos. As a rule, one single person carries a multitude of interwoven ideas simultaneously. If we assume that an idea is a self-contained entity striving to be manifested, then idea carriers are the place in which it is manifested. Idea carriers are interrelated because of their common responsiveness. These relationships organize themselves systemically. Family therapy has dealt especially with the organization of relationships in the system of the family, applying the general systems theory developed in 1962 by Ludwig von Bertalanffy for physical and biological systems. No matter how fruitful many of these thoughts are for therapy, it remains dangerous to assume that whatever parts of systems theory are valid for physical and biological systems must also be applicable to social psychology, as if the selfsame law governed everything. This may easily result in certain erroneous reflections, or at least in reductionism in psychological observation.

A *system* is defined as a complex of components in a self-regulating interaction, capable of preserving itself as a unity in an interaction of component parts and in an interrelation with the environment. Every system divides up into subsystems and is in itself a subsystem of the next higher system.

General Living Systems Theory, according to J. G. Miller (1978), regards the composition of the universe as a hierarchy of concrete systems that organize matter, energy, and information. It searches for laws that are equally valid for physical, biological, psychological, and social systems. It sees the hierarchy of systems in the universe in the fact that atoms consist of particles, molecules of atoms, crystals and organelles of molecules. Cells are the smallest units of living systems, and consist of atoms, molecules, and multimolecular organelles. Organs are composed of cells, which combine into tissues. Organisms consist of organs. Groups (families, working teams) consist of organisms (individuals), organizations (companies, communities) of groups, societies (states, nations) of organizations, supranational systems of states. Higher systems are composed of living and nonliving ones; they contain ecological systems such as solar systems and galaxies. For all these systems, the General Living Systems Theory has discovered the same organization, which has as its function to receive, process, and transmit matter, energy, and information, to demarcate, protect, and reproduce the system.

Let us restrict ourselves to human systems. The thought of drawing an analogy between society as a social organism and living organisms was developed and critically examined before: first by the Greeks, then by Christianity, later by the Romantics, by Auguste Comte (1798–1857), and by Herbert Spencer (1820–1903). Spencer, one of the founders of sociology, was the first to examine society systematically as an organism. He discovered important differences. In an organism, thinking and consciousness are concentrated in certain parts of the body, which is not the case in society. In a living organism the individual parts exist for the whole. In society the converse applies: the whole exists for the well-being of the individual members.

It is enticing to search for analogies between the series atom/molecule/crystal, the series cell/organ/organism, and the series person/family/society. This analogy is criticized by Ackoff and Emery (1972). Attempts to treat social groups like organisms keep on reappearing, although their unsuitability has long been proved. Both organisms and social groups are organizations, but the crucial difference resides in the fact that the elements that constitute an organism are not purposeful. In an organism only the whole can show a will; none of its parts can. The organs of which an organism is composed are doubtless necessary for the organism to function, but are not sufficient for the attainment of its aims.

Human systems are different from all other systems in that their components are capable of making decisions, formulating aims, and choosing between different aims (Zeleny and Pierre 1976). The system does not exist in itself, but is defined by persons making use of the system for certain unifying aims, functions, and purposes. The situation is fundamentally different in an organism. A leg does not use the nervous system or the organism in order to contract, but the organism makes use of its legs in order to walk. A muscle fiber will always remain just that, and never become a brain cell. It has its function without being able to choose or codetermine it, and without being conscious of the whole of the organism. The analogy of an organism applied to a social system would be most accurate for a strictly led armed force where, at least according to what officers regarded as ideal in times gone by, the soldier had to function like a cell, and only like a cell: he had to obey without participating in the decision-making process. It is also not true that social systems are structured according to the hierarchy of individual/group/organization/ society. Rather, the person is almost everywhere the sole subsystem of the social organism: the person is the sole subsystem of the family, of the working team, of a political party, of an ideological or religious movement, and, as a citizen, elector, and taxpayer, of the state.

The various systems of which the person is part largely exist side by side and are not integrated into a mutual hierarchic order. They have only little influence on one another, and often only indirectly have any on the person. Thus working team and family influence each other only through the working person, rarely through direct contact of all system members, and even then only to a limited extent. The person is a citizen of the state. It is not the family that is a citizen; the persons who make up the family are also the citizens of the state. A man may participate in various ideational systems simultaneously—in the family as father, in the working team as coworker, in a political party as a member, in the state as a taxpayer, in a supranational system as a supporter of the peace movement.

Now, what actually is a human system? A cell is a substantial system, as is an organism, but a human system does not tangibly exist as such. We can only ask: who constitutes a human system? who constitutes a family? who constitutes a working team? who constitutes a nation? A human system does not merely consist of persons. Rather, it also includes the persons' beliefs, which organize themselves in relation to the beliefs of other persons in order to carry out a common ideational process.

Family therapy has conducted intensive investigations into the systemic organizations of relationships within families. Whereas psychoanalysis maintained that the contents of relationships (fantasies, ideas, needs) determined their form, systemic family therapy regards the form of relationships (their organization) as determining their contents. Systemic family therapy argues that it is not so much individuals who are disturbed, but their relationships. Many conflicts occur as structurally false organizations of the system, faulty structures, unclear boundaries, ambiguous hierarchies, and paradoxical rules or regulatory mechanisms. Systemic family therapy has always consciously resisted a psychodynamic perspective. It does not want to know about fantasies, emotions, fears, or individual conflicts; instead, it wishes to direct all its concentration on the systemic organization of relationships. This may well have been necessary as a reaction to the formerly predominant psychodynamic perspective.

What are relationships? Relationships are the result of two or more persons' corresponding thematic responsiveness. A human system is not simply the organization of relationships; rather, it is based on common ideational processes. The nature of the family as a system is the organization of the family-related ideas of its members. Faulty systemic organization in the family is caused by a disturbed evolution of family ideas. Systemically self-organizing relationships are not ends in themselves but serve a purposive ideational process. The system is only the organizational form of this process!

THE EVOLUTION OF IDEAS

An ideational process is a purposive process growing out of the common anxiety of idea carriers, who jointly target and systemically organize their idea-related activities and energies. This systemic organization has certain structures and orders that coordinate the idea carriers' behavior toward the aim. The process can therefore also be seen as a succession of system states, of orders in a historical, irreversible sequence.

Just like living systems, ideational processes, too, are open systems: they must be engaged in a continuous exchange with culture and with competing ideas in order to stay alive. An ideational system withers if it demarcates itself too rigidly, but it also dissolves if it cannot define itself sufficiently. The evolution of an idea thus manifests itself as a sequence of occasional, stabilized organizations in the idea carriers. In this way, the ideational process controls the order of its own changes. Like every living system, the ideational process, too, shows a succession of phases of either preservation or modification. Excessive preservation as well as excessive modification endangers its chance of survival. "Two dangers threaten the world: order and disorder," says Paul Valéry (Jantsch 1982).

Like living systems, ideational processes exist only in a state of disequilibrium, in which they are continuously active. Once an idea is generally accepted and fully integrated into a culture, it no longer triggers processes. Copernicus's hypothesis (idea) that the Earth is not the center of the universe but is one among several planets circling around the sun virtually turned the world upside down and produced immense ideational processes. Today this idea is integrated into our culture and no longer triggers any processes. The ideational process of women's suffrage is nearing its end. Within a few years it will no longer produce sufficient imbalance to convert any more energies as a process. Thoughts and ideas are not in themselves permanent; they continue only insofar as they are thought by human beings again and again.

An idea evolves according to Hegelian dialectic. An idea is a thesis that can trigger a process only by interacting with an antithesis. The greater the tension between thesis and antithesis, the more intense and the more energetic the dialectical process. The process strives for the reduction of tension, and for the resolution of thesis and antithesis in a synthesis. Once the synthesis has been found, the ideational process dies, unless it further differentiates itself in new theses and antitheses. If it does so, the idea develops toward ever-higher complexity and differentiation. Such higher complexity and differentiation continually demand and create new organizational structures and systems.

Paradoxically, order in a systemic process is not caused by equilibrium, but is provoked by divergent fluctuations, by threatening chaos, by the necessity constantly to organize forces into a purposive process. In this process of growth, order is maintained by the state of disequilibrium, by the need constantly to re-create the system.

Ilya Prigogine (1976) discovered this principle of order through fluctuation in chemical reaction systems and called them *dissipative structures*. According to Prigogine, disequilibrium is a source of order and organization. For biological systems, equilibrium corresponds to death. The same applies to ideational processes: in the long term, stabilized equilibrium and rigid structures lead to the deterioration and the decline of a system. If world history is regarded as the evolution of a colossal ideational process, then the history of mankind results from continuous imbalance. People and peoples have always striven for order and its preservation, whereas ideational processes have always striven for further differentiation; in consequence, social structures have become correspondingly more complex. A higher degree of pluralism was achieved worldwide. There was the increasingly complex dynamic of present-day global evolution. Conventional, behaviorist-oriented world models have long been based on homogeneous states of equilibrium for which every fluctuation and every positive feedback looked like a danger to the structures. These models were postulated to be mechanistic systems, and assumed the existence only of processes that could preserve the structure. Newer systems theory, and therefore also newer forms of family therapy, however, are interested in modifying structures rather than in preserving them. These newer theorists are interested in encouraging evolution rather than in forced stabilization of states of equilibrium, and in processes rather than structures (Hoffman 1982).

Like Prigogine's dissipative structures, an ideational process, in itself far from being in a state of equilibrium, creates order. Either it maintains this order or, if the fluctuations become too violent, there will be a "catastrophe," the dissolution of the existing ideational structure, and a transition to an ideational reorganization. As long as idea carriers interact, they will always organize themselves systemically. A principle of order will always assert itself. Observed in too short a period of time, an ideational process often seems to stagnate or be misdirected through systemic organization. Seen over longer periods of time, however, ideational processes show an amazingly strong inherent tendency to correct and differentiate themselves meaningfully.

These "longer periods of time," however, often exceed a human lifespan. It is in a way tragic for those who have sacrificed their worldly goods, their well-being and health, even their lives, for an idea, that they cannot experience the breakthrough of their idea, and that they often die feeling that all their efforts have been in vain. What better solace, then, than the knowledge of being part of suprapersonal processes, and the certainty that in the long term what is true, good, and just will usually assert itself, and that the fruits of what was intended will be for the good of other people?

HOW IDEAS DEVELOP

As a rule, ideas develop in a dialectic of thesis and antithesis striving for synthesis. Those responding to an idea—that is, its representatives—polarize themselves at first against the representatives of an antithesis. In this phase of the development of an idea, those who respond to it are usually united by a high degree of solidarity. They have a defined external enemy against whom they direct their energies. They often have to make sacrifices and accept privation and humiliation, but gain substantial relief from their like-minded friends' mutual support. Idea carriers long to assert and to actualize the idea, and they think that the attainment of their aim will give them happiness and contentment. Usually the opposite happens. It is as if the idea knows that it can survive only as long as it can mobilize emotional energies and produce interactional tensions.

If idea carriers succeed in asserting themselves in society and in securing general recognition for their idea, their exultation is usually short-lived. The prevailing dynamic often undergoes a fundamental change even while victory is still being celebrated. Former comrades-in-arms become opponents, former friends bitter rivals. The idea carriers' originally external polarization against their adversaries has shifted to the inside. The system now divides itself into two or several competing factions, which begin to fight about one particular aspect of the idea. This course of ideational development is so fatefully preprogrammed that it happens to idea carriers no matter whether they want it to happen or not, no matter whether the group's members are ambitious or aggressive, unable to tolerate frustration or inclined toward narcissistic delusions of grandeur. It is not the idea carriers who create an ideational process; rather, the ideational process uses its carriers to fulfill its own needs for evolution and differentiation. It does not show any consideration for what a "decent idea" should owe its carriers.

As soon as the idea carriers have asserted themselves against their external adversaries, schisms inside their own system will occur. For those people concerned, these are often painful, but they are quite clearly in the interest of the idea. They contain the structure of disequilibrium necessary for the survival of the idea, and they cause a continuous dialectical evolution and differentiation of the idea by means of constantly renewed polarizations among the idea carriers.

There are some particularly felicitous examples of such ideational developments in the field of the development of psychotherapy. Basically, we would expect psychotherapists to be particularly good at directing ideational processes constructively and at coping with conflicts among idea carriers. The ideational process is stronger, however, and overcomes all the concentrated therapeutic competence. The development of Freud's psychoanalysis was marked by continual serious conflicts and schisms. First, Adler broke away, then Jung; both men then developed their own important schools. There were also other, less-well-known schisms, all of which, however, had stimulating repercussions on psychoanalysis and demanded from it a continuous readjustment and development.

I had a similar experience as an idea carrier of couples and family therapy. In 1968 Theodor Bovet expressed his vision of establishing a Faculty of Marital Studies at the University of Zurich, imagining interdisciplinary cooperation between a theological, a medical, and a legal department. Bovet introduced me to Josef Duss-von Wardt, who, as a philosopher and theologian, was at the time particularly concerned with anthropological aspects of marriage studies. As soon as Bovet sensed that the relationship between Duss and me had become strong enough, he withdrew, in order to grant us complete freedom in building up and actualizing his ideas. A kind of biological symbiosis developed between Duss and myself, a long-term relationship advantageous for both of us. We each needed the other's support, both personally and for professional development. I was not certain at that time whether I could develop any further in the University Hospital. He found access, through me, to the psychotherapeutic métier. From 1970 onward, we jointly organized training courses in couples and family therapy. Duss established an institutional basis in the Institute for Marriage and Family. I dedicated myself to the scientific formulation of the collusion concept, which was published in book form in 1975. We were each other's ideal complement, and supported each other in every possible way. We were both very much concerned with promoting couples and family therapy against the individual therapy predominant at that time.

Our efforts were crowned with success. The more general recognition we were accorded, however, the more difficult our relationship became. In the meantime, Duss had expanded his institute. As the University Hospital continued to be my workplace, I increasingly felt that my role in the courses organized by the Institute for Marriage and Family was that of a visiting lecturer. Conversely, through the publication of my books, I had found recognition in which Duss and his colleagues did not feel they shared. The separation occurred in 1979. My colleagues and I set up our own training courses at the Psychiatric Hospital, which immensely stimulated the development of couples and family therapy at our institute. On the other hand, the separation enabled Duss and his colleagues to achieve more of a scientific profile, and to gain more scientific recognition. The ideational cause for the separation seemed slight enough if viewed from the outside, but it deeply affected our mutual understanding. The members of the Institute for Marriage and Family who were responsible for training were identified with consistent application of systems theory in therapeutic practice, whereas I continued to strive for an integration of systemic and psychodynamic perspectives. The separation was a painful process for both parties. It clearly served to develop and further disseminate the idea of family therapy, however. Younger staff could move up into the position of lecturers. Psychotherapists of differing origins could identify themselves with the idea of family therapy. There is a fair, stimulating competition between the two institutes. Our experience as family therapists may well have enabled us to protect ourselves from destructive developments in this process. My friendship with Josef Duss has remained intact. I often had the feeling that the process was happening to us against our wills.

HOW IDEAS ARE STRUCTURED

The organization of an ideational process is identical with the organization of its carriers' intellectual systems, which can differ a great deal. Some carriers tend to identify themselves strongly with an idea and to commit themselves to its actualization. Others are interested in, or sympathetic toward, an idea without actively committing themselves to it. Varying commitment, varying degree of identification, but also varying competence in developing and disseminating an idea—these factors alone will ensure that different people will execute different functions in the dissemination of an idea, and that in actualizing it, some persons will earn more credit than others. These differences are especially relevant to those idea carriers who are highly committed to the idea, since these differences can affect their recognition, functions, tasks, roles, and status. If actualizing an idea requires organized work, and if the idea gains general recognition, then the holders of functions that confer prestige and power will be inclined to prevent changes in the systemic organization that could reduce their functions and status. Whenever the ideational system is questioned, their functions and jobs are under threat. Understandably, those who are established tend to restrict dissenting ideational fluctuations, and to resist

changes in the structure of the ideational process. Institutionalized ideas frequently tend to become closed systems,
no longer engaged in a flexible exchange with the environment, with culture, and with competing ideas; instead, they
become ends in themselves, preserving certain idea carriers'
positions of power, property, and honor. Thus such systems
move farther and farther away from a state of disequilibrium,
and approach a state of "inner equilibrium." Paradoxically,
this provides them with more stability for a certain time. At
the same time, they become more fragile, and less capable of
adapting and developing. Sooner or later a "catastrophe"
occurs, a revolution through which the rigid structures must
be blown up, and through which ideas are forced to crystallize
themselves into new shapes.

There are ideas, however, that cannot be permitted, in
the midst of personal fluctuations, tensions, and imbalances,
to assume different organizational forms again and again.
These are the state institutions. They require a continuing
structure, a great capacity for perseverance against fluctuations and cataclysms, because their working order affects the
existence of society. Every form of state administers social
ideas in areas whose efficient organization must continuously
be guaranteed, such as the functions of medical care, education, justice, the police, the economy, and state finances.
All these areas are institutionalized, and their functions defined by complex laws. Such a relatively rigid and fixed organization is necessary because different groups' tangible
interests clash in all these areas. In the health sector there may
be conflicts between health-insurance companies and doctors'
payment claims, between independent doctors and clinics,
between registered doctors and unregistered therapists and
healers. Institutionalization and laws are meant to avert gross
improper developments. On occasion, however, they also
threaten to protect improper developments, and to hamper
positive developments unforeseen at the time of legislation.

There is a danger nowadays that we might see every form

of institutionalization as a negative phenomenon. Institutions are essential wherever continual work must be done, and wherever definite functions must be fulfilled over a longer period of time. Institutionalization provides an idea with an official name. An externally visible system is constructed that defines its objectives, rules, and responsibilities, both internally and externally. Within an institution, the functions connected with an idea are subdivided into function areas, and the function carriers' responsibilities are defined. Extrasystemic checks supervise the objectives, which are fixed by statute and are supposed to prevent misuse of power. The institution must execute its function in a reasonable cost/benefit ratio, and as a rule is expected to give an account of its efficiency in an annual report. These checks and statutes make further development of an ideational process cumbersome, but they also prevent the collapse and dissolution that often occurs with noninstitutionalized ideational processes.

The claim to self-determination and independence cannot easily be brought into accord with the requirements of fitting into institutions. Carl Rogers (1977, pp. 266–68) says, "One of the deepest antipathies of emerging persons is directed toward institutions. They are opposed to all highly structured . . . institutions. . . . What will take the place of the institution for this new person? . . . One trend that I see is toward small, informal, nonhierarchical groups." I think that Rogers expresses an attitude that is particularly widespread among the intellectually active parts of the population.

After pointing out the dangers of institutionalization for the "development" of ideas, as well as the danger of power being misused by those who are established, I would also like to mention a different aspect: the actual aim of state institutions is to enable the individual citizen to live in justice and liberty, and to protect the weak and the helpless. State institutions depend on the commitment of the strong and the privileged. The concentration of one's energies on one's own self-realization threatens to bestow more independence and freedom upon the competent and assertive, because the weaker people are increasingly left to the care of state institutions. One cannot rationally delegate the care of children, old people, the disabled, difficult characters, and the mentally disordered to professionals and to institutions while simultaneously complaining about the increasing power of those institutions. Institutions are there for the citizens, and depend on active participation on the part of the citizens. It is easy for me to criticize institutions; it is harder to commit myself to finding better solutions to their functions. Such detachment increasingly saps the institutions, and they are turned into scapegoats: thus, it is the psychiatric clinics that make people psychically ill, the police that make youngsters aggressive, the prisons that turn their inmates into criminals, the teachers that make students dumb. Instead of voicing such criticism, we should encourage people to live with people who are mentally ill, to create living conditions and forms of communities acceptable to the young, to integrate criminals into society, and not to let the structuring of the educational system be dictated by the universities and by the economy.

If the danger of institutionalization lies in the paralysis and misuse of the ideational process, then rejection of all organization as such results in paralysis due to chaos and a decrease in productivity because of continual personal struggle for direction. Organization introduces a certain order into the interaction of forces in the ideational process. It is a widespread but dangerous (or at least often disappointing) illusion to think that ideational processes that avoid all institutionalization proceed more satisfactorily, more creatively, and more productively than do processes in which clear structures and areas of responsibility are negotiated.

An Idea That Failed for Lack of Organization

The *Zurich youth movement of 1980/81* will serve as an example here. This movement began with the so-called Opera House

Riot in May 1980, which in turn emerged from an anger, widespread in the population, that the government granted generous subsidies only to institutionalized culture in the theater, in music, and in art, which were often far from the real needs of the people. Since police intervention against the demonstrating crowd was very forcible from the outset, there was an explosion of collective rage, which motivated thousands of young, and of not so young, people to enter into a power struggle with government and police. Every few days there were massive demonstrations, with considerable damage to property and many injuries. Initially, the Zurich movement was supported by the mass media. The movement's actions were characterized by witty, provocative, and often genuinely comical ideas, which won them many sympathizers. The movement mobilized a hope in many circles of the population that this could be the advent of more motion, warmth, and spontaneity in this city. It was also a conscious attack on the money-ridden banking and economic metropolis, where the quality of life was increasingly being lost while economic coercion reigned supreme. The movement likened Zurich to Greenland and called it Pack-Ice. It published its own newspaper, *Eisbrecher* ("The Icebreaker"). It was characteristic of the original idealistic attitude that the editors resigned at their own request after some months because they were worried that their activities would give them supremacy inside the movement. The paper continued to be published, now as *Brecheisen* ("The Crowbar"). Gradually, the movement petered out because its "actions" became increasingly stereotyped as mere damage to property with subsequent brawls with the police.

Nonetheless, it won a struggle for a piece of real estate situated near the city center, the *Autonomous Youth Center* (AYC), and was granted the equivalent of approximately $570,000 in subsidies by the Municipal Council of Zurich, so that those in the movement could restore the building themselves. The responsibility of managing this center, and of working in and on it, soon overtaxed the movement with its creed of spontaneity in ideational processes. The claim to a place "out of bounds to the law" very soon attracted drug addicts, dealers, and escaped criminals, who found protection from police interference in the center. The problem was recognized, but no one had the competence to take efficient action against it. The police encouraged this destructive development by means of marked passivity. The large subsidies for the restoration of the building caused yet another problem. Here, too, no one had the competence to administer the money and to organize purposeful work that could have been paid for appropriately and justly. Morale became increasingly low as appeals for solidarity were either plaintive or wrathful; eventually, the movement gradually dissolved itself. When in April 1982 the building was razed to the ground, hardly anyone put up a fight.

The following description is taken from the May 1981 issue of *Kamikaze*, another journal of the movement. Under the heading "Autonomous Lemmings," it said:

> Sometimes the movement strikes me as a herd of lemmings, running and running behind an imaginary ideology instead of behind a leader. Autonomy, but no one knows exactly what that means for US, AMONG US; that's why we keep on running from action to action, from demo to demo, and when we don't know what to do next we make a new demand, bigger and more beautiful than all previous demands, and maybe we add another ultimatum for a change—and run on—on, right up to the cliff top and over, straight into the sea, into the collective suicide of self-laceration and self-mutilation. The death wish is fantastic, too, and if we all die together it'll almost be orgasmic.
>
> The experiences of last summer have somewhat called into question my political identity. I used to dream of how beautiful it would be if there was a new movement. I had all the ideals of anarchy, autonomy, self-government, and direct democracy without hierarchical structures. But it

didn't turn out like that. There was an enormous wrangling for power and influence, for a position in the pecking order of the active members. For example, the Red Factory Working Group [a group that had been using a disused, brick-built factory for alternative cultural events] was dissolved on the grounds that it should not dominate the movement. But in reality, nothing changed. On the contrary! When the formal structures were abolished, informal ones took their place (personal contacts; meetings to which only those people were invited who were willing to adapt themselves to the behavior and moral code of the inner clique—that is, toadies), and it is much more difficult for the vast majority to see through and check informal structures. What I find even worse is how the whole thing runs on a personal level. I have the feeling that the atmosphere is becoming more and more aggressive, the spokespersons and microphone suckers more and more dogmatic, and the plenary sessions more and more intolerant. Just as in bourgeois society, it takes one hell of a lot of energy, assertion, and elbow power to report something to, say, a plenary session or to a coordination meeting. I sometimes have the impression that it's as if I was in the middle of a screaming competition—and I'd often love to cut those rowdies' throats: always this powerlessness, the brutal pigs, the arrogant municipal council—but *what gets on my nerves more than anything else is the powerlessness against the mechanisms taking their course among us, that we can't manage any different behavior among us but this chaotic, self-lacerating hacking.* . . .

I reckon that nothing split the movement more than the 1½ million [subsidy] available for the AYC. As soon as the AYC was open again, the great wrangling for the money started. A whole lot of people turned up, in the renovation group and elsewhere, whose simple and overriding concern was the dough; they didn't care much for the AYC, but wanted, as simply as possible, to cut themselves the largest possible slice of the cake. The way in which such problems were dealt with in the plenary sessions again reminds me of the dogmatic behavior in a religious sect, where what must not exist does not exist. In concrete terms: the result of it all is the immense chaos that now prevails, and the fact that in the last few weeks, during which the AYC has been open again, appallingly little has been going on. . . . Meanwhile you've been able to hear more and more stories about what has been happening with "our" dough. . . . Some people of the Dive [the restaurant of the AYC] reckon the bar needs a new counter, marble. All right, I've always been for marble. But why not go to the junk shop and pick up marble slabs off old bits of furniture and then have them cut to size? No, it must be expensive, pink marble by all means. Without checking up on what it will all come to, you give some people five grand in cash, and they hie off to Italy to buy marble. . . . At one plenary session they decided that from the hourly wage of fifteen francs two should be set aside for the jail group. When on the following payday the site manager wanted to pay out thirteen francs, the kids attacked the guy with their hammers. They told him to cough up the whole lot, they were not interested in that plenary decision (they had not been there), it was all exploitation. It is hardly surprising that the site manager was fed up for a certain time after this incident.

But the worst thing is that a small group use their aggressive manner to walk over a large proportion of the people, who either can't or don't want to scream all that loud, and that the whole atmosphere is poisoned by this shifty behavior. In the end what it amounts to is that the guy who can assert himself is the guy with the strongest elbows, who talks more aggressively than anyone else, and who is the biggest crook—just like bourgeois society! And yet the renovation of the AYC is an opportunity to have experiences different from those on a normal building site; the traditional hierarchical structures could be modified, there could be something like a group feeling, there could be positive experiences and consciousness processes.

I have quoted from this report because it is valid for many similar developments in cooperatives, communes, cultural movements, and therapeutic communities. At the start there is a great deal of enthusiasm, willingness to make sacrifices, and much goodwill; at the end, months of tiring fights and of resignation. The reason for the failure of the enterprise is usually sought in middle-class education. A person cannot live in a capitalist society for twenty or thirty years, and then be able to live by completely different ideals in a few months. What remains is the belief that the necessary solidarity can be learned in a process of reeducation.

Because I use systems therapy in my work with families, I cannot endorse such accusations and reasons, because I can see much more apparent and banal causes of failure. A social system that intends to do purposive, concrete work needs a clear structure and a division of functions in order to function properly. If it does not have them the members will soon be plagued by mutual mistrust, rivalry, fear, and aggression. Above all, they will lose faith in themselves, because, despite their goodwill, they cannot live up to their high ideals. If at first they believe that they will be able to work together without structures and rules, without division of functions and organization, then they usually realize quite soon that, on the contrary, they plot behind one another's backs, manipulate one another, and mutually put on an act of solidarity. The group is tyrannized not by someone whose office invests him or her with power, not by demagogues or even thugs, but simply by those who know how to assert themselves most effectively, by means of an intellectual or physical law of the jungle. Clear rules and functions, clear areas of responsibility and structures, clear boundaries have nothing to do with capitalism or bourgeois power structures. Instead, they are a help to well-ordered cooperation. Additionally and particularly, they provide protection and security for the weak.

The dream of a cooperative without a hierarchical structure is another illusion. In every group discussion there are from the outset great differences between the participants in how long they can speak, how many ideas they produce, how competent they are, and how ready they are to listen to one another, and for how long, and with how much attention. A leader whose main concern is the process, not his own status, will consider it his task to coordinate the participants' activities in a manner that supports the strengths of the weaker ones and channels the strengths of the stronger ones, so that an optimal actualization of the group's potential becomes possible. The crucial question is not whether to have a hierarchy; what is decisive is how a group handles its own hierarchy.

There are bound to be inequalities between group members in competence, influence, and power. A declared hierarchy makes these differences visible and therefore also lays them open to attack. A rejection of a visible hierarchy often conceals the differences.

As a rule it is most favorable to a working process if the areas of responsibility are defined, but are at the same time interrelated, particularly from below toward above, in such a manner that criticism is possible at any time without fear and suppression. Working in an unstructured, nonhierarchical community can be substantially more frustrating, and especially more energy consuming, than working in a clearly structured organization, because in an unstructured group much energy is wasted on pointless personal wrangling. It should not be of any import whether one person has more power than another; it is the jointly created process that ought to be decisive. This process can be judged only by its effects. The question is whether the idea carriers' potential is used optimally in the process. One basic prerequisite for this is the participants' continuing identification with the ideational process. This identification is lost once too much energy is tied up in personal quarrels; but it is also lost when, in a declared hierarchy, corrective feedback is not constantly encouraged and permitted. Sadly, power is exercised by means of violence too often in political systems today. It has destructive effects on the ideational process of the system. Ideational processes can be suppressed by force, but constructive ideational process cannot be activated by force.

The use of military force to maintain domestic order points toward the development of ideational processes that endanger the prevailing form of power and call for new forms of organization.

CHAPTER 10

How the Joint
Unconscious Operates

I n the foregoing I have presented ideational processes as if
  their carriers consciously disseminate ideas. Since, however, most ideas, fantasies, and imaginings of a person are
unconscious or preconscious, we must ask whether there are
ideational processes that use unconscious processes in the carriers in order to actualize themselves; that is, *are there unconscious, suprapersonal ideational processes?*

As I mentioned previously, ideas can be exchanged only
by people who can communicate with one another. In order
to actualize itself, an exchange of ideas requires at least two
such persons, with a common language and mutual responsiveness to a common subject. They must establish a common
topic, out of which the ideational process can develop dialectically.

The psychotherapeutic situation as a field is especially well
suited to observing preconscious and unconscious suprapersonal ideational processes. Depth-psychological therapy
attempts to reduce conscious, rational control of communication, in order to gain access to deeper, partially unconscious

layers of the person. In this process, not only should the
patient renounce rational control, but the therapist must enter
into the process in such a way that something can actually
happen that rationally he can at first neither consciously recognize nor direct. Therapist and patients attune themselves
to a common topic, a common ground, out of which the
therapeutic ideational process strives toward a common solution as if by its own efforts; at first it is not clear who has
effected what. Often after a phase of therapeutic stagnation,
where everything looked hopeless, a solution presents itself
most unexpectedly, one that none of the participants had
thought of before. It is as if the forces had become attuned
to one another, had suddenly become coordinated, and now
run through all participants, at times like an electric shock.
It strikes me again and again how in therapy I say or do
something without knowing why; indeed, I am often dis-
concerted by the words coming out of my mouth, as well
as by the frequent subsequent realization that what I said
turned out to be correct in its effect. It is as if the situation
would have me act and speak, as if a process had developed
among all participants, a process independently striving toward a solution.

This may be illustrated with the help of an everyday example. In a student Balint group—a weekly group discussion
of (fifth-year) medical students attached to the hospital—the
first four sessions were characterized by the students' openness and commitment when talking about their fitting into
hospital hierarchy. I could easily accept that the students were
at first completely preoccupied with their own personal situation in the hospital, and did not have much energy left for
relationships with patients. In the course of the fourth meeting, however, I was becoming increasingly uneasy and had
the feeling that something was not going right in this group.
I asked why none of the students had so far reported on any
problems arising from relationships with patients. One of the
participants retorted that, after all, I had asked them to report

on how their first professional experiences moved them personally. Why, he asked, was I now rigidly adhering to the rule that Balint groups would have to deal with doctor/patient relationships? Rationally, I accepted that he was right; yet I insisted on expressing my uneasiness, which I could not quite explain to myself.

One of the students now declared that she could not experience any problems in doctor/patient relationships, because she did not have any relationships with the patients whatever. When taking down a medical record, for instance, she would proceed according to a framework demanded by the hospital, and would concentrate solely on asking everything correctly and omitting nothing. She said that she had the impression that she was already exercising this activity like a routine job, without inner participation, without pleasure, being concerned merely with making no mistakes. She proved her statement with an example of a patient with unclarified diarrhea. She had asked that patient precise questions about the nature of the diarrhea, about its frequency, about the precise appearance, consistency, and color of the stool, and so forth. The head of the clinic had been very pleased with the details she could report about this stool. When I asked the student about this, she explained that the stool occurred with irregular frequency; sometimes the patient could hardly leave the bathroom all day long; on other days the stool would be normal; on other days again she would tend to be constipated. The patient was sixty years old. No carcinoma had been detected, and the patient had been discharged into her local GP's care.

As our discussion showed, however, the student had failed to investigate this situational occurrence of the diarrhea. She had not asked the patient about the general condition under which the diarrhea occurred, or whether the patient suffered from any nervous tension that might express itself in diarrhea. As the student in fact knew, this sixty-year-old woman had been a widow for a year, and had been living with a friend for approximately four months. The diarrhea had lasted about four months, too. The student, because she was young and inexperienced, had not had the courage to speak to this woman about connections in greater detail. Thus this woman was discharged without having been examined for possible emotional causes of her illness.

Yet what had happened to us in this group process? At the beginning of the session, I had been wondering about the students' relationships with the patients. This had mobilized the group's resistance to this topic. One student then wanted to justify their common resistance to me by means of a practical example. In order to achieve this, however, she chose a case that in fact revealed how a possible treatment may have been missed because she had not been thinking about doctor/patient relationships. The students were embarrassed. By presenting this case, the student had described the situation of the whole group. All the students subsequently admitted their fear of more personal involvement with patients. They thought they would invade the patients' privacy, and were afraid of not being competent enough to give medical advice. At first, however, they were not willing to speak about this fear, but defended it behind their assertion that there were no problems between themselves and their patients. In this dialectical tension, an unconscious process developed, one that carried out the purpose behind such Balint groups.

This is a simple, not very spectacular, example from daily life. It shows how a common topic crystallizes in the different participants in such a manner that a purposive process results. I was not completely aware of why I asked about the apparent lack of relationships with patients; the student was even less aware that she was providing me with precisely the example that would make my point in a manner that got under all the participants' skins.

According to Enid Balint and her team (Balint and Norell 1976, p. 8), the doctor should let himself be used by the patient. If the doctor succeeds in "tuning in," then a "flash" may occur, a lightninglike elucidation of the situation and of an aspect important to the patient. This understanding is the patient's as well as the doctor's achievement, because in this technique "the therapist's role is to 'tune in,' to follow the patient's lead, to allow the patient to use the therapist, even to make use of him." The "flash" is not restricted to the doctor; it can occur to the patient or to the doctor, or to both simultaneously. It is a communication on a common psychotherapeutic wavelength. Therapy does not happen in the doctor, or in the patient, but between both of them. It is an experience of a spark suddenly flying between two people. This presupposes that the doctor can identify strongly with the patient because of great similarities in their character structures. A doctor or a therapist can allow such identification, however, only if his or her ego is strong enough for him or her to be able to regulate the identification so that no fusion or clinch with the patient occurs, but the I/You differentiation is maintained.

At the beginning of his or her working life, a therapist will usually concentrate on diagnosing the facts of the case or on the textbook application of a therapeutic technique. Only in the course of time will he or she become able to forget what the textbooks said and simply be moved by the process, without surrendering too much to the patient. In becoming part of a common process, the therapist will intervene less and less in ways already learned to be correct, and more and more in a manner that results from the situation and from the patient's receptivity. It is no longer so much the therapist who acts as it is the situation that lets the therapist act. Carl Rogers describes this experience as follows.

> When I am at my best, as a group facilitator or as a therapist, I discover another characteristic. I find that when I am closest to my inner, intuitive self, when I am somehow in touch with the unknown in me, when perhaps I am in a slightly altered state of consciousness, then whatever I do

seems to be full of healing. Then, simply my *presence* is releasing and helpful to the other. There is nothing I can do to force this experience, but when I can relax and be close to the transcendental core of me, then I may behave in strange and impulsive ways in the relationship, ways which I cannot justify rationally, which have nothing to do with my thought processes. But these strange behaviors turn out to be *right*, in some odd way: it seems that my inner spirit has reached out and touched the inner spirit of the other. Our relationship transcends itself and becomes a part of something larger. Profound growth and healing and energy are present.

This kind of transcendent phenomenon has certainly been experienced at times in groups in which I have worked, changing the lives of some of those involved. One participant in a workshop put it eloquently: "I found it to be a profound spiritual experience. I felt the oneness of spirit in the community. We breathed together, felt together, even spoke for one another. I felt the power of the 'life force' that infuses each of us—whatever that is. I felt its presence without the usual barricades of 'me-ness' or 'you-ness'—it was like a meditative experience when I feel myself as a center of consciousness, very much a part of the broader, universal consciousness. And yet with that extraordinary sense of oneness, the separateness of each person present has never been more clearly preserved. [Rogers 1980, pp. 129–30.]

It is as if a joint unconscious formed between the participants, a subterranean process in which all kindred souls partake, although no one steers this process singlehandedly, or could often even state its aim. The process makes use of the participants in order to express itself. Each participant senses that he or she is not acting as a mere individual, but is at the disposal of the process, without, however, losing the sense of self in the process. A strong sense of relatedness is felt by all the participants in this process, an intensification of their energies and wakefulness.

A therapist experiences again and again that he or she acts "wrongly," and in doing so does the right things intuitively. Therapeutic training often becomes a schooling of "correct" behavior in therapeutic situations. Experienced therapists continually confirm that in a concrete therapy situation, all that has been learned and acquired must be forgotten and left behind, and that breaking the rules of "correct" behavior is actually often the right thing. This schooling of "correct" behavior may be necessary, for it appears to take a great deal of experience to be able to sense when and to what extent "wrong" behavior may be right. It takes experience to let a therapeutic process develop in a "wrong" direction, while at the same time the therapist retains enough of an overview to be able to intervene if a correction does not come from the patient. Therapy frequently develops into a process in the course of which patients express by themselves what the therapist has just been about to say. In other cases, the patients experience important changes between sessions that were not previously talked about at all.

SYNCHRONICITY

Tuning in to a common process, acting and feeling on the basis of a joint unconscious, may assume the form of simultaneous internal processes going on in two or more interrelated persons without their having communicated consciously by means of their five ordinary senses. A synchronicity of ideational development is established—not by direct communication, but, as it were, through the harmony of two souls, through vibrations of the same wavelength.

I am using *synchronicity* here to refer to a simultaneity of several persons' mental processes that cannot be traced back to direct communication by means of the five ordinary senses. I am therefore using this term in a more restricted way than did Jung, who defined synchronicity as a meaningful but not causal coincidence of several incidents, understanding *incidents* as including not only mental processes but also objective, external events in the environment that do not seem to be mental or emotional in nature, but which correspond to the observer's internal state. Jung adduces the following example.

> On the morning of April 1, 1949, I noted down an inscription, a figure whose upper part was man and whose lower part was fish. That day, we had fish for lunch. Someone mentioned the custom of the "April fish." In the afternoon a former patient, whom I had not seen for months, showed me some pictures of fish. In the evening, someone showed me some embroidery representing sea monsters and fish. Early the following morning I saw a former patient for the first time in ten years. She had dreamed about a large fish the previous night. When a few months later I used this series in a work of considerable size, and had just finished writing, I went out in front of the house, to a place by the lake where I had already been several times that morning. This time, a foot-long fish was lying on the lake wall. Since nobody could have been there, I do not know how the fish got there. [Jung 1952]

Thus Jung regards synchronicity as a correspondence between what moves us personally and matching *external* counterparts. For a time, concepts such as the Gnostic principle of *fullness* or *pleroma* played a part in Jung's reflections on synchronicity. In some Gnostic writings, *pleroma* seems to refer to the dwelling place of God, the source of all revelations. If an intermediary space is assumed, neither internal (mental) nor external (environmental), then the synchronistic phenomenon could be understood as a participation of both internal and external realities in the occurrences of this intermediary world (Bonin 1981, p. 477).

For an assumed synchronicity of mental processes between several persons, it is of course not easy to rule out unconscious communication completely. I assume that there are smooth borderline transition states between conscious communication, unconscious communication, and the actual synchronicity of mental processes with any communication.

W. Furrer (1969) has described the tuning in of therapist and patient in psychoanalysis very well. One of his analysands, who suffered from chronic depression, was at times unable to speak. During a session in which she had been silent from the outset, he suggested that she try to draw a little. He passed her paper and colored pencils, saying, "Just let your hand move around on the paper without thinking; just doodle without producing an actual drawing." The analysand, who felt inhibited toward him, agreed on condition that he, too, should draw something, so that he could not watch her. Thus he, too, began to doodle (at the same time but turned away from her) on his own sheet of paper, just like that, without reflection. This kind of separate doodling by analyst and analysand was repeated a few times over several months. Later, such doodlings in pairs were done with five more analysands, but only when they appeared to be therapeutically meaningful, and when in that session no verbal interaction had occurred that would have informed the therapist about the analysand's inner state. The result was highly interesting. The doodles that had been produced by analyst and analysand in the therapeutic situation of silence were, despite the lack of verbal information, so similar to each other that any layman could recognize with certainty which two belonged together. Furrer arranged two rows of ten doodles each, one row with his own, the other with his patients', and presented them to various judges, asking them to assign similar doodles to each other, so that corresponding pairs would be formed. Amazingly, the accuracy with which the doodles were rearranged into the correct pairs, in more than a hundred verification tests, was 100 percent. It was evident that in psychoanalytic situations of silence, both partners had unconsciously brought related kinds of mental states into resonance. This was not a transference of individual thoughts or of conceptually expressible contents, but a synchronic activity arising out of common attunedness.

Personally, I am most likely to experience such synchronicities in interhuman processes in supervising therapists. The following process occurs fairly frequently. A therapist joins me for a therapy discussion; he is depressed and complains about not getting anywhere with a therapy, about feeling paralyzed and not knowing how to proceed. This phase of paralysis has lasted for weeks, possibly even several months. We then discuss the therapeutic process in great detail (in the patient's absence; indeed, without the patient's knowledge of the discussion). We try to fathom what the patient triggers off in the therapist, and what the reasons could be that both have gotten into this dead end. Sometimes the discussion produces an "Aha!" experience in the therapist. He can suddenly see what he wants to do differently in his next session with the patient, and may even decide how to start the next session. But then the following happens: the therapist does not get a chance to carry out this decision, because the *patient* starts off the session with the same words. The therapist is completely baffled, and cannot explain how this is possible. Evidently, the same process went on synchronically in both patient and therapist; the patient, too, has suffered from the therapeutic stagnation for weeks or even months; the patient's uneasiness, too, culminated at the same time in the easing of something, so that a new therapeutic phase could be started.

Once a man over forty was being treated by one of my colleagues in our inpatient Psychotherapy Unit. The patient had got into a depressive development that led as far as suicidal intentions. In our unit he blossomed relatively rapidly; he became cheerful, indeed often quite boisterous. His entering into a relationship with a female fellow patient substantially contributed to this stimulation. This, however, did not suit his wife, who was staying at home, particularly because he constantly went into raptures over this fellow patient. In our supervision group, the therapist showed a videotape of a conversation between the patient and his wife (recorded with their knowledge and consent). The therapist was convinced of the successful course of the therapy, and was therefore surprised to see that the tape caused uneasiness in the rest of us. We had the impression that the therapist concentrated too much on the patient, ascribing the abatement of the depression, and the patient's blossoming, to his therapeutic efforts, and did not sufficiently take into consideration how disadvantageous the wife's position was, alone, at home, with no therapy, while her husband was well looked after in the unit, surrounded by fellow patients of both sexes, equipped with the therapist's support and blessings, in a situation that was comfortable in every respect. Evidently, the therapist had little sympathy for the wife, whom he felt to be possessive and restrictive. We asked him to what extent he reinforced this behavior on the wife's part.

The therapist responded positively to our reservations, and decided to discuss the problem with the patient during the next session. To his great surprise, however, the patient began this session with the remark that he had the impression that the therapist's behavior toward his wife was unfair, and that his wife's irritation at his inpatient treatment should be viewed with more sympathy because, after all, she was at a disadvantage, and excluded from all this.

Another therapist was depressed because he was unable to proceed in the treatment of a young girl. This girl had made two serious suicide attempts, and continued to be seriously depressive. During therapy she would sit in silence and hardly ever speak a word. Only when he asked her specific questions would she give brief, monosyllabic answers. The therapist felt increasingly under pressure. On the one hand, the serious danger of suicide continued, so that the patient needed care. On the other hand, the therapist had the impression that his care did not set anything off in her. He and I discussed why he did not dare talk openly with the patient, and what was going on between them that obstructed progress. He had avoided discussing this last question with her for fear that she might do something to herself. After our talk he decided to raise this topic openly with the patient during the next session. He could not do so, however, because, to his great amazement, the patient took the initiative and broached the subject at the beginning of the session, for the first time in this therapy. She spontaneously recalled a dream: "I am by a river with you. You keep preventing me from diving into the water. I manage to slip away from you, though, and dive into the water, but I realize only then that the sheer cliffs are much higher than I thought. I look up and see you standing there in amazement, and I swim away from you and laugh at you."

Such synchronicities occur not only in the field of psychotherapy but also wherever strong emotional energies are mobilized in interhuman processes. In a Balint group, for example, a student desperately reports on the difficulties she has in integrating herself into hospital life. She finds the hierarchic organization inhuman, and has the feeling that as an assistant she is a nobody; she feels exposed and sadistically tormented when the senior consultant questions her about a specific case in front of all the staff. She feels so strained that her relationship with her boyfriend, with whom she lives, is threatening to break up. In this crisis she seriously asks herself whether she does not want to give up her studies. The group listens to her with compassion, but is unable to give her any help. At the next meeting, she surprises us by saying that on the day after that session, the senior consultant's behavior toward her was completely different. Although she had not said anything to him, he spontaneously offered her half a day a week off so that she could recover better. Again, although she had not said a word to him, he had refrained from publicly questioning her. Obviously, the senior consultant had indeed noticed how much this student suffered from her situation.

He synchronically experienced the same process, which aimed at a change in the relationship and in the situation. Such examples are so common that everyone can experience them, if only they keep their eyes open. Experiences such as the following are more curious, however.

In October 1979 a colleague applied for the position of assistant doctor in our Psychotherapy Unit, which was then run in two departments. I told him that I could not notify him until March 1980, because it had been planned that a colleague from the United States, who was also interested in working with us, would come to introduce herself, and that I might prefer to give the job to her. Meanwhile, however, I decided to restructure one of the two departments of the Psychotherapy Unit into a Teaching and Research Department for Psychosocial Medicine. The beds of this department would be removed, and the corresponding position of assistant doctor would become unnecessary. I communicated this plan to the staff of the Psychotherapy Unit at the beginning of March 1980. One of my colleagues, who was acquainted with the applicant of October 1979, wonderingly related the following story. Two weeks before, this colleague had phoned him because he had been disturbed by a dream. In fact, he had dreamed that there were no patients anymore in that department of the Psychotherapy Unit, but a group of black Africans with a tribal chieftain. He had wanted to know whether any changes were planned for this department. My colleague denied this, because at that time no one knew yet about my plans. It is inexplicable to me how that colleague could come by this information in a dream.

Psychoanalytic literature, particularly of the 1930s, abounds with works on such synchronic phenomena. They were triggered off by the interest in "telepathy" that Freud developed in his later years. Psychoanalysis is ideally suited to the appearance of such phenomena, because it creates a situation that the literature describes as favoring telepathy.

Analyst and analysand are in an altered state of consciousness; according to Freud's instructions, the analyst should achieve a state of balanced attention, and the analysand should associate freely; both strive for a state in which conscious, rational control of the flow of ideas is largely excluded. Freud, in "A Child Is Being Beaten" (1940b, vol. 12, p. 477), gives the instruction that the analyst should passively expose himself to the patient's unconscious; this instruction is similar to that which a medium receives in a telepathic experiment. According to Freud, the analyst should turn his own unconscious as a receptive organ toward the patient's unconscious. Just as the receiver of a telephone set transforms back into sound waves the electric fluctuations originally caused by sound waves, the doctor's unconscious is able to reconstitute the contents of the unconscious that have been communicated to him.

Yet it is not only the analyst who "channels" a patient's unconscious messages like a medium. In literature, many examples are mentioned where patients seem to receive the analysts' unconscious messages. This is even more astonishing because analysts take pains to behave impersonally, and to reflect the patients' projections back to them. They think that by avoiding personal statements, they are protected from their patients' intimate perception. The psychoanalyst I. Hollos (1933) reports that his patients often uttered precisely what he was thinking at that moment, without any assistance by the senses, without any conversation. He would, for instance, think certain thoughts on his way to work, which were then uttered by the first patient in his or her first sentences. The literature also mentions dreams that specifically represent the analyst's private situation, which is not known to the patient. Helene Deutsch (1926) was celebrating her eighth wedding anniversary and was therefore somewhat distracted during an analytic session. In this consultation, a patient related the following dream. A family is celebrating an eighth wedding anniversary. The married couple are sitting at a round table.

The wife is very sad, the husband angry and irritated. The wife is sad because of her childlessness, which she now finally has to accept. In fact, the analyst was particularly sad on that day because of her childlessness.

E. Servadio (1956) reports on a patient's dream. The patient is near the analyst's house, which, however, looks different—in fact, like a house by the sea with a little garden. A domestic brings a bowl of noodles, which she deposits near the garden gate. The analysand is very hungry and would like to appropriate the noodles. At that very moment, however, the analyst and his wife arrive by car, so that the patient has to disappear. He is now suddenly inside the house, where the analyst's wife turns her back on him and attends to three children, two of them pretty blond little girls aged four and eight. The analysand feels frustrated, unhappy, and deserted. This dream precisely matches the analyst's present situation, for his wife has gone on holiday to the seaside with their own daughter and two nieces, two blond girls aged eight and four. The analyst is frustrated at this time because he feels deserted by his wife. He has therefore invited colleagues round to have a dinner of noodles, and has sent the domestic to the patient in order to cancel the therapy session.

Servadio interprets the dream as follows. Everything happened as if the analysand had expressed, in the affective language of his dream, "Don't I know that you think about your wife more than you think about me? Don't I know that you offer agreeable food to strangers and not to me? Don't I know that your wife devotes her love and feeling to little girls, whereas I have no maternal person who looks after me and whose attention I can claim? Don't I know that you neglect my needs and send a domestic to take my food from me? Don't I know that all this corresponds to emotions and similar reactions in you, which are your own, however, and must not thwart my treatment?"

This is not the place to explain the nature of such phenomena. My personal opinion is that we should exercise great restraint in assuming the existence of paranormal extrasensory perceptions such as telepathy. In my view, parapsychology deals one-sidedly with extraordinary phenomena, whereas I am interested in the "parapsychology of everyday life." Astonishingly, parapsychological research has neglected this field so far. Most of the phenomena described as telepathic or paranormal seem to me to be explicable in terms of normal psychology. In parapsychology, *psi* denotes a mental capacity that is supposed to enable a person to establish contact with the environment without normal sensory or muscular activity (Bonin, 1981, p. 409).

I think that many phenomena that seem to be telepathic correspond to synchronicities. The harmony of two hearts on the basis of similar responsiveness and attunement creates corresponding, mutually related mental processes, without direct mediation by the sensory organs. Any observant person can repeatedly experience being part of suprapersonal processes in such daily incidents. In other cultures this sort of consciousness is taken in stride, whereas we ward it off for fear of inner dependence. In our Western culture we are inclined to view the individual as being merely the body and the conscious activities of the sensory organs. Whatever does not correspond to immediate sensory perception is rashly described as a psi phenomenon.

HOW THE JOINT UNCONSCIOUS
CAN MALFUNCTION

Synchronicities and actions arising from the joint unconscious may be pleasurable experiences, and convey a feeling of increased closeness and of the significance of one's own actions. There are also sinister developments, however, in which collectively unconscious elements lead to disaster, with an inevitability following its very own laws.

Georges Simenon is a master of the description of such processes, which seem to begin as banal, everyday situations that are experienced by everybody; gradually, however, it emerges that the protagonists are being caught in a net, which is slowly being pulled together toward one particular point, while the protagonists, move by move, behave in such a way that the inevitable is bound to happen. Destructive collusions develop, in which several persons' corresponding needs and fears amplify one another, and no one can muster the courage to resist this development.

In Simenon's novel *La mort de Belle*, the following happens. Ashby, a respectable schoolmaster who leads a peaceful and harmonious life in a small city, is suddenly confronted with the following situation. Belle, an eighteen-year-old girl, has been living as a lodger in his household for a month. He has not had any contact with her; indeed, he has hardly taken any notice of her presence. On the night in question his wife is out playing bridge with friends, and Ashby is at home alone, pottering about in his workshop in the cellar. Belle looks in through the door for a moment, apparently to say good night. The following morning Ashby is called home from school. Belle has been found dead in her room, strangled and probably raped. In a flash, Ashby is struck by a thought that occurs to all around him, too, a thought that is dismissed by all, but inevitably becomes more and more irresistible: that he himself must be the murderer. He was alone in the house with Belle. There were no traces to indicate that someone else had entered the house. No one besides him can know that he did not kill her. Now a cruel process sets in: Ashby, obsessed with the thought of being considered the murderer, increasingly works himself into behavior that confirms these suspicions. Gradually, a collective unspoken agreement about his guilt develops among his wife, his headmaster, his colleagues, his students, his neighbors, and the whole city. As if in a trance, Ashby, too, now begins to identify himself with these fantasies, which increasingly resemble those of the murderer. In harmony with his environment, the erstwhile philistine of moral strictness and flawless reputation fantasizes about being a strangler, and works himself up into an intolerable state, to which he puts an end by raping and strangling his examining magistrate's secretary. Thus any man could be turned into a murderer if he lets himself be sucked into the whirlpool of an unconscious ideational process.

Something similar happens in Simenon's novel *La veuve Couderc*. Jean, a young man who has just been discharged from prison, becomes a lodger at the widow Couderc's farm. At first he feels carefree and liberated in his work as a farmhand. There are serious tensions between the widow Couderc and her relations, who live in the neighborhood. These have a girl, grown up and pretty, who already has a child and who follows Jean around. He does not know exactly what she expects of him. The widow Couderc, who suffers from her loneliness as a woman, senses what is going on between the girl and Jean, and wants to place Jean under an obligation to be with her all the time. She checks up on his every movement, and jealously reacts to every glance that Jean casts at the girl. More and more he finds himself in a clinch with the widow Couderc, until finally he does what she, and all her relations and neighbors, were always afraid that he would do: he kills her. Thus he confirms himself as the criminal he was held to be.

In social psychology such processes are known as the *labeling approach* and as *stigmatization*. Labels diverging from a norm—as *criminal* and *mentally ill* are both perceived by the environment—are integrated by those concerned into their images of themselves. The often-unconscious expectations shared by those concerned and the others in their life fix the development of a diverging "career," although professional helpers (such as psychiatrists and social workers) and institutions (such as the police and the prison system) appear to do all they can to prevent such developments.

Processes in whose course each makes of the other something that apparently nobody wants can be seen particularly frequently in the destructive developments of married couples. I have described this in great detail in my book *Couples in Collusion* (Willi 1982a) and will not repeat it here. The *collusion concept* described in that book denotes the following process. Similar unconscious fears and unrealizable wishes may cause two partners to enter into a long-term relationship with the expectation that together they will be protected from all previous frustrations and injuries. The similarity of the fears and irrational desires, however, will sooner or later maneuver the partners back into their former difficulties. The rage caused by this disappointment first causes them to get the expected happiness by way of blackmail, and later to revenge themselves on the partner by means of destructive behavior. Such unconscious destructive developments can also occur in larger collectives; indeed, they can include whole peoples, as the history of National Socialism demonstrates particularly impressively. Often the process is experienced as if it were controlled not by those concerned, but by a foreign power. The fatal development happens *to* them. No wonder that primitive cultures often associate such cases with enchantment or witchcraft, or with possession by a strange spirit.

Psychological mass phenomena have again and again resulted in appalling catastrophes and injustice. They are therefore feared, and rightly so. The individualistic self-realization, appealing to autonomy and self-responsibility, after World War II may partially be understood as a reaction to the mass phenomena of the Third Reich. This is the fear, also expressed by Jung, that in collective processes human beings tend toward primitive reactions, lose their control, and can easily be seduced into surrendering their ethical attitudes and into acting purely emotionally. Mass phenomena are often experienced as highly pleasurable. They may be a substantial motivation for people to be part of the seething public at sports events. The regressive behavior of spectators at sports events is a particularly good example of actions arising from the joint unconscious; rock and pop concerts are similar events. The subject of unconscious ideational processes is a wide and fascinating field, which, however, I cannot treat here in any more detail.

In its constitution, the joint unconscious is similar to the individual unconscious. According to psychoanalysis, the contents of the unconscious represent instincts. Fantasies and imaginary scenarios derive their energy from instincts. The unconscious acts according to the primary process, the pleasure principle. Emotional energy wants to flow freely, without having to encounter obstacles, without postponing or restricting instinctual satisfaction. Psychoanalysis endeavors to make unconscious tendencies conscious, and therefore strives for greater mastery and control in order to use these instinctual energies rather than suppress them. I believe that the same is valid for common unconscious tendencies. Our Western aspirations to individualism, conscious personal boundaries, and independence from fellow human beings threaten to suppress and repress the tendencies of the joint unconscious. These, however, become operative in a proportionally more primitive form. By analogy to what psychoanalysis endeavors to do for the individual, the instinctual forces combining into suprapersonal processes should not be unacknowledged or disowned, but should be made fruitful for suprapersonal processes. Since at present we tend to dismiss instinctual forces that strive for suprapersonal processes as regressive and primitive, uncontrolled and destructive developments may occur—for instance, in religious groups: shameless exploitation of the readiness to join a community and to be available for suprapersonal processes, tyranny extending to collective suicide.

CHAPTER 11

How the Individual
Helps Universal
Consciousness Evolve

An ideational process is made up of its carriers' ideological systems. For its ecological growth, it requires a suitable environment—a culture. The structure of a culture as a fertile soil, however, is not fundamentally different from that of an ideational process; rather, a culture is the totality of the ideational processes in a certain place at a certain time. A culture represents a wealth of ideas, divided into layers of brief idea waves (that can, however, cause violent fluctuations), into longer-lasting gradual developments, and finally into a foundation of ideas that are integrated, that change only gradually in the course of time, and that constitute the ground and the treasure of a culture. All these various ideas are interrelated and engaged in continuous exchange. But the various cultures, too, are interrelated and engaged in a continuous exchange, and thus form a world culture. Thanks to present-day communication technology and the internationalization of the economy, this global culture is becoming more and more comprehensible and dominant.

Persons' relationships to culture can be imagined as follows: persons' ideological systems organize themselves into ideational processes, which in turn organize themselves into cultures. Ideational processes are interrelated not only spatially but also temporally. Present ideational processes derive from former ones and aim at future ones. This results in a cultural history in which every epoch is interrelated with, and derives from, previous epochs.

The person experiences culture as an external environment to which he or she must adapt. The individual also experiences world and cultural history as if exposed to it, as if it were happening to him or her. Yet history is the totality that results from the combination of all the idea carriers' shares in it. The protagonists of world history act as representatives of such ideational processes. A Hitler, a Stalin, a Khomeini are representatives of their cultures, not simply unpleasant individuals whom one would like to make disappear so that everything would be nice again. In its longer-term developments, world history is dominated far less by individual politicians than the man in the street would assume.

There is a continuous transition between this idea of a layered culture, which rests on a foundation of integrated, more constant images and ideas, and Jung's idea of the *collective unconscious*. Jung assumed that our mental world contains an immeasurable wealth of images, which have been accumulated and organically condensed by millions of years of living development. These images are condensations of thousands of years' experiences of the struggle for adaptation and existence. Again, it is only a small step from Jung's views to *Plato's theory of ideas*, according to which ideas are self-contained (divine) prototypes that manifest themselves in individual things and shapes.

In my view the differences derive from a temporal perspective: should centuries or tens of thousands of years be taken into account? Plato speaks of a world soul, Hegel of a world spirit. Hegel assumes a self-actualization of the spirit.

I regard this actualization of the spirit as an immense global evolutionary process of ideas, produced by the carriers of these ideas. The systemically organized totality of spirit makes us speak of "the Spirit" or of "God," which may also be understood as *a cipher* that describes the totality of the common ground of human ideas. This common ground is often experienced as if it were a central guiding and directing power, as if it were a "God" confronting us, who may permit the bad to happen in order to make the good win through again and again, a "God" who rewards good and grants justice the final victory. This aspect of what is meant by "God" need not differ in quality from the organized totality of conscious and unconscious human longing and aspiration. Much of what is described as a quality of "God" need not transcend the totality of what is human, but could be inherent in it. The term *God* might be an image enabling us to confront this otherwise incomprehensible whole.

The totality, which consists of the organized sum of all aspirations to improve the world, is an immense force capable of correcting extreme historical movements toward the middle again and again, capable of restoring justice and humaneness in a continuous process of differentiation, despite all imperfection. If the totality constituted by the psychological foundation of all human beings is understood as the God to whom we pray, whom we implore for help, and on whom we call to guide history and fate, then this is perfectly sensible in my opinion. Prayer, here reduced to the aspect of common pleading, directs the mental powers of the praying toward a goal. A people's common belief in the efficacy of their pleading can "move mountains." The purposive organization of the ideas and energies of many human beings can be a tremendous power that can influence world events decisively and that creates circumstances in which extraordinary incidents and actions may occur, which present themselves as fulfillment of the prayers. Much of what is perceived as a specific influence of God, whom we have asked for something, can be understood on the basis of the effectiveness of the suprapersonal unconscious, too. All of this says something about certain aspects of ideational processes, but not about the nature of God as such.

Man is not a being fundamentally different from nature, but is part of it. He is not pervaded by a different spirit, but is a vehicle of an all-embracing spirit. A universal consciousness crystallizes itself in all that lives and nourishes all spiritual movement. The individual's consciousness constitutes a great joint consciousness, of which every one is only part. There is a circular movement from individual to cosmos and back to individual, from the human spirit to universal consciousness and back to the human spirit. According to Govinda (1976, p. 253), the world is a system of infinite relationships, an organic whole in which every individual part is determined by every other part. To live is to integrate oneself into the rhythm of life. Any man who refuses to use his individual voice, because he is not willing to coordinate himself and to fit into the whole, will detach himself from the choir in splendid isolation and will die a spiritual death.

In the consciousness of a sense of belonging to a creative cosmos, prayer thus assumes additional dimensions. It is also a way of listening to the whole, which communicates itself to us and shows us the way. In *The Prophet* (pp. 78–81) Khalil Gibran says about prayer:

> For what is prayer but the expansion of yourself into the living ether? . . .
> When you pray you rise to *meet in the air those who are praying at that very hour*, and whom save in prayer you may not meet.
> Therefore let your visit to that *temple invisible* be . . . sweet communion. . . .
> God listens not to your words save when He Himself utters them through your lips.
> And I cannot teach you the prayer of the seas and the forests and the mountains.

But you who are born of the mountains and the forests
and the seas can find their prayer in your heart,
And if you but listen in the stillness of the night you
shall hear them saying in silence. . . . [My italics.]

Govinda (1976, p. 165) assumes an all-embracing, ever-present depth consciousness as a source of all divine powers, in which the experiences of a past without beginning are stored, and through which every human being can partake in a greater life that encompasses the whole universe and interrelates all human beings.

All forces and capacities of the universe are contained in us. If, however, they are not awakened and activated in us through constant practice, they will not be real. An idea has taken deep root in us Western people, according to which the individual is the center and the source of instinctual forces, of consciousness and unconsciousness, of his or her own processes and activities. It is difficult for us to consider individuals to be not self-contained, bounded units, but the means of expression and points of crystallization of a universal stream of life. This universal stream of life assumes shape in us, expresses itself through us, and actualizes itself in our behavior and action. It is not only an individualized self that manifests itself in us but also an immense suprapersonal process of which the individual can be only a part. Ecological self-realization means to be available for the actualization of this process.

The individual can participate in this universal stream of life even without being able to own it. The universe assumes consciousness in individuals, and the individuals become conscious of their universality. The universal requires the individual in order to manifest itself, and the individual draws his or her energies from the universal. Nothing exists independently in itself, but only in relation to others and ultimately in relation to the entire universe.

Self-realization is not possible in every form of life.

Everyone makes certain irreversible decisions in life. Just as every railroad network has switches that offer a choice between various directions, so every human being is offered the decisions of following this road or that. But once we have opted for one road, the journey is only forward; we cannot go back. We must enter into a relation with all that comes toward us on our journey, with all that manifests itself as part of the human environment and the culture of which we, too, are part. Our actualization is always becoming, never being. We can become part of reality only by interacting with our immediate environment, so that it will in turn make us real. We must actualize ourselves together so that our culture will become real, manifest, embodied, actual.

Notes

For detailed source data, see Bibliography.

Chapter 1

5: On the influence of the mother, see also the criticism by the psychoanalyst M. Wangh (1983).

6: On alienation, see especially Erich Fromm, *Marx's Concept of Man* (Ungar, 1961) for a translation (by T. H. Bottomore) of and commentary on Marx's "Economic and Philosophic Manuscripts of 1844." —Ed.

18: On borderline disorders, see, among others, Kernberg 1975 for a detailed description.

Chapter 2

29: Husserl is quoted in Böckenhoff 1970 (Kern, "Das Problem der Intersubjektivität in der phänomenologischen Philosophie Edmund Hesserls," lecture, 1963).

30: Regarding psychoanalysis and the human environment, exceptions are the family theories derived from psychanalysis, such as Stierlin 1975b and 1978, and Richter 1970 and 1976.

32: On children and their parents' expectations, see, among many others, Laing 1960 and 1961, Miller 1981, and Richter 1976.

46–47: Sartre is quoted in Böckenhoff 1970.

59–60: Feuerbach is quoted in Böckenhoff 1970, p. 111.

60: "Our human essence. . ." quoted in Böckenhoff 1970, p. 109.

Chapter 3

74: This derivation of the word *individual* is in Hoffmeister 1955.

74–75: On relative constancy of individuality, see Buchholz in Rexilius and Grubitzsch 1981, p. 487.

76: Regarding Yannaras's discussion of *person* and *pros-opon*, I am indebted to A. Berner for pointing this out to me.

77: On systems theory, see Jantsch 1982.

90: Regarding Jung's letter to Kirsch, I am indebted to Verena Kast for this information.

93: "I comprehend myself. . ." is from Jäger, *Vorlesung zur poetischen Sprache*, 1980/81; quoted in Thamm 1982, p. 275.

100: On industrial psychology, see Ulich 1978a and 1978b.

100: McGregor and Theory X are discussed in Bruggemann, Grosskurth, and Ulich 1975.

102: The quotations from Frisch in this section are found in Thamm 1982, pp. 270–71.

102: Michaux is quoted in Schelling 1983, p. 37.

105: The quotations from Marx are found in Böckenhoff 1970, pp. 86–87.

Chapter 4

120: On surviving partners, see, among others, Parkes, Benjamin, and Fitzgerald 1969.

126: On species and natural habitat, see Weizsäcker 1975; quoted in Jantsch 1982, p. 269.

145: For more about the collusion concept, see Dicks 1967, Willi 1982a, and Lemaire 1979.

Chapter 6

177: On the influence of dead family members, see Paul and Paul 1975, Boszormenyi-Nagy and Spark 1973, Wirschung and Stierlin 1982, and Sperling et al. 1982.

200: On the scapegoat, see, among many others, Allport 1951, Boszormenyi-Nagy 1975, Richter 1976, Stierlin 1975a and 1975b, Sperling et al. 1982, and Hoffman 1982.

203: On Dürkheim and the outsider, see Hoffman 1982, pp. 57ff.

209: On the hidden task, it is used here as understood by Stierlin (1975b); see also Richter 1976.

Chapter 7

230: "Only the similar . . ." (*Simila similibus comprehendi*) is quoted in Grassi and Schmale 1982, p. 26.

231: Kimura is quoted in Grassi and Schmale 1982, p. 35.

Chapter 8

247–249: These examples from the history of science are all found in Störig 1954.

Chapter 9

289–290: Regarding differences between participants in a group discussion, compare the results of the joint Rorschach test in groups (Willi 1973).

Bibliography

Ackoff, K. L., and E. E. Emery. 1972. *On Purposeful Systems.* Chicago: Aldine Atherton.

Allport, G. 1951. *ABC of Scapegoating.* New York: Anti-Defamation League of B'nai B'rith.

Bach, G., and P. Wyden. 1969. *The Intimate Enemy: How to Fight Fair in Love and Marriage.* New York: W. Morrow.

Balint, E., and J. S. Norell, eds. 1976. *Six Minutes for the Patient: Interactions in General Practice Consultation.* London: Tavistock Publications.

Balint, M. 1965. *Primary Love and Psychoanalytic Technique.* London: Tavistock Publications.

Barz, H. 1981. *Stichwort: Selbstverwirklichung. Ehrenrettung eines Modewortes.* Stuttgart: Kreuz.

Bateson, G. 1972. *Step to an Ecology of the Mind.* Novato, Calif.: Chandler Publications.

Berman, M. 1981. *The Reenchantment of the World.* Ithaca: Cornell University Press.

Berner-Hürbin, A. 1974. *Psycholinguistik der Romanismen im älteren Schweizerdeutschen.* Frauenfeld: Huber.

Biermann-Ratjen, E. M., and J. Schwartz. 1981. "Zum Empathiebegriff in der Gesprächspsychotherapie," *GwG-info* 43:42–48.

Binswanger, L. 1962. *Grundformen und Erkenntnis menschlichen Daseins.* Munich: Reinhardt.

Bittner, G. 1980. "Gruppendynamik—ein ziemlich sicherer Weg, sich selbst zu verfehlen." *Psychosozial* 1:41–65.

Blanck, G., and R. Blanck. 1968. *Marriage and Personal Development.* New York: Columbia University Press.

Blenkner, M., M. Bloom, and M. Nielsen. 1971. "A Research and Demonstration Project of Protective Services," *Social Casework* 52:483–99.

Böckenhoff, J. 1970. *Die Begegnungsphilosophie.* Freiburg: Alber.

Bonin, W. F. 1981. *Lexikon der Parapsychologie.* Frankfurt am Main: Fischer.

Boss, M. 1953. *Der Traum und seine Auslegung.* Bern: Huber.

Boszormenyi-Nagy, I. 1975. "Dialektische Betrachtung der Intergenerationen-Familientherapie," *Ehe* 12:117–31.

Boszormenyi-Nagy, I., and G. Spark. 1973. *Invisible Loyalties.* New York: Harper & Row.

Bovet, T. 1969. *Kompendium der Ehekunde.* Bern: Haupt.

Bowers, K. S. 1973. "Situationism in Psychology: An Analysis and a Critique." *Psychological Review* 80:307–36.

Braunmühl, E. von. 1975. *Antipädagogik.* Weinheim: Beltz.

Bronfenbrenner, U. 1979. *The Ecology of Human Development.* Cambridge: Harvard University Press.

Bruggemann, Grosskurth, and Ulich. 1975. *Arbeitszufriedenheit.* Schriften zur Arbeitspsychologie no. 17. Bern: Huber.

Buber, M. 1973. *Das dialogische Prinzip.* Heidelberg: Lambert Schneider.

Buddeberg, C., and B. Buddeberg. 1982. "Familienkonflikte als Kollusion—eine psychodynamische Perspektive für die Familientherapie." *Praxis der Kinderpsychologie* 143–50.

Bühler, C. 1932. *The First Year of Life.* New York: John Day.

Capra, F. 1982. *The Turning Point: Science, Society, and the Rising Culture.* London: Wildwood House.

De Mause, L., ed. 1974. *The History of Childhood.* New York: Psychohistory Press.

Deutsch, H. 1926. "Okkulte Vorgänge während der Psychoanalyse." *Imago* 12:428–33.

Dollard, J., L. W. Doob, N. E. Miller, O. H. Mowrer, and R. R. Sears. 1939. *Frustration and Aggression*. New Haven: Yale University Press.

Döpp, H. J. 1981. "Narziss: Ein neuer Sozialisationstyp?" In *Narzissein neuer Sozialisationstypus?*, ed. H. Häsing, H. Stubenrauch, and T. Ziehe. Bensheim: päd-extra Buchverlag.

Dürkheim, K. 1983. "Der Körper, den ich habe—der Leib, den ich bin." Paper no. 33, Lindau Psychotherapy Weeks, April 27, 1983; on audiocassette.

Eisenbud, J. 1964. "Telepathy and Problems of Psychoanalysis." *Psychoanalytical Quarterly* 15:32–87.

Endler, N. S., and D. Magnusson. 1976. "Toward an Interactional Psychology of Personality." *Psychological Bulletin* 83:956–74.

Erikson, E. H. 1956–57. "Das Problem der Identität." *Psyche* 10:114–76.

Ferguson, M. 1980. *The Aquarian Conspiracy. Personal and Social Transformation in the 1980s*. Los Angeles: J. P. Tarcher.

———. 1984. "Beziehungen." *Sphinx* 25:17–23.

Feuerbach, L. 1903–11. *Sämtliche Werke*. Ed. Bolin and Jodl. Stuttgart: Frommann-Holzboog.

Fischer, C. 1978. *Der Traum in der Psychotherapie*. Munich: Minerva Publications.

Freud, S. 1940a. "Bemerkungen zur Theorie und Praxis der Traumdeutung" (Remarks on the theory and practice of dream interpretation). In *Gesammelte Werke*, vol. 13, pp. 299–314. London: Imago.

———. 1940b. *Gesammelte Werke*. London: Imago.

———. 1940c. "Neue Folgen der Vorlesungen zur Einführung in die Psychoanalyse" (New introductory lectures on psychoanalysis). In *Gesammelte Werke*, vol. 15. London: Imago.

———. 1940d. "Psychoanalyse und Libidotheorie" (Psychoanalysis and libido theory). In *Gesammelte Werke*, vol. 13, pp. 211–33. London: Imago.

———. 1940e. "Traum und Telepathie" (Dreams and telepathy). *Gesammelte Werke*, vol. 13, pp. 163–91. London: Imago.

———. 1946a. "Psychoanalyse und Telepathie" (Psychoanalysis and telepathy). *Gesammelte Werke*, vol. 17, pp. 27–46. London: Imago.

———. 1946b. "Zur Geschichte der psychoanalytischen Bewegung" (Toward a history of the psychoanalytic movement). In *Gesammelte Werke*, vol. 10, pp. 163–91. London: Imago.

Frisch, M. 1975. *Stichworte*. Frankfurt am Main: Suhrkamp.

Fromm, E. 1961. *Marx's Concept of Man*. New York: Ungar.

Fuchs, W., R. Klima, R. Lautmann, O. Rammstedt, and H. Wienhold, eds. 1973. *Lexikon zur Soziologie*. Opladen: Westdeutscher Verlag.

Furrer, W. 1969. *Objektivierung des Unbewussten: Psychotherapeutische Kommunikation, sichtbar gemacht in Zeichnungen von Analytiker und Patient*. Bern: Huber.

———. 1972. "Unbewusste Kommunikation zwischen Arzt und Patient." *Imago Roche* 51:14–17.

Gibran, K. [1926] 1980. *The Prophet*. Reprint. London: Heinemann/ Pan Books.

Govinda, L. A. 1966. *The Way of the White Clouds*. London: Hutchinson & Co.

———. 1976. *Creative Meditation and Multidimensional Consciousness*.

———. 1984. *Mandala*. Bern: Origo.

Grassi, E., and H. Schmale. 1982. *Das Gespräch als Ereignis*. Munich: Fink.

Haley, J. 1976. *Problem Solving Therapy: New Strategies for Effective Family Therapy*. San Francisco: Jossey-Bass.

———. 1980. *Leaving Home: The Therapy of Disturbed Young People*. New York: McGraw-Hill.

Hartmann, H. 1964. *Ego Psychology and the Problem of Adaptation*. New York: International University Press.

Häsing, R., H. Stubenrauch, and T. Ziehe, eds. 1981. *Narziss— ein neuer Sozialisationstypus?* Bensheim: päd-extra Buchverlag.

Hayek, F. A. von. 1975. *Kinds of Order in Society: Studies in Social Theory*. Menlo Park: Institute for Human Studies.

Hegel, G. W. F. 1955. *Philosophie der Weltgeschichte*. Reprint. Hamburg: Meiner.

Hell, D. 1982. *Ehen depressiver und schizophrener Menschen*. Berlin: Springer.

Hentig, H. von. 1976. *Was ist eine humane Schule?* Munich: Hanser.

Herbst, P. 1975. "The Product of Work Is People." In *The Quality of Working Life*, ed. L. L. Davis and A. B. Cherns, vol. 1, pp. 439–42. New York: Free Press.

Herrmann, T., P. R. Hofstätter et al., eds. 1977. *Handbuch psychologischer Grundbegriffe*. Munich: Kösel.

Hitler, A. 1935. *Mein Kampf*. Unabridged German popular edition.

Hoff, R. 1978. "Wilhelm Reich and Body-Oriented Psychotherapy." In *Berkeley Holistic Health Handbook*. Berkeley: And/Or Press.

Hoffman, L. 1982. *Grundlagen der Familientherapie*. Hamburg: ISKO-Press.

Hoffmeister, J. 1955. *Wörterbuch der philosophischen Bergriffe*. Hamburg: Meiner.

Hollos, I. 1933. "Psychopathologie alltäglicher telepathischer Erscheinungen." *Imago* 19:529–46.

Holzhey, A. 1983. "Jenseits des Bedürfnisprinzips." *Schweiz. Montashefte* 63:997–1006.

Humboldt, W. von. 1903. *Ueber die Verschiedenheit des Sprachbaues und ihren Einfluss auf die geistige Entwicklung des Menschengeschlechtes*. In *Gesammelte Schriften*, vol. 7. Berlin: Preussische Akademie der Wissenschaften.

———. 1968. *Grundzüge des allgemeinen Sprachtypes*. Berlin: de Gruyter.

Jacobson, E. 1964. *The Self and the Object World*. New York: International University Press.

Jantsch, E. 1982. *Die Selbstorganisation des Universums*. Munich: Deutscher Taschenbuchverlag.

Jones, E. 1956. *Sigmund Freud: Life and Work*. Vol. 1. *The Young Freud 1856–1900* London: Hogarth Press.

Jung, C. G. 1952. Natureklänung und Psyche. Zurich: Rascher.

———. 1954. *Von der Wurzeln des Bewusstseins* (On the transformation of consciousness). Zurich: Rascher.

———. 1960a. *Gesammelte Werke*. Zurich: Rascher.

———. 1960b. "On Psychic Energy." In *Collected Works*, vol. 8. New York: Pantheon.

———. 1960c. *Psychological Types*. In *Collected Works*, vol. 6. New York: Pantheon.

———. 1960d. "Synchronicity as a Principle of Acausal Connectivity." In *Collected Works*, vol. 8. New York: Pantheon.

————. 1966. *Two Essays on Analytical Psychology.* In *Collected Works*, rev. ed., vol. 7. New York: Pantheon.

————. 1967. *Psychology and Alchemy.* In *Collected Works*, rev. ed., vol. 12. New York: Pantheon.

————. 1972. *Briefe I, 1906–1945* Olten: Walter.

Kast, V. 1982. *Trauern.* Stuttgart: Kreuz.

Kernberg, O. F. 1975. *Borderline Conditions and Pathological Narcissism.* New York: Aronson.

Kimura, B. 1971. "Mitmenschlichkeit in der Psychiatrie." *Zeitschrift der Klinischen Psychologie und Psychiatrie* 19:3–12.

————. 1974. "Ueber die wahnhafte Herkunftsablehnung und deren kulturanthropologische Bedeutung." In *Die Wirklichkeit des Unverständlichen*, ed. J. M. Broekman and G. Hofer, pp. 184–215. The Hague: Martinus Nijhoff.

————. 1982. "Die Bedeutung der Atmosphäre für das Gespräch." In *Das Gespräch als Ereignis*, ed. E. Grassi and H. Schmale, pp. 35–44. Munich: Fink.

Kohut, H. 1971. *The Analysis of Self: A Systematic Approach to the Psychoanalytic Treatment of Narcissistic Personality Disorders.* London: Hogarth Press and Institute of Psycho-analysis.

————. 1977. *The Restoration of the Self.* New York: International University Press.

König, K., and R. Tischkau-Schröter. 1982. "Der interaktionelle Anteil der Uebertragung bei Partnerwahl und Partnerveränderung." *Zeitschrift für psychosomatische Medizin* 28:266–79.

Krähenbühl, V., H. Jellouschek, M. Kohaus-Jellouschek, and R. Weber. 1984. "Stieffamilien: Struktur, Entwicklung, Therapie." *Familiendynamik* 9:2–18.

Krüll, M. 1978. "Freuds Absage an die Verführungstheorie im Lichte seiner eigenen Familiendynamik." *Familiendynamik* 3:102–29.

Laing, R. D. 1960. *Divided Self.* London: Tavistock Publications.

————. 1961. *Self and Others.* London: Tavistock Publications.

Laplanche, J., and J.-B. Pontalis. 1967. *Vocabulaire de la psychanalyse.* Paris: Presses universitaires de France.

Lasch, C. 1979. *The Culture of Narcissism.* New York: Norton.

Lemaire, I. G. 1980. *Das Leben als Paar.* Olten: Walter.

Lévi-Strauss, C. 1980. *Mythos und Bedeutung.* Frankfurt am Main: Suhrkamp.

Lilly, J. C. [1972] 1979. *The Center of the Cyclone: An Autobiography of Inner Space*. Reprint. New York: Bantam Books.

Lowen, A. 1970. *Pleasure, a Creative Approach to Life*. New York: Coward McCann.

———. 1976. *Bioenergetics*. New York: Penguin Books.

Mahler, M. S. 1968. *On Human Symbiosis and the Vicissitudes of Individuation*. New York: International University Press.

Manika, C. 1978. "Sind Frauen 'fraulicher' und Männer 'männlicher', wenn sie in der Paarsituation aufeinander bezogen sind. Untersuchung mit dem Individuellen und Gemeinsamen Rorschach-Versuch." *Familiendynamik* 3:91–100.

Maslow, A. H. 1968. *Toward a Psychology of Being*. New York: Van Nostrand Insight Books.

Masters, W. H., and V. Johnson. 1961. "Orgasm, Anatomy of the Female." In *Encyclopedia of Sexual Behavior*, ed. A. Ellis and A. Abarbanel, vol. 2. New York: Hawthorn Books.

May, R. 1977. *The Meaning of Anxiety*. New York: Norton.

———. 1982. "The Problem of Evil: An Open Letter to Carl Rogers." *Journal of Humanistic Psychology* 22:10–21.

McGregor, D. 1960. *The Human Side of Enterprise*. New York: McGraw-Hill.

Meissner, W. W. 1978. "The Conceptualization of Marriage and Family Dynamics from a Psychoanalytic Perspective." In *Marriage and Marital Therapy: Psychoanalytic, Behavioral, and Systems Theory Perspectives*, ed. T. J. Paolino and B. S. McCrady. New York: Brunner/Mazel.

Merleau-Ponty, M. 1945. *Phénoménologie de la perception*. Paris.

———. 1966. *Les relations avec autrui chez l'enfant*. Paris: CDU.

Mertens, W. 1984. *Vom Ich zum Selbst*. Paper, Lindau Psychotherapy Weeks, 1984.

Miller, A. 1981. *The Drama of the Gifted Child*. New York: Harper.

Miller, J. G. 1978. *Living Systems*. New York: McGraw-Hill.

Millet, K. 1969. *Sexual Politics*. New York: Doubleday.

Minuchin, S. 1974. *Family and Family Therapy*. Cambridge: Harvard University Press.

Minuchin, S., B. Rosman, and L. Baker. 1978. *Psychosomatic Families: Anorexia Nervosa in Context*. Cambridge: Harvard University Press.

Mischel, W. 1973. "Toward a Cognitive Social Learning Reconceptualization of Personality." *Psychological Review* 80:252–83.

Moore, B. E., and B. D. Fine, eds. 1968. *A Glossary of Psychoanalytic Terms and Concepts.* New York: American Psychoanalytical Association.

Neumann, E. 1963. *Das Kind: Struktur und Dynamik der werdenden Persönlichkeit.* Zurich: Rhein.

Parkes, C. M., B. Benjamin, and R. G. Fitzgerald. 1969. "Broken Heart: A Statistical Study of Increased Mortality among Widowers." *British Medical Journal* 1:740–43.

Paul, N. L., and B. B. Paul. 1975. *A Marital Puzzle.* New York: Norton.

Perls, F. S., R. F. Hefferline, and P. Goodman. 1973. *Gestalt Therapy: Excitement and Growth in the Human Personality.* Harmondsworth: Penguin/Pelican.

Piaget, J., and B. Inhelder. 1966. *La psychologie de l'enfant.* Paris: Presses universitaires de France.

Popper, K. R. 1957. *Die offene Gesellschaft und ihre Feinde.* Vol. 1, *Der Zauber Platons.* Bern: Francke.

Prigogine, I. 1976. "Order through Fluctuation: Self-Organization and Social System." In *Evolution and Consciousness,* ed. E. Jantsch and C. Waddington, pp. 93–133. Reading, MA: Addison-Wesley.

Rapaport, D. 1959. *Structure of Psychoanalytic Theory.* New York: McGraw-Hill.

Reich, W. 1949. *Character Analysis.* 3d ed. New York: Farrar, Straus & Giroux.

Rexilius, G., and S. Grubitzsch, eds. 1981. *Handbuch psychoanalytischer Grundbegriffe.* Reinbek: Rowohlt.

Richter, H. E. 1970. *Patient Familie.* Reinbek: Rowohlt.

———. 1976. *Eltern, Kind und Neurose.* Reinbek: Rowohlt.

Richter, H. E., and D. Beckmann. 1969. *Herzneurose.* Stuttgart: Thieme.

Rieger, G. E. 1981. *Henrik Ibsen.* Reinbek: Rowohlt.

Rogers, C. R. 1961. *On Becoming a Person.* Boston: Houghton Mifflin.

———. 1977. *On Personal Power, Inner Strength and Its Revolutionary Impact.* New York: Delacorte Press.

———. 1980. *A Way of Being.* Boston: Houghton Mifflin.

Sartre, J.-P. 1980. *L'etre et le néant*. Reprint. Paris.

Satir, V. 1981. "Networking: A Viable Model for the New Age." *Newsletter*, Association for Humanistic Psychology, San Francisco, November.

Scheler, M. 1948. *Wesen und Formen der Sympathie*. 5th ed. Frankfurt am Main.

Schelling, W. A. 1983. "Symbol und 'innere Welt.' " *Neue Zürcher Zeitung*, March 5/6, 1983, p. 37.

Schepank, H., H. Hilpert, H. Hönmann et al. 1984. "Das Mannheimer Kohortenprojekt—Die Prävalenz psychogener Erkrankungen in der Stadt." *Zeitschrift für psychosomatische Medizin* 30:43–61.

Schmid, H. 1981. *Jeden gibt's nur einmal*. Stuttgart: Kreuz.

Schoenebeck, H. von. 1982. *Unterstützen statt Erziehen*. Munich: Kösel.

Selvini-Palazzoli, M., L. Boscolo, G. Cechin, and G. Prata. 1975. *Paradosso e controparadosso*. Milan: Feltrinelli.

Servadio, E. 1956. "Ein paranormaler Traum in der analytischen Situation." *Zeitschrift für Parapsychologie und Grenz-gebietspsychologie* 1:155–65.

Simenon, G. 1971. *La mort de Belle*. Paris: Presses de la Cité.

———. 1971. *La veuve Couderc*. Paris: Gallimard.

Sperling, E., A. Massing, G. Reich, et al. 1982. *Die Mehrgenerationen-Familientherapie*. Göttingen: Vandenhoeck und Ruprecht.

Stierlin, H. 1975a. *Eltern und Kinder im Prozess der Ablösung*. Frankfurt am Main: Suhrkamp.

———. 1975b. *Von der Psychoanalyse zur Familientherapie*. Stuttgart: Klett.

———. 1978. *Delegation und Familie*. Frankfurt am Main: Suhrkamp.

Störig, H. J. 1954. *Kleine Weltgeschichte der Wissenschaft*. Stuttgart: Kohlhammer.

———. 1969. *Kleine Weltgeschichte der Philkosophie*. 2 vols. Frankfurt am Main: Fischer.

Tart, C. T. 1975. *Transpersonal Psychologies*. New York: Harper & Row.

Thamm, A. 1982. "Poesie und integrative Therapie." *Integrative Therapie* 4:267–85.

Tomazewski, T. 1978. *Tätigkeit und Bewusstsein*. Weinheim: Beltz.

Ueda, S. 1982. "Das Gespräch und das 'Mon-Dô' im Zen-Buddhismus." In *Das Gespräch als Ereignis*, ed. E. Grassi and H. Schmale, pp. 45–57. Munich: Fink.

Ulich, E. 1978a. "Entwicklungsmöglichkeit des Menschen in der Arbeit." *Managementzeitschrift* 47:281–86.

———. 1978b. "Ueber mögliche Zusammenhänge zwischen Arbeits-tätigkeit und Persönlichkeitsentwicklung." *Psychosozial* 1:44–63.

Varela, F., H. Maturana, and R. Uribe. 1974. "Autopoiesis: The Organization of Living Systems, Its Characterization, and a Model." *Biosystems* 5:187–96.

Walsh, R. N., and F. E. Vaughan. 1980. "Beyond the Ego: Toward Transpersonal Models of the Person and Psychotherapy." *Journal of Humanistic Psychology* 20 (no. 1): 5–32.

Wangh, M. 1983. "Narzissismus in unserer Zeit: Einige psychoanalytisch-soziologische Ueberlegungen zu seiner Genese." *Psyche* 1:16–40.

Watzlawick, P., J. H. Beavin, and D. D. Jackson. 1967. *Pragmatics on Human Communication*. New York: Norton.

Weizsäcker, C. U. von. 1975. "Die umweltfreundliche Emanzipation." In *Internationale Tagung für Humanökologie*. Vienna: Georgi.

Whitehead, A. N. 1933. *Adventures of Ideas*. New York: Macmillan.

Wickler, W., and U. Seibt. 1977. *Das Prinzip Eigennutz*. Hamburg: Hoffmann und Campe.

Willi, J. 1972. *Die Kollusion als Grundbegriff für die Ehepsychologie und Ehetherapie*. Sonderheft und Gruppenpsychotherapie und Gruppendynamik. Göttingen: Vandenhoeck und Ruprecht.

———. 1973. *Der Gemeinsame Rorschach-Versuch*. Berne: Huber.

———. 1978. *Therapie der Zweierbeziehung* Reinbek: Rowohlt.

———. 1982a. *Couples in Collusion*. New York: Jason Aronson.

———. 1982b. "Treue heisst auch, sich selbst treu zu bleiben." In *Lebenswandel*. Weinheim: Beltz.

———. 1984. "Gemeinsames Wachstum—Möglichkeiten und Grenzen *Psychother. Psychosom.* 29:222–233.

Willi, J., and S. Grossmann. 1983. "Epidemiology of Anorexia Nervosa in a Defined Region of Switzerland." *American Journal of Psychiatry* 140:564–67.

Winnicott, D. W. 1965. *The Maturational Processes and the Facilitating Environment.* London: Hogarth Press.

Wirschung, M., and H. Stierlin. 1982. *Krankheit und Familie.* Stuttgart: Klett-Cotta.

Yannaras, C. 1982. *Person und Eros.* Göttingen: Vandenhoeck und Ruprecht, 1982.

Zeleny, M., and N. A. Pierre. 1976. "Simulation of Self-Renewing Systems." In *Evolution and Consciousness,* ed. E. Jantsch and C. H. Waddington, pp. 150–66. Reading, MA: Addison-Wesley.

Zimmer, D., and A. Uchtenhagen. 1982. "Fixerehen—Fixerpaare." *Familiendynamik* 7:211–27.